ArtMachine

A Reinvention of Photography, 1959–1999

ArtMachine

A Reinvention of Photography, 1959–1999

Clark Worswick

Midnight Books, LLC

Clark Worswick/Midnight Books LLC
1283 "A" Fruitville Road,
Sarasota, FL. 34236

Publisher's Note: This is a work of history and biography.

All Photographs Copyright© Clark Worswick & Joan Worswick

Book Layout © 2014 BookDesignTemplates.com

The kindest mention and thanks is made by the author to Tony Korner, Jennifer Milne and to Sabra Besley for their astute and passionate editing of this manuscript. Huge credit is given as well to Jeff Gaydash, who has labored now for years on our Ethiopian pictures, and other projects. In this work he has pioneered new printing technologies in his own unique reinvention of photography.

Library of Congress Cataloging-in-Publication Data.

Worswick,Clark.
ArtMachine: A Reinvention of Photography 1959-1999/
Clark Worswick.
Includes biographical refereneces.
ISBN 978-0-9969280-0-7
1.Photographic History. 2.Biography. 3. Exploration.

DEDICATION

This book is dedicated to Terry Moore, Lynn Johnson, Dan
Budnik and to Adelaide de Menil, who during fifty year careers,
have yet to gain wide acceptance of their work creating
incandescent photographic art-documents in over two hundred
years of individual work.

PREFACE

This is a book about a mechanical art that was born in 1839 as the radiant child of the Industrial Revolution.

This is also a book about love, dangerous travel, and photography.

***

At its birth photography was hurled into the firmament of the nineteenth century. In its first years it literally changed the way man viewed the natural world.

By the late 1840s, the art of photography had been adopted by both the intellectual and artistic establishments of Europe. So stunning and unique was photography that it gained the patronage of the greatest royal houses of Europe as "the newly created art of the century."

Then, as things go in the art world, the seasons changed.

In the universe of art, patronage for photography slowly began to wane in the 1860s. In the many decades that followed, photography took a long walk toward oblivion and a century in the dying.

***

For decades, I've been preoccupied with the difficulties of first becoming a photographer, and then learning about the tangled and almost forgotten history of photography.

The later chapters of this book are my memoir of the art world and how photography became part of that world. In detail, they describe how photography was brought back and reinvented. They describe how photography beginning in the 1960s, like Lazarus, was resurrected then validated by the art world.

Make no mistake about how forgotten photography was by the art world at the end of the 1950s. In both Europe and America, photography, apart from a few bright moments, had been forgotten for almost a century.

When I began taking photographs in 1959, for the most part the medium was used as a memento of love, a record of war, and for identifying the faces of criminals in police custody or morgues. In the world of commerce, newspaper and magazine photo journalists held steady employment positions, while both fashion photographers and advertising photographers created alluring models of business-oriented societies at work.

Apart from these modest occupations, there was no gainful employment for a photographer. An additional fact: at the beginning of the 1960s, not a museum in the world had a dedicated photography curator, nor any interest in collecting photographs.

When one is pressed to give examples of exactly how low the state of photography fell in the long century of its artistic exile, consider the contents of a parcel delivered by mail to a poorly lit building in Midtown Manhattan.

In 1961, that parcel, received at the New York office of the Magnum photographic cooperative, elicited little interest. Upon eventually opening this unsolicited box, the picture agency discovered the life's work of a California photographer named Edward Weston.

In due course the heirs of Weston were contacted. A sale was arranged. Then, set out on tables, the prints of Edward Weston and his life's works were put up for sale. In honor of these works, as one of the few "artists" in American photography, the

Weston estate was identified by a small sign. It stated: "Prints for Sale. $25 each."

Few prints sold to anyone.

With little notice and ceremony, the contents of the parcel were wrapped up. They were then shipped back to Weston's sons in California. It's worth noting that today, in the second decade of the twenty-first century, Edward Weston prints, both transcendent and otherworldly works by one of the greatest artists of twentieth-century America, have sold regularly for more than $2 million each.

In a second example of how low the estate of photography was in 1976, I arranged the sale of another penurious photographer's life's work.

Included were his prints, some 3,400 of them, plus this artist's negatives and the publishing rights to create limited editions of his work. At the time of this sale, this photographer was perhaps one of the five most famous photographers in both Europe and America. This entire artistic patrimony was sold for $200,000.

After the sale in New York, I walked along Madison Avenue with the man who had purchased this artistic estate. At the intersection of Madison and East 74th Street, the man turned to me.

He said that it was now his intention to destroy the prints that he'd just purchased. He wanted to create instant rarity for a set of limited-edition photographs, which he intended to produce from the photographer's negatives now in his possession.

I recall I'd stood there in the frozen wind of early February.

I told the man that in the distant future of photography, perhaps someday there might be a market for older prints, or "vintage photography," as it was then called.

A few days later, the man agreed to postpone the great burning. And that is why the prints that comprise the life's work of a photographer named Robert Frank still survive.

***

A few additional facts about photography as an art in 1959:

On the planet Earth, there was not a single dealer who represented a single photographer's work in any known art gallery. Not even for a millisecond did art dealers, or art museums, consider the strange idea that photography could someday be considered an art.

Alternatively, were this sad trajectory not dismal enough, there was not a single university that taught either a studio course in photography or the history of photography as part of its curriculum.

It would not be until eleven years later, in the early 1970s, that the first Ph.D. in photographic history was granted. And it would not be until fifteen years later, in 1975, that the first art gallery in Tokyo exhibited photography on a regular basis.

***

In 1959, I took up photography. It was a hobbyist's avocation. It was unimportant *craftwork*.

In that year, I began to wander the periphery of the art world, and I settled on traveling a road full of difficulties. When I look back at the moment I took it up, photography seemed a fatally damaged medium. Beyond the commercial worlds of journalism and fashion, I went the opposite direction from everyone else. In time, as the 1960s aged during a tumultuous moment in America, I took a walk on the wild side. I came of age in a period of war, civil chaos, sex, drugs, and rock and roll. I made photographs of places slated for cultural demolition.

Once, when he was asked what his own photographs were about, Walker Evans, perhaps one of the greatest artists of twentieth-century America, answered, "I make 'art documents.'"

My photographs were similar to Walker Evans's "art documents."

In the last quarter of the twentieth century, it seemed to me that only "art documents" could memorialize a period where a new world culture began to emerge and sweep away national identities as well as entire millennial landscapes. I traveled to India, the Middle East, Asia, and Ethiopia. As I watched, the cities of the world were enveloped then erased by suburbanization.

It seemed to me that mankind's fate was to inhabit a world that was both familiar and similar everywhere. I photographed a world disappearing in front of me. As the artifacts of mankind's past were subsumed, it seemed a sort of cataclysm, and I thought back to Walker Evans's prescient intuitions about photography.

Of all the arts, only photography could create true-to-life "art documents," with the unique ability to exactly and precisely preserve what the world was.

In the wastage which time wreaks on man's civilizations, will photographs remain as the enduring artifact of our period? Perhaps in some remote future, only our photographs will be able to excite curiosity as to who we once were.

To the end of my life, I will always remember the moment when I saw a photograph emerge on the surface of a blank piece of paper that was soaking in a developing tray.

It was a miracle.

***

CHAPTER ONE

Ethiopia

From the beginning of time, perhaps, and in a place seldom seen and scarcely traveled, the Danakil Desert in Ethiopia has always been one of planet's most extreme environments.

It is an area of violent volcanoes.

It is also an area of blistering air with some of the hottest temperatures ever recorded on Earth.

It is a place that, until recently, held a great secret that remained to be discovered.

This secret was that the Danakil Desert was, and is today, quite literally being ripped apart by enormous planetary events.

In an area now termed the Afar Triangle is an unusual triple junction of gigantic tectonic plates. They meet uneasily along a geological fissure called the East African Rift System. In a place of shaking, boiling earth, a large part of Africa is coming apart. At the center of this zone is the Danakil Desert, where both the Arabian Plate and two parts of the African Plate meet. Then, traveling to different places, they part .

In an event measured in eons, the huge African tectonic plate pulls away from the Arabian Plate.

This is a colossal geological event.

An additional fact: in the nineteenth and twentieth centuries the Danakil Desert was dubbed the cruelest place on Earth. One entered the Danakil cautiously and at one's own peril. In the 21st Century, the following news articles sourced from the British press, detail just how lethal the Danakil Desert remains today:

***

SAS joins search for Britons abducted in Ethiopia"

The Times, March 5, 2007 Rob Crilly and Michael Evans, Defence Editor

A substantial special forces team, including SAS troops, is being assembled to plan for the rescue of the five Britons abducted by militant rebels in northeast Ethiopia. The Foreign and Commonwealth Office asked the Ministry of Defence to draw up a hostage-rescue plan soon after the five Britons, four of them staff members of the British Embassy in Addis Ababa, the Ethiopian capital, and the wife of an official with the British Council, were seized while on a tourist geological expedition in the Afar region of the country.

The military team includes the Armed Forces' most experienced hostage-rescue experts, as well as specialists trained in negotiating with kidnappers.

Details of the special forces team, its numbers and its whereabouts were a closely guarded secret.

No one has so far admitted the kidnappings to the Ethiopian or British governments. Five Ethiopians said to have been in the same party were reportedly found by guards near the disputed border with Eritrea yesterday. It was not clear whether they had been freed or escaped. At least another eight Ethiopians were also taken hostage.

***

"Desert telegraph brought first word on Ethiopian hostages"

The Times, March 9, 2007 Philippe Naughton

The first clear indication as to the hostages' fate, had trickled back via nomadic herdsmen passing through the desert region, who traditionally greet each other as they pass each other in the desert and, having sat down together, painstakingly swap news under the system of *dagu*.

Dagu is one of the few things binding the society together. The Afar is a region where fathers buy their sons Kalashnikovs at the age of 10 or 11 so they can protect themselves against rival tribesmen when they are sent off to herd their camels. Poverty is almost universal, tuberculosis is endemic. "They learn about what has changed in a changeable land, and in the world at large, and from all this they pick a course of action.

"Those who pay the closest attention to the news, they say, may go on to survive, Inshallah—God willing."

The Times columnist Matthew Parris, who visited the region last year, wrote: "Hell lies 3,000 meters below Mekele, below sea level, in the deserts of the Danakil Depression. A hundred miles over dry mountains and down the other side is an inferno of a place: one of the hottest and most inhospitable on Earth."

***

"Five European tourists killed in attack in Ethiopia" *The Guardian*, January 18, 2012, David Smith_

Gunmen in northern Ethiopia have attacked a group of European tourists, killing five, injuring two, and kidnapping four people, according to a government official. Two Germans, two Hungarians, and an Austrian are dead in the remote northern Ethiopian Afar region. An Italian and a Hungarian were wounded in the attack, with two Germans and two Ethiopians who were kidnapped.

Bereket Simon, the Ethiopian communications minister, said the attackers struck before dawn on Tuesday.

The tourists were visiting the volcanic Afar region, which is one of the hottest places in the world and a known haunt of rebels and bandits from Eritrea and Ethiopia.

Simon said the attack occurred 12 to 15 miles from the Eritrean border. A German media report said the group of tourists had been close to the Erta Ale volcano, one of Ethiopia's most active.

Speaking about the latest attack an Austrian foreign ministry spokesman, Peter Launsky-Tiefenthal, said two foreign groups totalling as many as 22 people may have been attacked, though he said the numbers were unconfirmed.

"The problem is there is no infrastructure in the area. No telephone lines; satellite phones barely work." He likened Afar to "the surface of Mars."

***

The Danakil Desert, on the edges of Eritrea and Ethiopia, Dawn, May 1968

I'd dreamed I drowned in blowing sand.

Was this my nightmare?

In my dream my eyes are glued shut with sand and sweat.

I feel weightless. I wake up. The storm died last night.

I'm disoriented.

Dawn again. I look upward. I see daylight through the pinpricks stitched into the tent seams above me.

My last moments of sleep.

***

I open the tent flap. I've been in the Danakil four days.

How is it possible for human beings to live in this place? I'd entered this place incautiously.

Like the surface of the moon, the leaden smoldering desert stretches away into the distance. I'm totally exhausted after my night's sleep.

I don't want to think about another day in the Danakil.

***

In the early 1930s, a man named Ludovico Mariano Nesbitt published a book about this desert. Nesbitt related a journey through the borderlands of this wasteland and into the molten heart of the Danakil.

He called his book *The Hell-Hole of Creation.*

Turning 360 degrees outside my tent is an immense empty vastness. I've been in the Danakil too many days.

A few starved trees cling to life 400 yards away. East, west, south, and north, this trackless inferno tilts toward distant mountains that appear to be the edge of the world. In the anticipated inferno of another day, the mountains shimmer there like a hallucination.

In far eastern Ethiopia, bordering the Red Sea, the Danakil Desert is occupied by a people called the Afar.

The only vegetation in this place are the low scrub trees and the occasional thornbush. Coating every dirt-covered barb, these bushes are filled with a violently infectious poison. Once lodged in your arms or legs, the thorns create septic trenches in human skin. If they lodge in an eye, blindness follows.

One hundred and fifty years ago, the two discoverers of the source of the Nile in central Africa, John Speke and Richard Burton, barely got out of this place alive. Speke had four spears thrust through his legs. Burton survived the same attack with a barbed spear lodged in his face. The spear had passed through both of his cheeks and destroyed his rear teeth. To this day, one can see Sir Richard Burton's wounds in an oil painting that now hangs in the National Portrait Gallery in London.

What else can one say about this place?

For some reason, I remembered the introduction to Nesbitt's book *The Hell-Hole of Creation*. It had been written in 1929, and it said:

> The real untouched Danakil lies westward...within the borders of Abyssinia. It forms an irregular rectangle, some 400 miles long from north to south, by 150 miles wide, and is an old upraised seabed, like the valley of the Jordan and Wadi Musa, of which indeed it is probably a continuation.

> In some parts it is still between 300 feet and 400 feet below the level of the Red Sea, and my companions and I frequently experienced in our tent a shade temperature ranging between 140 degrees F and 156 degrees F. Before our journey, three expeditions had been launched for the exploration of this territory or parts of it: namely, that of Munzinger in 1875, that of Giulietti in 1881, and that of Bianchi in 1884. All these expeditions met with disaster, and no European member of any one of them ever returned.

> We (ourselves) lost three loyal and excellent fellows among our native attendants. They were assassinated by the Danakils. Ten camels and three mules died of thirst, starvation and fatigue. *L.M. Nesbitt, The Hell-Hole of Creation, The Exploration of the Abyssinian Danakil*, pp. 6–7.

Next to me inside another tent was my companion Robert Gardner. He was the architect of our joint journey toward oblivion.

When we first came into the desert, I'd been warned not to go beyond the village. If I moved beyond sight of the village, I had to have armed guards or be armed myself. My companion was not awake yet. He slumbered onward.

Set among the low scrub thornbushes, the village of the Afar beyond my tent was comprised of seven squat skin-covered huts surrounded by a ring of thornbushes to keep carnivores from attacking at night. The huts' short humped shapes protected the Afar people from the huge winds of the Danakil.

Robert Gardner and I had come here to make the first film of the interior of this desert. The film we were making was on the Afar. It had been conceived as a record of perhaps the most lethal and elusive people on earth. No doubt, inside his tent, my companion was dreaming his own visions of the naive and the utterly feckless.

What amazed me about the Danakil Desert was that people actually inhabited this place. It was almost devoid of life. During a longer acquaintance with the Danakil in the last few weeks, I'd come to think of this place as the natural, fitting home of the Afar people. Each Afar seemed to live out his own particular, terrible version of hell. Every Afar was a killer. In my wildest imagination, I never believed that someday I'd wake up in a kind of topographical nightmare. In addition, the Afar were known for their intense and abiding hatred of foreigners.

For one moment, the sun wasn't there. The next moment, full of malice, it suddenly appeared. Across a flat, dried wadi were the two dusty white Toyota Land Cruisers that had brought us into this desert. In the distance, as the sun struggled out of the desert, you saw how bleak this place was.

In front of me, six Afar materialized. They stood there, staring at me without speaking. They were dressed in earth-colored thin cotton cloth. They'd become the hues of this place, their worn rags the shades of the desert. Below huge heads of dusty hair, they had angular mocha-brown faces.

They watched me the way vultures watch a dying camel. In this desert, there was nothing freely given, nothing extra. The Afar's sole preoccupations were raiding other Afar clan groups and picking off stragglers from the hapless yearly salt caravans, which crossed the edges of their terrible desert kingdom.

The Afar are, first, family units. A group of Afar families then form a clan group. Every Afar has only one thought. Born into the desert, they are possessed by a terrible darkness which deforms each one of them. To the Afar, murder is a kind of devotion. Anyone who enters their desert is an enemy. When an Afar moves in to kill you, your only hope should be that you die quickly. Next comes emasculation. As a sort of prize, your genitals will be hung around your murderer's neck.

Upon my first acquaintance with the Afar, they seemed a people of smiles. Only later did I learn what the smiles were about.

Upon longer acquaintance, their chief preoccupation seemed to be the desire to kill you quickly. Each male member of the tribe, or female member of a clan, practiced a living version of homicidal Islam.

In 1968, by my count, only four Europeans had ventured into this land and then emerged alive.. They were Sir Richard Burton, John Speke, Ludovico Mariano Nesbitt, and the strange British specimen of the exotic named Wilfred Thesiger.

The six Afar, my bodyguards, stood there. They walked down into a wadi in front of me as I descended a dirt scarp to make my morning toilet.

Behind me, each of the Afar guards carried long curved knives. Strapped across their chests were bandoliers of ammunition. Polished to a dull sheen, the leather of the bandoliers had been burnished by generations of use. In the desert, nothing is wasted.

Nothing is discarded. Some of my guards were equipped with vintage 1898 Martini-Henry rifles. Two other guards were supplied with magazine-loaded Lee-Enfield rifles from World War I. Every Afar went armed at all times. They were miraculously adapted to intense heat and thirst. But above all, they were indomitable trackers. The Afar could cover immense distances in search of prey that, in most cases, was another man.

In the Danakil, it was amazing what one got used to.

Fear was ever present. The heat was unbearable until you got used to it.

It's hard to imagine it. Every drop of water we swallowed had to be excavated out of a dry riverbed. That is what we drank each day. The bottom of our water hole contained a sort of brownish sandy goo. We managed to drink sixteen glasses of water a day flavored with dirt. It was startling what the ordinary became when there were no choices.

I climbed out of the wadi.

In the dawn, I looked back toward our two Kenyan heavy canvas expedition tents. There was movement inside the tent of my companion. There were thumping noises on canvas as he stood up. A groan. Cursing.

How could anyone willingly seek out this place? I wondered. My cameras filled with sand. The lenses were coated with a perpetual film of dust. I hoped this fine grit didn't get into my film cassettes and scratch my films. I was using a black German Leica M2. It had been my companion on my journeys everywhere in the last six years. In my camera bag was a black Nikon F that I'd used in police riots in Berkeley, then during the California period of acid and rock and roll in the mid1960s.

I watched the tent of my companion. Nothing moved inside now. I wondered if my companion, on this joint visit to the dawn of mankind, had become unstrung by regret during the night? On the other hand, perhaps during the darkest part of the night, he'd rolled over and inadvertently been wounded by a lethal snake?

At that moment, a four-foot-five-inch man appeared from one of the huts of the village.

His name was Abdullah. His skin was espresso black. He was our passport into, and hopefully out of, this desert. Abdullah was our Afar factotum, our go-between. He was our bridge across mankind's past on the edges of the Great Rift Valley to our immediate present, as long as that lasted.

The people of this village were Abdullah's clansmen. He was the unlikely facilitator of our presence. He was our translator. He was our arranger of Afar tribal matters. He guaranteed our precarious continued existence.

Abdullah was the collateral and the tribal "fixer" for Alimirah Hanfere, then the Sultan of the Afars, who ruled the Danakil.

From 1734 onward, the royal Imamate of Aussa governed the Danakil Desert. During the last few years, the Sultan had lived on his best behavior as a prisoner-pensioner of Haile Selassie, the Emperor of Ethiopia. They lived a few miles from each other in cool, eucalyptus-shrouded Addis Ababa, the capital of Ethiopia. Both the Emperor and his prisoner, the Sultan of the Afars, lived in fear of their assassination by members of their own communities.

I clapped my hands and smiled. I nodded toward a portable camp table set with three settings.

"Abdullah," I called. "A pleasant night I hope! Breakfast awaits." And now another wonderful and incommunicably awful breakfast to look forward to.

Each day began with another adventure. Another day of unending terror.

Abdullah looked worried, but then he always looked worried. "Good morning, sir," he whispered.

In the distance behind me were the faint bluish outlines of the Tigrinya Highlands of Ethiopia. Below these mountains was the Danakil Desert simmering in a giant frying pan.

Carefully, Abdullah checked the sand underneath the table for things that bit and stung. Settling himself into a collapsible canvas chair, he took a deep breath then looked up and smiled. Abdullah's genuine smile would light up his face.

I joined Abdullah at the table, turned, and beamed at him. "The comforts of home. All of your relatives nearby. What a joy life must be for you here?"

Irony was not part of Abdullah's limited English skill set. His smile faded. He looked puzzled. I supposed Abdullah was hungry.

Out of his tent 150 feet away, Robert Gardner appeared. With luck, perhaps we'd both live to film another day, trapped in this desert nightmare.

My companion stared up at the sun. He looped a pair of aviator glasses over his eyes

Two hundred miles away to the south from where we sat was the town of Harar. In the late nineteenth century, the Imamate of Aussa had given refuge to Arthur Rimbaud, the displaced French poet.

On the fringes of the Danakil, Rimbaud turned from rhymes to the profession of European arms smuggler. After living eleven years of running armaments into Somaliland, he didn't escape this place. He left Ethiopia with an inflammation of his knee, which led to an amputation of his leg, then later death in Marseille as a fever-ridden East African wreck.

In the first rays of day, Robert looked like a kind of Abercrombie & Fitch explorer or matinee idol. As he moved toward us, he had a kind of ambling Gary Cooper gait. He had movie-star looks. In his rumpled bush jacket tied casually by a cotton belt, he looked the outrageously brave Marine Corps officer that he'd once been.

Before we'd come into this sandy wasteland, Robert had built a filmmaking reputation. A few years earlier, he'd led a Harvard-sponsored filmmaking expedition into the highlands of New Guinea to film the Dani tribe. They had only been recently discovered by anthropologists and academics. On film, the Dani were a strangely compelling group. My companion had demonstrated their special Neolithic tribal life with cinematic virtuosity: the women of the tribe suckling young pigs at their breasts; the Dani men devoting themselves chiefly to almost ritualistic warfare with other clan groups, as they stabbed their neighbors with cruelly barbed spears.

Robert retreated back into his tent.

He emerged a few moments later with his loaded Arriflex 16mm camera. In a theatrical way, he raised the camera to his right eye.

Squinting upward at the rising sun, he began shooting film while he tilted the camera downward from the sun into the Afar village. Then, for a splendid filmmaking effect, he began a long shot walking toward the Afar village, filming as he went.

Following him now were a comic group of Afar men.

They moved, bent over almost double, squinting between Robert's legs as he walked and filmed simultaneously.

This procession continued for ninety seconds as the quite baffled Afar followed him in single file trying to see what he was doing.

As many times as I'd tried to explain to Abdullah the process of filmmaking, our marvelous camera art seemed to elude him and his relatives. Their interest in filmmaking usually lasted a minute or so before they began twittering and hooting like demented birds. This didn't ruin Robert's shots. It simply wrecked the sound recordings I tried to make in addition to my photography.

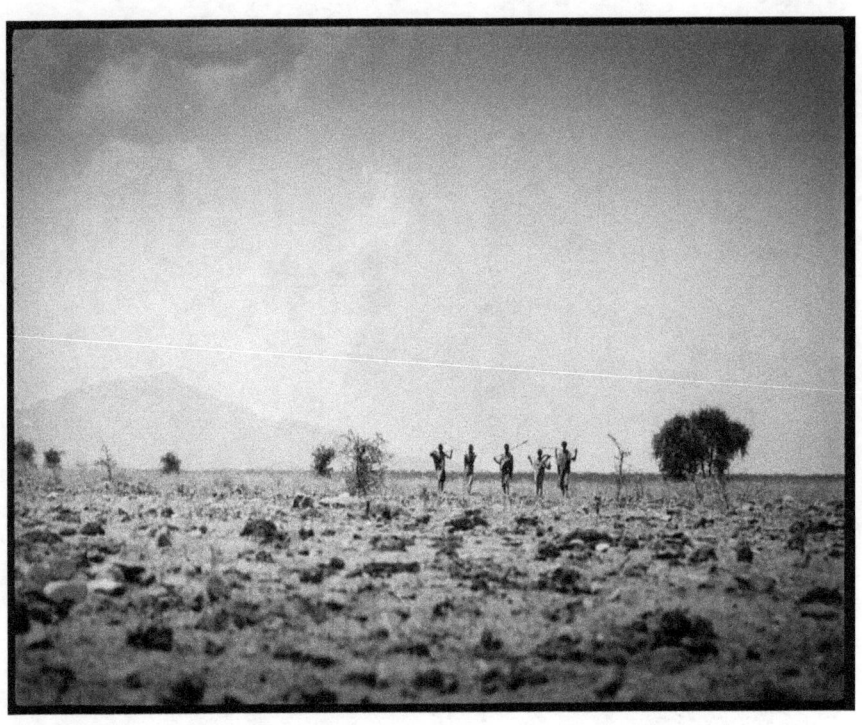

The Danakil Desert, Warriors, Afar

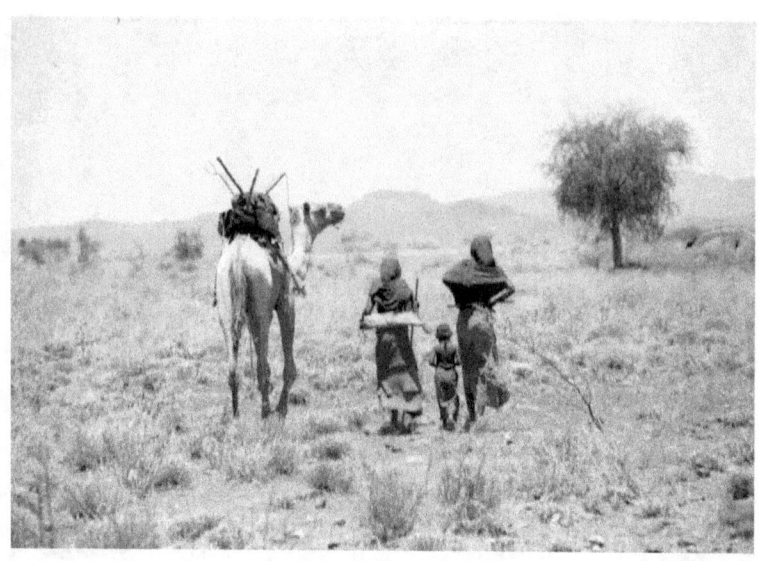

Afar Women, the Danakil Desert

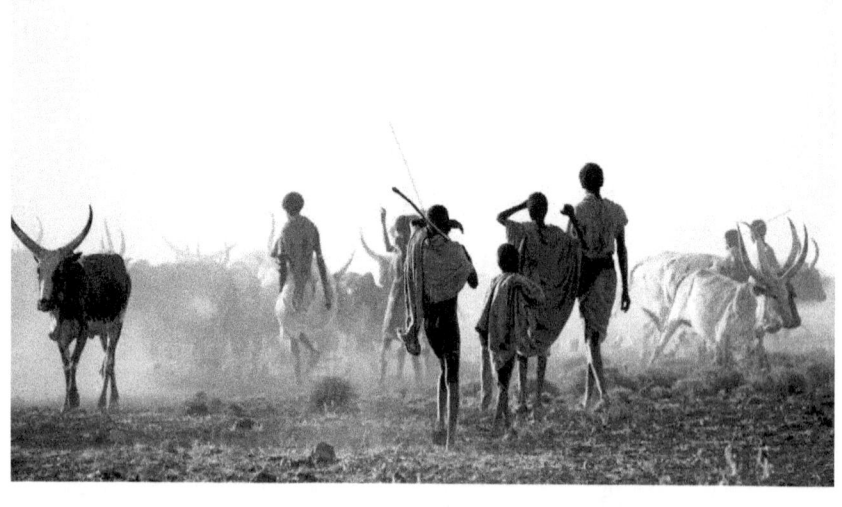

Ancient Long-Horned Egyptian Cattle, the Danakil Desert

Robert had now approached one of the huts.

Taking advantage of his preoccupation, I picked up the two pieces of Spam on Robert's plate. It seemed that Robert didn't really care about food. Many times after the creative spark seized him, he'd forget his breakfast and I'd be able to augment my meager rations by theft.

Another day. A lot more terrible juju.

From a hut, the figure of an old woman emerged out of the interior darkness.

She raised her clenched fists with handfuls of dirt. Next, she proceeded to dribble dust through her fingers as she screeched curses at Robert who was filming her. Today, as Robert moved through the village filming, it looked like she meant to kill us both, with her hideous black-magic incantations.

Abdullah looked over at me. "She still doesn't like him, I think."

Oblivious to any shred of horror, Robert circled around the old woman. The woman almost glistened with hatred and malice. His filming seemed to further enrage her.

I noticed that today Robert was using a set of lenses that had been given to him by a German filmmaker from another era. They had been made by Cooke Optics of England. The great German filmmaker was Leni Riefenstahl, Robert's friend. She had used these exact same lenses to create her monumental four-hour epic on the Berlin Olympics of 1936.

I took out my own cameras. My Leica. My Nikon F. I began to take pictures of the village and the desert.

The reason we were still alive in this village, baking in this desert inferno, was the adroit, nearly virtuosic Ethiopian political manipulations of my companion.

Robert had managed to obtain the services of Abdullah, and an entire Afar clan, to people our own personal desert film set.

Robert had high-level Harvard and U.S. government contacts which translated into other contacts with the Emperor of Ethiopia. The various services rendered to us in the Danakil had been bought and paid for by a transaction involving U.S. dollars paid to the Sultan of the Afars, with the approval of the Emperor.

In this exchange of political jujitsu, poor Abdullah and his services were offered to us for the duration of our stay in Ethiopia. If anything happened to us in the Danakil Desert, the Sultan of the Afars would doubtless be upset.

The sultan was a very basic man. I'm sure that it had been very carefully explained to Abdullah in lifelike Technicolor detail that his mother and his sisters, as well as his clansmen, would be punished.

That morning, I thought about the literally hundreds of photographers just then roaming around Vietnam documenting the meat grinder at work. At the same moment I was taking the first photographs of the Danakil, I thought back to an offer I'd had to shoot photographs in Vietnam for *Look* magazine.

In the heat that morning in the Danakil I shuddered, remembering that photographers and journalists were dying in Vietnam month by month in a long series of fatalities.

I resisted thinking about the foolhardiness and sheer audacity of our undertaking.

A hundred miles away from where I ate breakfast were the Red Sea and the Suez Canal. Was there an ulterior motive in America's abiding concern and passion for the tribal people of Ethiopia? The Danakil was just a hop, skip, and a jump from the most vital shipping artery in the world.

Was that too cynical? Perhaps I'd been traveling too long. I'd been traveling at this point for nine years taking pictures.

My own presence in Ethiopia was accidental and unlikely.

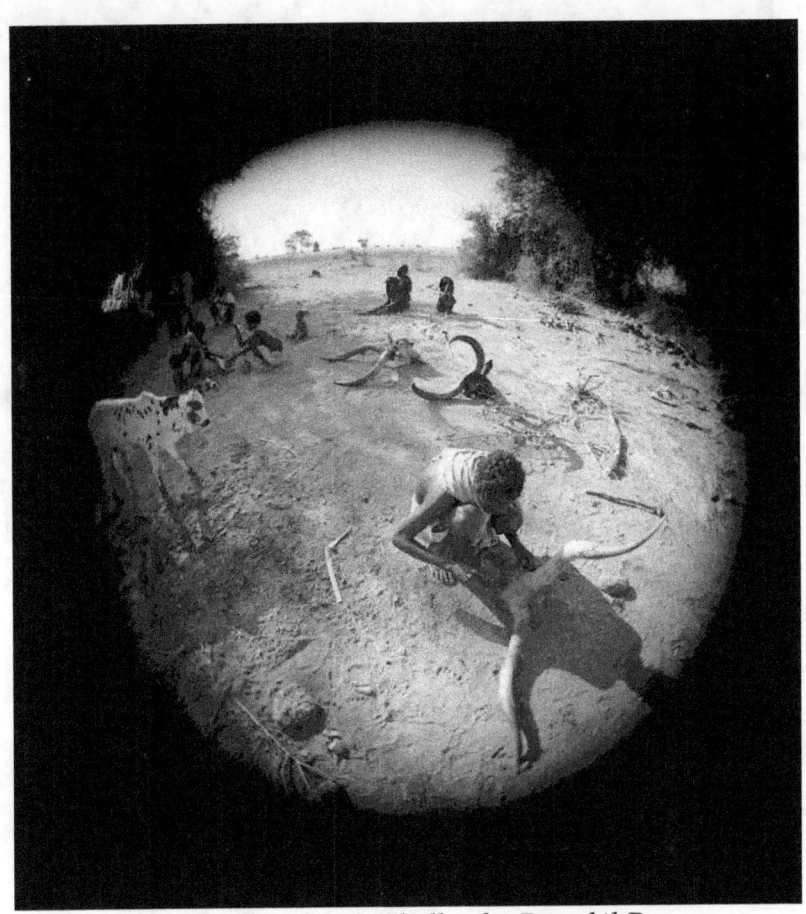

Afar, Rending Cow's Skulls, the Danakil Desert

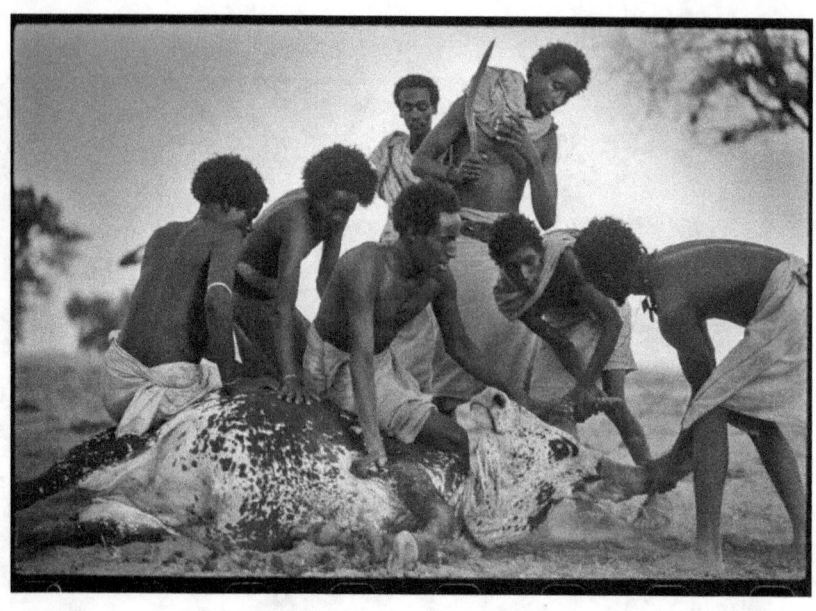

Cow Slaughter, the Danakil Desert

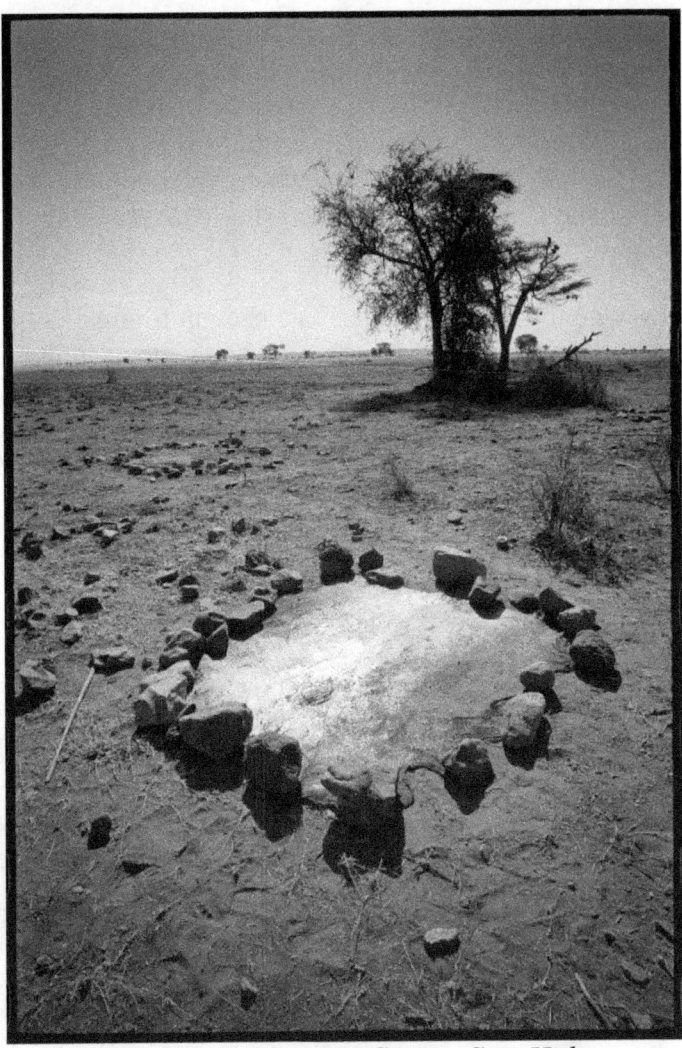

The Danakil Desert, Curing Cow Hide

At that moment, I was one of the few people engaged in ethnographic filmmaking. During the last five years, I'd made a film on tribal people in India, another on California, and still another on the Kotah Rajputs of central India. As a result, I was invited to join this unlikely project and given my very own Toyota Land Cruiser for this increasingly lovely Ethiopian adventure.

To sweeten the project further, as a backup filmmaker in case of sickness or any emergency, I was given the opportunity of photographing the interior of the Danakil Desert.

Lately, however, I'd come to think that my only real challenge in this project was to walk out of this place alive.

***

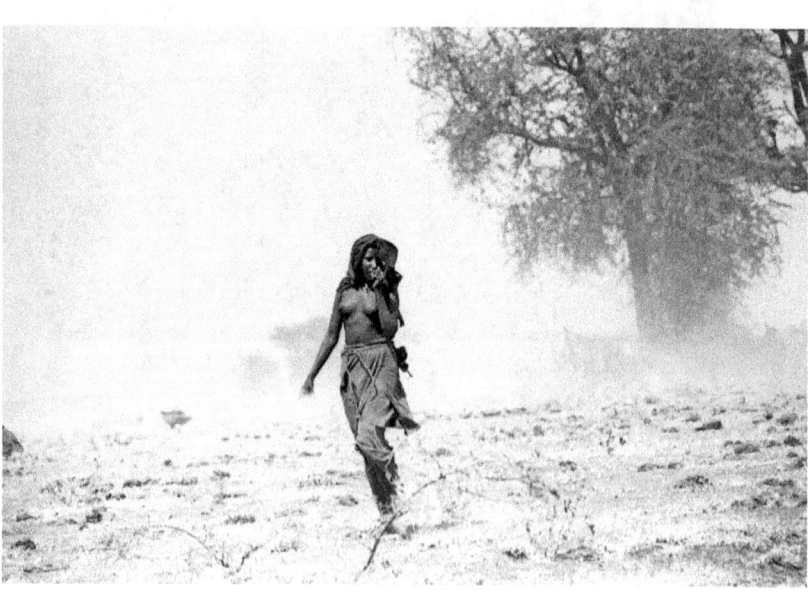

Afar Woman, the Danakil Desert

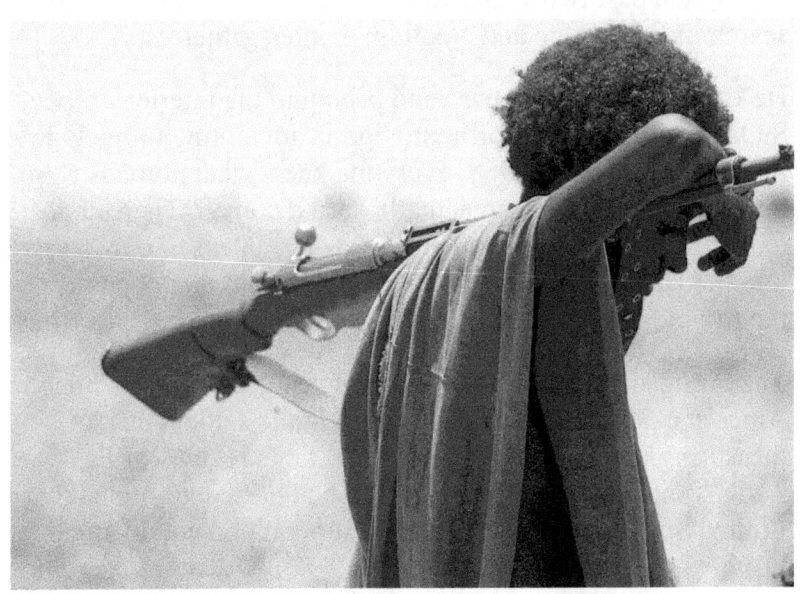

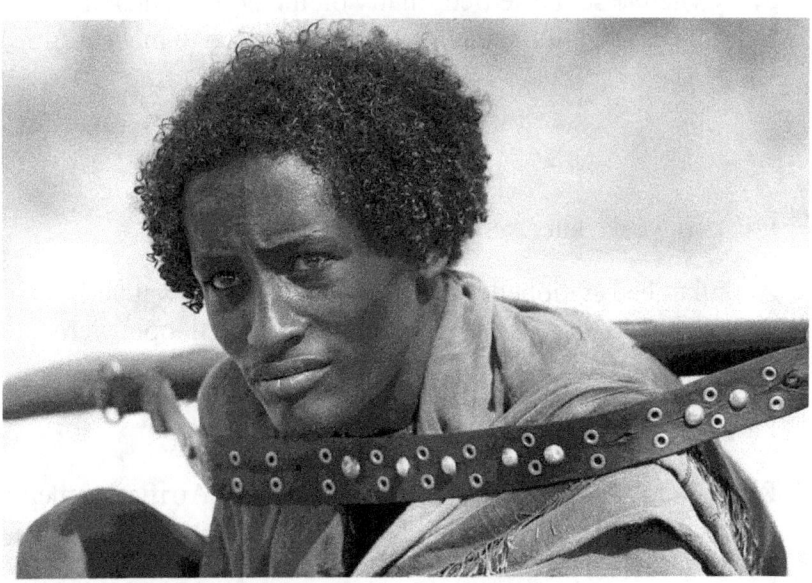

Afar, Warriors, the Danakil Desert

During the past two years, Robert had traveled the world in search of Paleolithic and Neolithic hunter-gatherers.

He'd crossed central Africa and been into the interior of the Sudan. He'd covered northern Nigeria attempting to track down nomadic peoples. In 1968, everyone knew what nomads were, but not many people had actually seen a nomad. There appeared to be few left anywhere in the world. The intent of our journey into the Danakil was to film nomadic peoples and document their lives.

The Smithsonian Institution was financing our work, while the American government was involved in the selfless task of measuring, then mapping, the most remote regions of East Africa. Somehow, in Washington it had been determined that a filmmaking project was worthy of support and would augment this gigantic mapping effort.

Robert rose to the challenge. In time, having gone seemingly everywhere else, he settled finally on the borderlands of Ethiopia as the unimaginably wonderful place to make a film.

***

It is two weeks later.

Abdullah had stationed himself so that he could watch the approaches to the village. The mountains of Ethiopia were behind Abdullah, the desert in front of him.

I always watched Abdullah watch us.

Robert had returned to his tent to pack up his Arriflex camera with its precious Nazi-period lenses.

Emerging from his tent, and now accompanied by his armed guards, he walked to the left, beyond our breakfast table, to tend to his morning necessities. He disappeared into his own chosen personal wadi a quarter of a mile away.

Robert's father was head of one of the largest corporations in America, General Electric. His brother headed the United Fruit Company, the august and hallowed company that currently controlled the destinies of several Central American countries. Propelling the Gardner clan toward the most elevated levels of Boston society was the fact that the matriarch of the clan, Isabella Stewart Gardner, had founded one of the most important art museums in America from her private collection. Robert had, in fact, been born at Fenway Court, his aunt's gigantic house, constructed to resemble a fifteenth-century Venetian palace, that later, as a museum, had become one of the chief cultural destinations in the art world.

Actually, Robert and I didn't speak very much these days.

What was there to talk about? A new goat or camel appearing to be butchered? Another evening of the spitting and the grunting of the Afar? I had the feeling that the longer we stayed in this place, the more our powers of communication would become diminished.

Robert returned to our rickety wooden table for coffee. It seemed to me, having just eaten Robert's Spam, that his breakfast now consisted now of orange-flavored Tang soaked in cow-piss water and our two-week-old bread, roasted upon an open fire, fueled by ancient wooden sticks. The resulting sandy toast was then smeared with gelatinous New Zealand butter that seemed strangely impervious to the heat.

I thought that only someone from Boston without taste buds could ever pretend this was a delicious meal. As unvarying as this monotonous, horrorific breakfast was, somehow, quite unbelievably, my companion attempted to create the idea that each morning his breakfast was delicious. He would rub his hands and pat his stomach.

I drifted off into a coma as I watched him, and he began talking to Abdullah.

That morning, I had finally abandoned my own interminable private speculations about how to animate the film that we were making. It seemed to me, in this poor village stalked by the millennial tragedies of this place, that nothing except another cattle raid or another murder would ever happen here.

The unremitting boredom and the horror of this desert had worn me away. I'd photographed prayers, tribal meetings, gigantic desert wind storms, and the slaughter of camels, cows, and goats. Very little else happened in the village. The children herded the goats and camels. The women fought an endless battle to gather enough water and firewood for the clan to survive.

After weeks in the Danakil Desert, Robert and I faced a narrative crisis in our film work and with each other.

Each day we watched as the men prayed five times a day facing Mecca. Other than that, sleeping was the daytime favored occupation of the men. Occasionally, these thin men rose from their sleep and watered the desert with thin streams of urine. Meanwhile, the women excavated for water in the rock-strewn wadis.

When the men weren't sleeping, they sat on the small wooden stools each of them carried everywhere. Under sparse scrub trees, they stared into the distance with 10,000-yard stares.

***

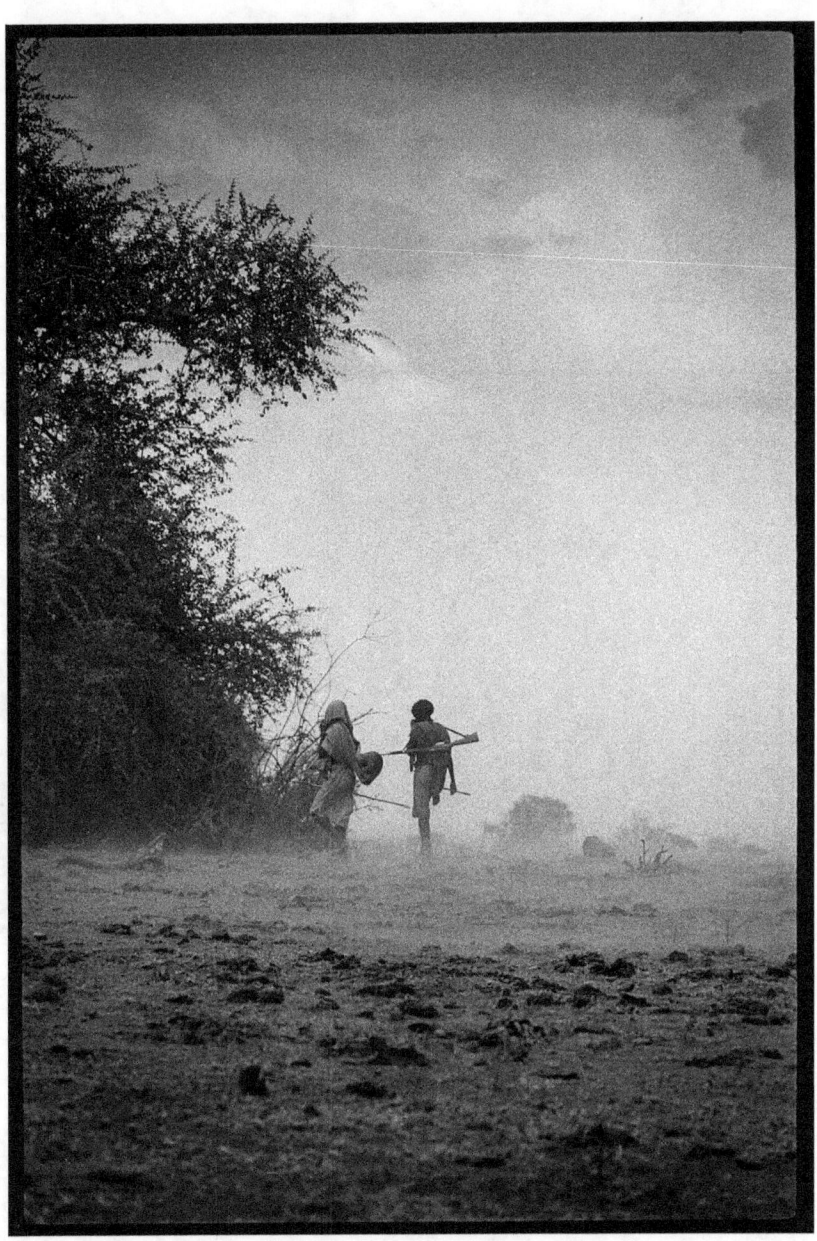

The Danakil Desert

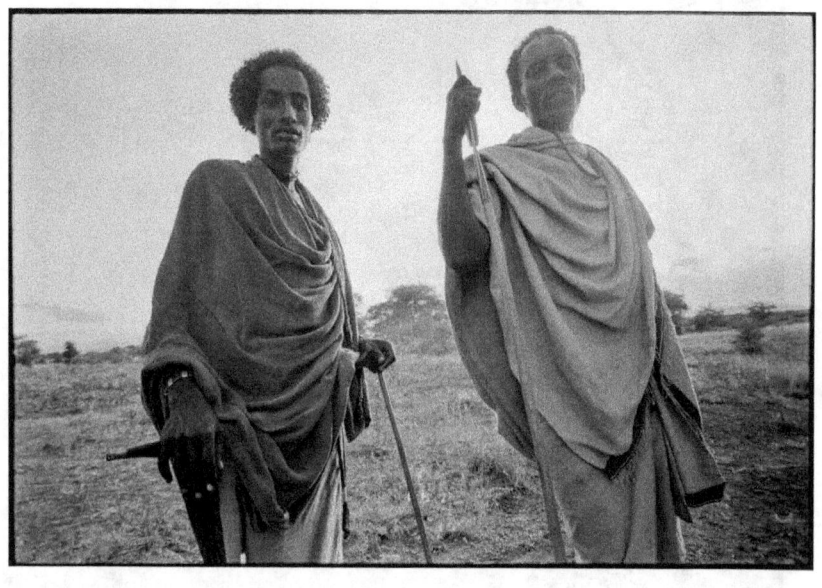

Afar Tribesmen, Danakil Desert

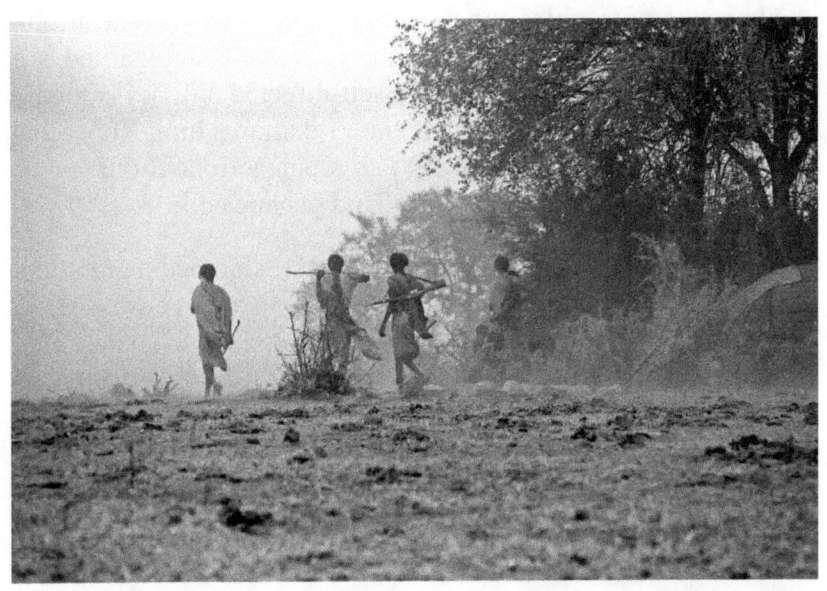

Afar and Village Hut, The Danakil

It is two days later.

Yesterday, my companion admitted that his film wasn't going anywhere; however, I'd shot thirteen rolls of 35mm black-and-white film—468 photographs.

I hoped my photographs were better than Robert's film. His admission of troubles appeared to be a rare chink in the armor of such a famous ethnographic filmmaker, one who regarded filmmaking as a single-minded, self-directed military campaign. Damn the casualties. In all the time I'd known him, Robert had seemed incapable of admitting either defeat or doubt. It probably wasn't in his New England genetic code.

In a kind of trance after breakfast, Robert slumped there in his collapsible camping chair. He looked up in a brave way. He gave me a weary smile.

"Trouble sleeping?" I asked brightly.

"We're having trouble getting this together, aren't we?" My filmmaking companion watched me for a long moment, then slowly he continued. "Being here isn't enough, is it?"

Cryptic. Very cryptic. Poetic. But cryptic. Suddenly it was "we." "We" were having trouble. I wasn't having any trouble. I was simply terrified night and day.

On the other hand, was this a rare admission of defeat? Too early to tell.

"So we go back to Addis? We start somewhere else?" I asked. "There have to be nomadic people somewhere around this gigantic, never seen and mysterious country."

My observation didn't seem to cheer him.

I continued, "I think I've come to the conclusion that Ethiopia is an utter puzzle. Think about that. No one even knows the tribes of people who live two mountain valleys away. Usually they have a completely different religion. They speak different millennial languages. Even to the people trying to map Ethiopia, like the CIA-sponsored U.S. Mapping Mission, no one here can tell you where rivers begin and where the rivers end, can they?"

Robert considered carefully what I'd just said. "You're not supposed to know anything about the funding of the U.S. Mapping Mission," he said tiredly.

At this point, even with his unnamed Washington contacts, my companion *had* traveled the length and width of Africa in a heroic attempt to hunt his nomads. When I thought about it, his fruitless journeys had a sort of epic, manic quality to them. Perhaps Sisyphus, and his labors of pushing a gigantic rock up an unending mountain, was Robert's spiritual template. The trouble with people from Robert's background, I suppose, was that they never learned to quit.

"We start again. Somewhere else," Robert said heavily, as if he were in pain. He nodded in agreement with himself.

I sat there and simply watched him.

This was so fantastic. Was he going to ask me to join him and come along with him? No, of course not. If I knew anything about him, I knew that he'd never ask me my opinion about our joint fate.

"Well, let us look at the bright side here," I said as a friendly observation. "After all, we haven't yet been hacked up into little tiny pieces by the Wuzzies, have we?"

"You've spent much too much time in India in the rotting tropical shades of the British Empire. When was the last time anyone called these people Wuzzies? In 1893?" Across the rickety portable table, the worn-looking, sleep-deprived filmmaker shook his head in disgust.

I didn't argue. Arguing might cause Robert to stay on longer in the Danakil in some kind of untoward funk.

"I think it's time to pack," I said cautiously. "It's time to drink our last quart of piss-flavored Tang. Then we can retire beaten, but unbroken, to the delights of the Fillowa baths in Addis. We can wash for the first time in seventeen days. I think that's an exceptionally grand plan, don't you?"

Across the table, Robert stared at the Danakil Desert. He stared for perhaps a minute at the village without speaking. "We're out. Time to wrap it. Time to switch off the lights."

My companion stood up. He stood there, swaying in the heat.

That morning, our journey into this awful place ended.

From where I sat, I looked up at Robert. I hoped he wouldn't change his mind. I wondered if he was coming down with heatstroke? Was it possible to get heatstroke at 6:10 in the morning?

***

An hour and a half later, we sat in our Toyotas. I glanced over at Abdullah in the passenger seat.

I wondered about Abdullah's strange homecoming. I wondered if there had been any happiness for him in his journey back to his village in the past seventeen days?

Abdullah tilted his head slightly. I'm sure he read my thoughts. He was staring at the mountains rising above the desert.

I turned on the ignition of my vehicle. The Land Cruiser fired up.

As the vehicles moved, Abdullah turned toward me and permitted himself the slightest trace of a smile. No longer would Abdullah be responsible for us in this godforsaken place. As I took my foot off the clutch and we began to move, Abdullah didn't look back at his village. No longer would his whole clan be under threat of extinction from the Sultan of Aussa if we were murdered.

Five minutes later, we were bumping over the desert toward the faint blue outlines of the highlands. I was thinking of the rains and the promise of cool, wet days. The sweat ran down my face. I exhaled slowly, gripping the slippery steering wheel.

"Jesus Christ," I whispered to myself. "How in hell did I get out of this alive?"

At that moment, I also wondered why I'd ever gotten involved in taking photographs of this place. I knew what I'd gotten out of: Robert and I had avoided being slaughtered.

Somehow I'd chosen ethnographic hell instead of Vietnam. Instead of being killed on assignment from *Look* magazine on a hilltop with a company of troopers in Vietnam, like my friend Sam Castan, I landed up here.

Instead of being a war photographer, I'd just trod a narrow pathway between living and dying in the Danakil. Perhaps the *Life* or *Look* photographer covering Vietnam had a life-insurance policy? I certainly didn't.

It was definitely time to limit danger in my life. Thinking about the pageant of my life during the past few years, I realized what I needed to do was to stop consorting with crazed people, like the insane filmmaker in the Land Cruiser ahead of me. I was tired of risk. I was tired of both my crazed work ethic and the places I traveled to.

I thought about earlier in 1968, when I'd been in India making a film on a warrior clan of Rajput princes. During this exercise in artistic creation, I'd spent three weeks with my girlfriend, Joanie Mitchell, under house arrest in what I learned too late was a Bombay whorehouse. The Indian Criminal Investigation Department seemed intent on my three-foot-thick file of unsubstantiated lawbreaking, which claimed making unauthorized movies in India and smuggling art. My crimes spanned the Indian subcontinent.

Before that, Joanie and I had both been in Pakistan and Sicily. The year before I'd photographed the infinitely depressing World War I battlefields of France. Before that, I'd been in California, where I'd photographed not only sex, drugs, and rock and roll, but also the American Nazi party.

When I thought about it, in the last few days I'd finished my ninth year of living in a never-ending free fall of constant travel. Lately, however, I felt I was too spread millimeters thin across too many landscapes. Perhaps my own life, like a low-budget Hollywood movie, had become filled with day-for-night shots filmed with an increasingly dark filter.

Staring at Robert's Land Cruiser in front of me, which now climbed across the rocky track toward the mountains beyond us, I thought about the future. It was an exercise I normally avoided. Joanie and I had another two months working in Ethiopia in front of us. She was in Addis working in the university library, trying to define, and hopefully discover, tribal groups immediately north of the Kenya–Ethiopia border.

In the Danakil, I realized that there were dangerous consequences to an out-of-control life when you loved someone who wanted to share that life with you. In September, I'd be twenty-eight years old. In the Danakil, I realized that for almost a decade, I'd off-loaded the risks that I'd taken in my life onto people who associated with me.

Sometimes, like now, people a price for this association.

In Addis, Joanie had an eye infection that she'd picked up on the Omo River while I went into the Danakil Desert. Joanie had gotten this infection when she'd let one of the tribesmen she was photographing look through her Nikon camera viewfinder. The first rule of photography in remote places is this: Never, *ever* let indigenous people look through your camera.

The only doctor who could treat Joanie's infection, specific to lowland Ethiopia, was a Czech doctor in Addis. He said the infection was curable. Joanie was the love of my life, but presently she was living on elephant-sized portions of antibiotics.

In the low foothills ahead of us, the track wound upward then downward. Next to me, Abdullah was mute watching the vehicle ahead that was drowning us in dust.

It was unforgivable. I was a total monster to leave Joanie alone in Addis.

***

As the road moved upward through a barren set of foothills populated by tufts of burnt-looking grass, ahead of me I saw the red brake lights wink on.

The Toyota ahead stopped abruptly. The door flew open.

Robert bolted out of the vehicle. He appeared to be running on his very long legs as fast as he could eastward, back down into the utter desolation of the Danakil Desert.

Abdullah and I got out of our Toyota just as my companion disappeared over the low rise of a hill. Below us, the hills were cut into innumerable wadis.

Once Robert got lost down in the wadis below the hills, we'd never find him.

What would I say to his wife? Usually, she hung out sunbathing at Bailey's Beach Club in Newport, Rhode Island, at this time of year. The kind of life Lee Gardner lived didn't fit in conveniently with the prospect of telling her that her husband had unexpectedly gone insane in the Danakil Desert.

"He ran. I couldn't catch up. Sorry." I could just hear my feeble explanations.

"Christ," I cursed softly.

Surveying this sudden disappearance, I had grave doubts, given Robert's head start, that anyone would be able to catch him. The way Robert was running flat out, he seemed to have been abruptly seized by an evil djinni.

Abdullah joined me looking down into the maze of barren wadis. "This is very bad, sir. What are we to do? There is no way we can ever find him down there before he is done harm by bad people...."

The only armament we had was a shotgun that we used for hunting guinea fowl for dinner. I wasn't about to go back into the Danakil armed with a ten-gauge shotgun looking for a maniac.

Out there in their wastelands, the Afar were equipped with almost century-old Martini-Henry rifles. In 1879, during the Zulu war in South Africa, these rifles had been sighted to an unbelievable 1,800 yards. What hope did Robert have in this vastness, surrounded by homicidal religious maniacs who were also some of the best shots in the world?

This was truly weird.

Next to me, Abdullah whispered, "Sir, I don't know how to explain this...but this is extremely, very bad for me. Having lost our friend, the Sultan will be very, very cross with me."

I ran a hand across my sweating forehead. "Somehow he's just completely lost his goddamned mind, Abdullah."

In the leaden blue sky, two vultures appeared. For five minutes, they circled and circled. Chewing his lip, Abdullah glanced over at me.

It was at this exact moment that my filmmaking companion appeared over the lip of the hill below. I stood there shaking my head. I watched him as he climbed out of a wadi.

Robert appeared to have something under his arm. Clutched in the crook of his left elbow, I saw that he had a baby ostrich.

Running his right hand slowly over the head of the baby ostrich, he came up to us. The ostrich settled on watching me with unblinking, metallic dinosaur eyes.

For the first time in days, Robert smiled. "His mother's gone. He's lost."

Right then, I wasn't happy. I pointed toward the Danakil, which stretched away into a smudged brown oblivion below. "Do you have any idea what I was thinking as you ran down there?"

For a long moment, Robert stared at me. "You know, you don't look your usual perky self this morning, do you?"

I laughed. Then, I laughed again.

"I can admit," Robert said, "seen from your point of view, that you probably thought I'd lost my mind."

"Not exactly," I said. "What I was thinking was that I'd totally lost *my* mind. Joining you on this trip, I'm the one who's flipped out. I'm the one watching you catch ostriches."

Robert looked at me brightly. He said something I didn't hear because I turned my back to him.

Back at my vehicle, I slammed the door angrily.

I looked in the rearview mirror and muttered, "I swear to god. There's no way back to where I began."

I had more months of filmmaking and photography in Ethiopia. I wondered right then, who was crazier, Robert or myself?

I wondered if I wasn't becoming progressively unhinged by Ethiopia. Actually, at that moment, I worried about slipping away into darkness.

***

A Place Seldom Seen, Ethiopia, 1968

The country of Ethiopia in 1968 had a population of about fifty eight million people. It is a place of diverse languages and the multihued practice of different religions. Ethiopia is also the second most populous country in Africa and the largest landlocked country on earth. The country also possesses one of the most varied populations extant with more than eighty different tribal groups.

 Finally, Ethiopia contained the longest mountain chain in Africa, with peaks that rise to over 15,000 feet in altitude, then disappear into cloudscapes formed by the interchange between extremes of heat and cold.

In the trackless vastness of the Simien Mountains, linked only by narrow paths connecting hundreds of almost inaccessible villages, in the third century CE the Ethiopian Kingdom of Aksum became the first major empire in the world to officially adopt Christianity as a state religion. In the twelfth century, amid these mountains, the emperor Lalibela built a series of Coptic Christian churches hewn out of living rock.

For most of its history, Ethiopia has been a monarchy. In 1968, the country was ruled by Emperor Haile Selassie, who claimed ancestral roots in the second millennium BCE as a direct descendant of the Queen of Sheba. Additionally, Ethiopia was the site of the oldest Muslim settlement in Africa, which staged the first Muslim pilgrimage, or hegira in Islamic history.

It seemed strange to me that still in 1968 most people had heard of Ethiopia, but no one had ever been there. In Europe and America few people could locate Ethiopia on a map.

***

I arrived in the town of Lalibela the painless way: by air.

Unlike my journey into the Danakil Desert, I was dropped off at the new tourist hotel in Lalibela by a taxi. The hotel had a dining room. Hot water. Flush toilets. It contained a tastefully decorated lobby, which in turn had an incomparable, quite astonishing view of the mountains of central Ethiopia. Surrounded by these mountains I measured the actual pitch and steepness of them. Around me, above me, they climbed upward into jagged rock scarps before disappearing into the clouds.

Twenty minutes after I arrived in Lalibela, the rains began. They continued for the next four days. The rainy season had arrived in Ethiopia.

I retreated to my room.

On the bed, I settled my back against the wall. My Ethiopian guidebook presented a meager meal when it came to facts about this country. Published two years before, the guidebook stated that as late as the 1950s, the only way to reach Lalibela was a month long slog, by means of steep paths up and then down the Simien mountain chain. In some places during this journey, the peaks of the Simien rose into regions of ice and snow. The book warned that paths disappeared into impassible ice fields.

If you were unlucky and caught in the mountains above the tree line as ice storms swept in during the rainy season, you would be fortunate to escape the mountains alive.

Luckily for me, in the central area of the Simien Mountains, Ethiopian Airlines had recently begun a new service from Addis Ababa to Lalibela. It took a sixty-minute flight from Addis to reach Lalibela, if things went perfectly. In 1968, Ethiopian Airlines flew repurposed twenty-five-year-old World War II Douglas DC-3s. In Ethiopia, many things were still very uncertain, like airport arrivals and departures, and strange things that happened in between.

According to my guidebook, treks involving days or weeks to remote villages in the mountains could be arranged. But if you trekked during the rainy season, you had to be prepared for rockslides, trail washouts, and traveling scores of miles on hair-raising, dangerous mountain paths. Between the huge mountains were rushing rivers spanned by impermanent bridges. The article on trekking in the Simien Mountains pointed out that the trails themselves crept alongside bottomless chasms, and they were threatened at all times by momentary collapse.

There was a knock on my door.

Crossing the room, I picked up my bag where I kept my cameras. My guide stood there. He was a scruffy, middle-aged Ethiopian Coptic Christian priest. He had a magnificent smile and a painfully thin body that looked almost wraithlike. As we walked out of the hotel toward the caves at Lalibela, the priest began to narrate the salient facts of this strange and wonderful place now hidden by wisps of passing clouds.

In 1187, after the capture of old Jerusalem by Muslims, Emperor Lalibela had seen Jerusalem in a vision. As a result of his mystical vision, determined in the darkest part of the Christian night, he vowed to build a new version of Jerusalem amidst the almost inaccessible Simien Mountains.

Claiming descent from the Queen of Sheba some 2,000 years before, Emperor Lalibela traced a biblical line from King Solomon, who had seduced the Queen of Sheba and sired a son, Menelik, the first of 225 emperors of Ethiopia descended from King Solomon.

***

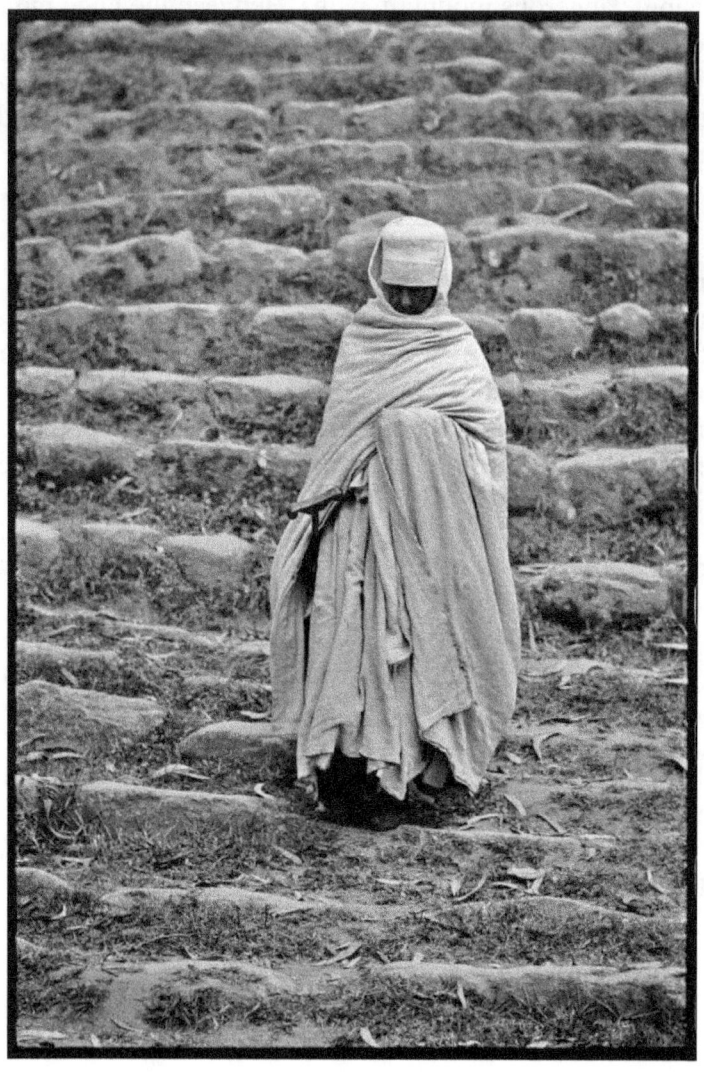

Ethiopian Coptic Christian Nun

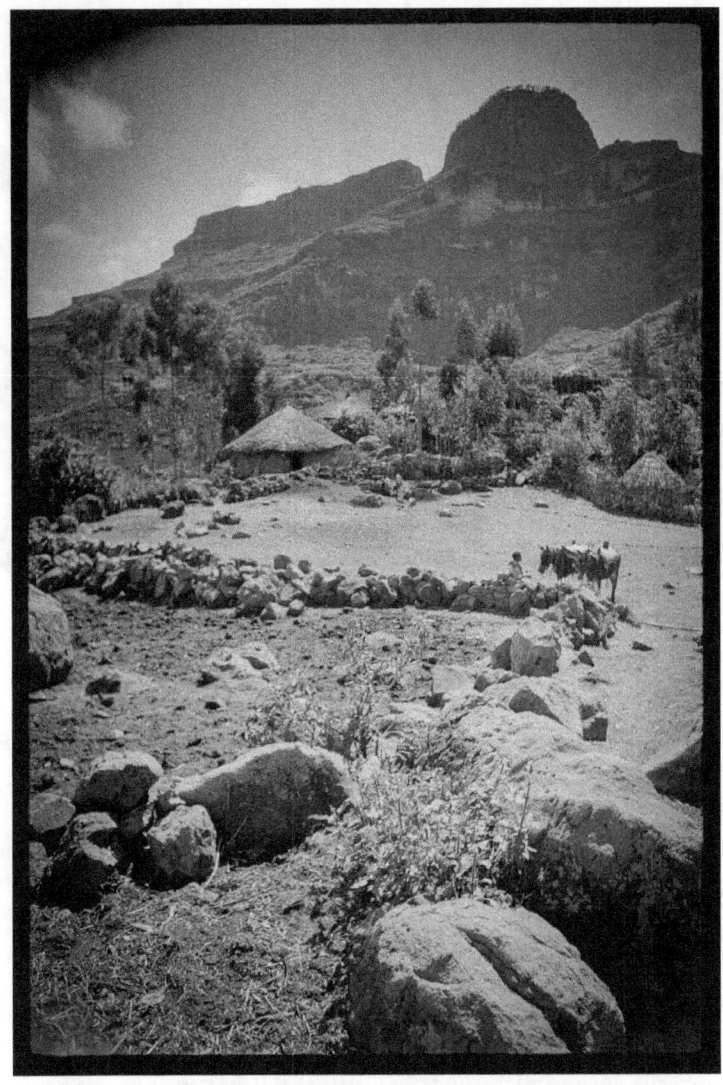

The Siemien Mountains, Lalibela

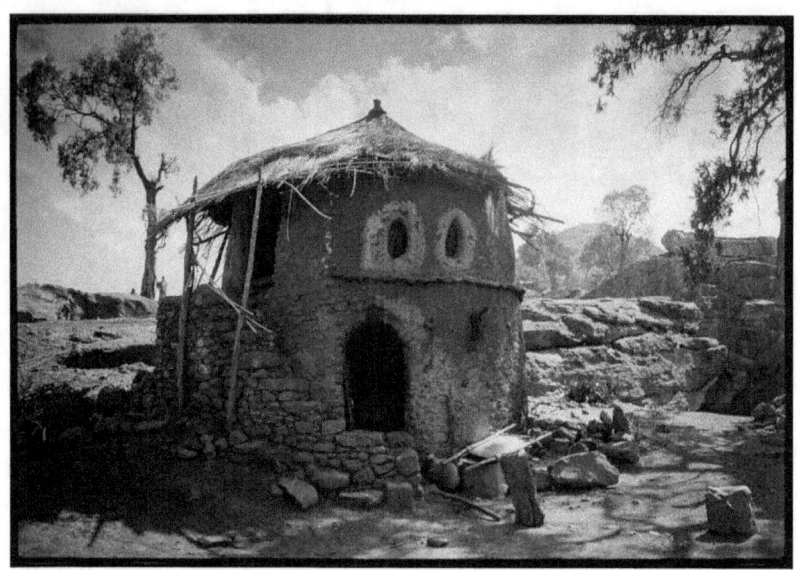

House, Simien Mountains, Lalibela

As part of his new kingdom of Jerusalem, Emperor Lalibela named many of the town's surrounding topographic features after biblical references. This included the renamed River Jordan, which flowed below the town of Lalibela toward the source of the Blue Nile.

To the Coptic Christians of Ethiopia, the town of Lalibela was second in holiness only to Aksum, the capital city of the ancient Kingdom of Sheba.

From the late twelfth century into the thirteenth century, Lalibela remained the capital of Ethiopia. Today, Lalibela is one of the holiest cities in the Christian world.

The rain fell in torrents now. Below me was the church of Saint George, or Bete Giyorgis. Hewn entirely out of living rock, the church was carved in the shape of a cross.

I took a deep breath.

Bete Giyorgis, as it was called in Amharic was the last church built of the eleven churches hewn at Lalibela. Among the least photographed major religious sites in the world, the rock-cut churches of Lalibela were gigantic. They were absolutely formidable human accomplishments.

I stood there staring down at the church. This was one of the holiest places on earth. Yet no one was here, few Europeans had ever come near this remote village. In the silence of this place, the only sound was the rain.

How very curious that in the mountains of central Ethiopia, an Imperial Roman tribune who had been tortured, then decapitated, for his refusal to denounce his Christianity would be venerated, then memorialized, in this fantastical work of art 900 years later, carved out of a mountainside.

Cautiously crossing patches of slippery moss, I approached the gigantic hole out of which Bete Giyorgis had been carved. One met a vertical plunge—a sixty-five-foot drop—into this extraordinary excavation.

Above the pit I stood there, staring.

Underfoot the mossy red lichen was exceedingly slippery. In the rain, it was like standing in a puddle of grease, as you perched at the edge of oblivion.

Next to me, my guide grabbed me and gently pulled me backward. Cautiously, together we moved toward the entrance to this miraculous church.

Bete Giyorgis was six sheer stories tall. The excavation in which it rested was ninety feet wide.

The eleven churches created by Emperor Lalibela were not constructed as much as excavated. First, a deep rock hole was dug into living rock, and then this hole was widened into a trench. Next, each church was eventually squared on all four sides as it was chiseled out of the living rock.

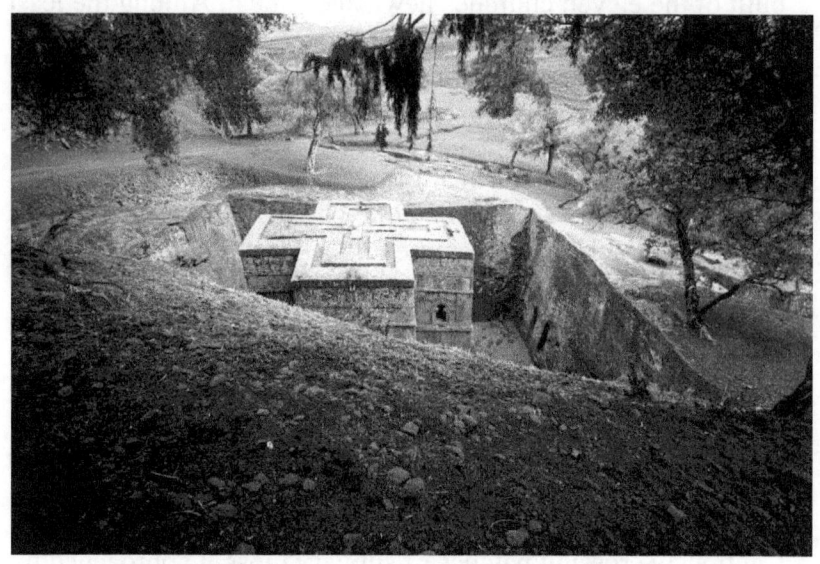

Bete Giyorgis, Twelfth Century Coptic Church, Lalibela

This form was cut into a freestanding obelisk, which in turn would become a church.

Over months and years, each obelisk was painstakingly carved down into a place of worship. The artisans involved in these constructions then turned to chiseling out the interior of each of the churches.

In the twelfth century, it must have been hard enough to enter these mountains, let alone create buildings like this. The site of Lalibela was so remote that even in 1968, only a few people had ever traveled there to see these astonishing churches or take photographs of them.

I wondered at the gigantic task of completing the eleven churches with only hammers and chisels to work with. It was an unbelievable labor of decades, and given the labor involved, it was perhaps akin only to the construction of the Great Pyramid in Egypt or the Kailasa Temple at Ellora in India.

Finally, I thought about the precarious nature of carving one of these churches.

If an artisan ran into a rotten seam of rock during the excavation or an earthquake damaged the structure, the men carving the structure would have to completely start over again in another place.

In India, I'd spent years photographing Buddhist, Hindu, and Jain caves built from the second century CE to the eighth century CE and carved out of solid rock. These were the lineal ancestors of Emperor Lalibela's caves. I'd learned in India that there were tricks to taking pictures of devotional rock-cut churches and temples. After many mistakes, I'd worked out that the best pictures always seemed to be taken from inside the caves looking outwards toward daylight.

You picked up the interior of the cave, but also the external details of cave construction.

Balancing my camera on rock ledges at Lalibela, I made long exposures then "bracketed" my several different exposures. I'd learned in India the idea of shooting from low angles, which gave interior architectural details a sense of their monumentality.

At Lalibela, one stood *inside* some of the most amazing sculptures ever created by man. They were carved by the bare hands of some of the greatest artisans who have ever lived.

Climbing out of the entrance tunnel, I looked upward at Bete Giyorgis.

The church absolutely filled the whole sky above me.

No one else was here. In the gently falling rain, the whole world seemed deserted.

As I passed from one church to the next, my only companion was the thin priest who guided me. Our conversation became a single word, *come*, as my guide-priest led me through dark corridors and more churches.

One by one we moved through courtyards, past places where a cliff had fallen away, and then into darkness and finally sunlight where you had views of the surrounding mountains. In sunlight Lalibela seemed to possess a shimmering almost unsubstantial reality.

***

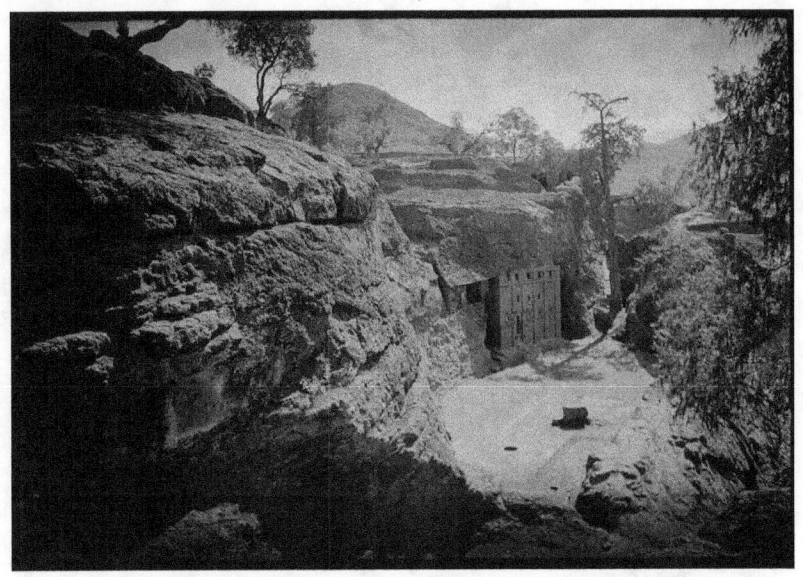

Rock-Cut Twelfth-Century Church, Lalibela

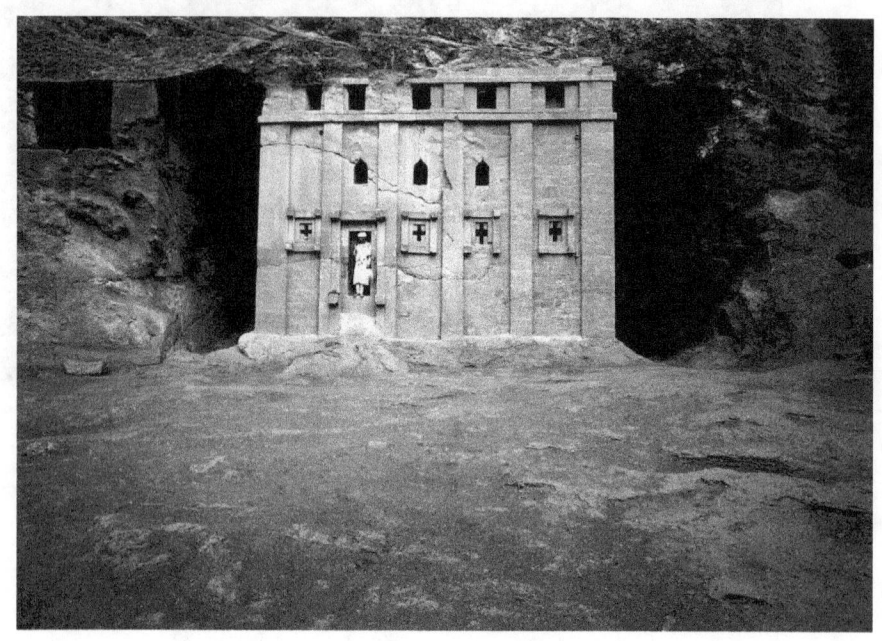

Rock-Cut Church, Lalibela

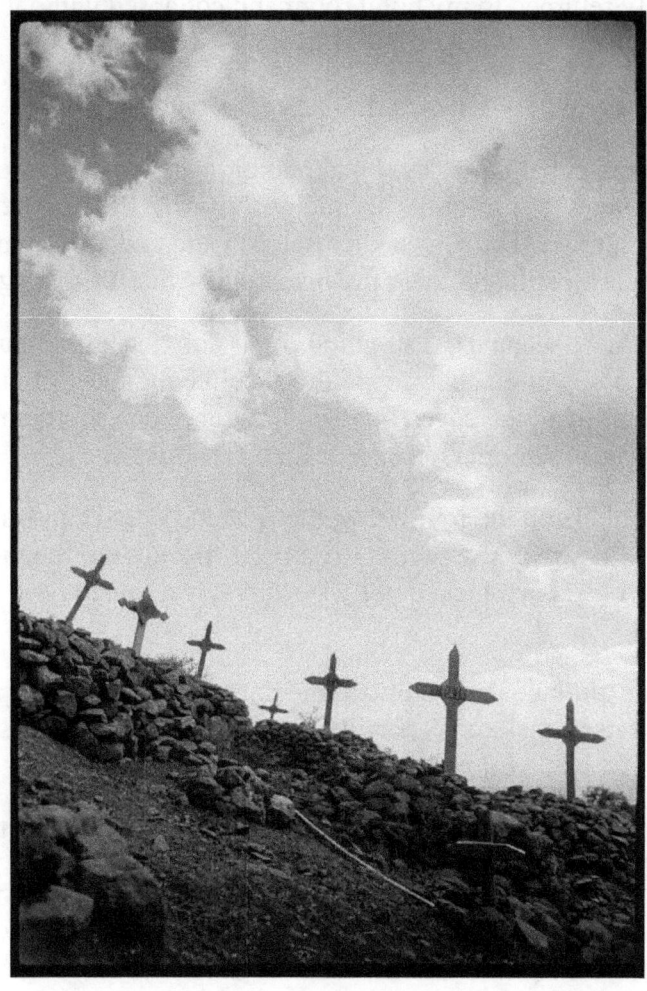

Coptic Graveyard, Lalibela

At the end of my third day photographing the caves at Lalibela, I finally returned to my hotel room and collapsed without eating dinner.

I was absolutely finished. Exhausted. Done.

At sunrise that third day, I had photographed what to me looked like graveyards from the second century CE. Each grave had a modest cross. The graves themselves were underneath mounds of stones. I still shot only my black-and-white Tri-X negatives.

Color here seemed a distraction. I felt only the chiaroscuro of black and white could record the absolute miracle of this place on film. In all the caves I passed through, I don't remember meeting another person except for a few priests.

At Lalibela on the fourth day, the first and only Douglas DC-3 since I'd arrived came into the airport. Because of the rains, the airport had been locked in by storms. It had rained heavily every day.

As the airplane taxied toward the huts serving as the airport, and while its propellers were still turning, the passengers descended quickly. Not a European came off the aircraft.

Five minutes later, it was revving its engines and about to take off. Twelve Ethiopians and myself had boarded the DC-3.

Outside the windows, it looked like another storm would break over the town at any moment.

Then the airplane hurtled down the runway and suddenly it lurched upward into the air. Fifty feet off the ground, the pilot violently turned the airplane away from a rapidly nearing mountainside ahead of us.

The DC-3 bucked against the change of direction. Staggering forward, it tilted now at an extreme gradient as it began to turn.

Slowly, ever so slowly, we gained altitude at right angles to the mountain, and then we were passing down into the valley beyond the town. Just as we reached the end of the valley, a truly monstrous rainstorm struck the airplane.

The storm hit so hard, I wondered if the aircraft would simply disintegrate. The winds jerked the whole plane upward, like a rubber ball bounding up a steep flight of stairs.

Then, suddenly, hail began pounding into the metal skin of the aircraft like gunshots.

Everything seemed to stop. It was as if we were frozen in time. We floated.

The storm began shaking the aircraft violently from side to side, like a huge dog had it between its teeth. Around me, all the Ethiopians were throwing up and simultaneously crying out in terror.

The shaking at that moment was replaced by something even more terrible when the pilot pulled back the stick to almost vertical. Now we fought for altitude. Slowly, ever so slowly, we climbed.

Five minutes later, it felt like I'd just swum off a huge waterfall and we were free-falling downward off a gigantic cliff. It was at that moment we broke into sunlight.

Lalibela and Ethiopia. A place of miracles. We were still somehow alive.

As the aircraft cut back its howling engines, I reached out slowly in a cold sweat. I patted the sides of this gorgeous airplane.

During World War II, 15,000 of these fantastic airplanes had seen service in every theater of the war. Each was an example of the greatest aircraft ever produced. How else could anyone describe these leftover remnants from another time in aviation, how enduringly reliable these superbly beautiful airplanes were?

How could you ever describe the renegade European and American pilots who flew these aircraft in places like Ethiopia? Was it even possible to describe the incredible men who had seen service and flown in every valley on earth that was flyable, and some that were not?   Thirty minutes later, we landed in Addis.

***

The Emperor of Ethiopia, Hailie Selassie I.

The returned messiah of the Bible, God incarnate to four million Rastafari

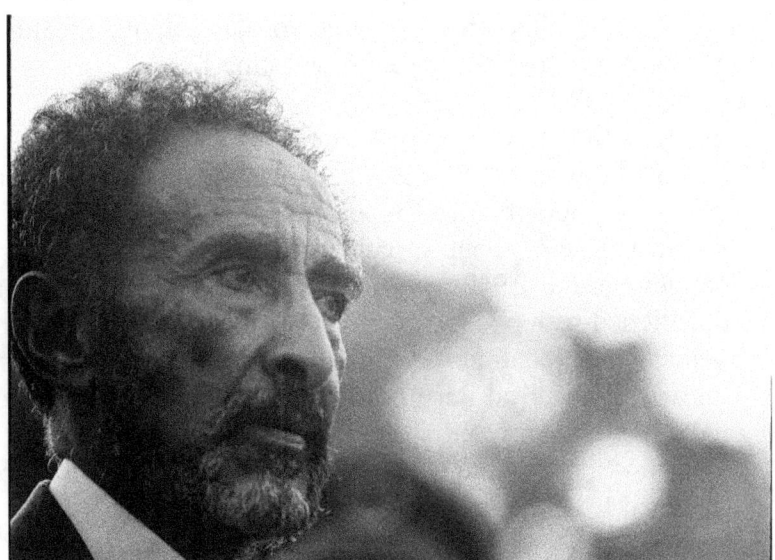

Ethiopia, Addis Ababa, June 1968

Addis Ababa was a city spread out over green, rolling highland hills.

In the center of the city was the main market, which was part Italian neorealist and part Middle Eastern souk. In the market were shops that mixed East African tribal goods with refrigerators, air conditioners, and electric fans.. Addis Ababa was the modern Amharic-speaking locus of an ancient Solomonic kingdom that had millennial connections to the central highlands of Ethiopia. The people of Ethiopia and Addis had soft chocolate-brown complexions and aquiline features. They were handsome, graceful, arresting

In India, the month before I came to Ethiopia, wedging myself past his bodyguards at a conclave of nonaligned nations in New Delhi, I'd photographed Emperor Haile Selassie.
When I thought about it, with the uncertain irony of nonaligned nations in the 1960s, the Ethiopians had been the original nonaligned nation since the period of Pharaonic Egypt. The few lamentable exceptions to Ethiopians' isolation from the rest of the world occurred during a British invasion of the country in the 1870s, then a grinding Italian invasion during the late 1930s. In a flip-flop of history, in the 1940s the Ethiopians were then liberated from the Italians by the British.

In Addis, little remained of the British incursions into the country, but the lasting effects of the Italian legacy were more long-lived. In 1968, 75 percent of the city of Addis Ababa dated from the period of Italian occupation. Even stranger were the scores of wonderful Italian restaurants sited in unlikely places and dotted around the country. Oddly, this same Ethiopian-Mediterranean hybridization gave the Ethiopians a unique Continental outlook. The always eclectic Ethiopian-

Mediterranean cuisine came if one wanted with pasta dinners and red wine.

Definitely, Ethiopia was a different version of Africa.

***

The stunning Joanie Mitchell and I had been in France, Germany, Italy, Sicily, the deserts of Pakistan, and then India for the last six months. We flew into Ethiopia from Bombay on a brand-new Ethiopian Airlines 707 jet with perhaps four other passengers. There was no one to meet us at the airport.

I had a crumpled piece of paper on which there was written an address in Addis. Studying the paper, we got into a taxi and arrived at the run-down house Robert Gardner had rented above the town. What struck one about Addis Ababa was how simple and basic Robert's needs were, and how basic our own needs would become. Most of Addis was one-story buildings. The people moved slowly with no hurry. No one seemed to possess any urgency in his life. The weather was in the mid-70s even in the rains.In the courtyard in front of Robert's house were two more or less functioning four-wheel-drive Japanese Toyota Land Cruisers. The personnel of our Ethiopian off road journeys were three Americans and two Ethiopians. Joanie was an art history student of Professor Ernst Gombrich at the Courtauld Institute of Art in London and a photographer.

Robert was a filmmaker affiliated with the century-old Peabody Museum at Harvard University in Cambridge, Massachusetts. I was a filmmaker-photographer. Among the Ethiopians who took care of us was Abdullah, our aforementioned translator-facilitator-factotum, who was an ethnic Afar and a Muslim. Our cook, Tekle, was Tigrean Christian from the highlands of Ethiopia. He specialized in Italian cooking of a miraculous Ethiopian sort.

What I discovered about Ethiopia the moment we arrived was that both physically and culturally it was one of the most diverse places on earth. It was also a place that virtually no one had photographed in any full-scale project of wide-ranging art documentation. We weren't photojournalists who traveled to distant and remote places staying a week making pictures. Cumulatively, Joanie and I were to stay in Ethiopia for six months.

The expedition Joanie and I joined, and our purpose for being in Ethiopia, was an odd sort of mongrel.

During the mid-1960s, few expeditions anywhere were staged to document tribal people in film and in photographs. The stated purpose of our expedition, staged from the Program in Ethnographic Film at Harvard University and the Smithsonian Institution, was to create a document of nomadic peoples. As Robert had previously found out in his wide-ranging travels, nomadic people, with few people paying any particular attention, seemed to have disappeared into extinction.

The intellectual academic rationales of our expedition were thus minimal and depressingly spare.

Seen in another way, perhaps, with a scarcity of human migratory groups, our expedition supported by Harvard University appeared to me to be an attempt to do the Indian rope trick without the rope.

While Robert and I were in the Danakil Desert, Joanie had been asked by Robert to do research in the university library in Addis. Joanie discovered that southern Ethiopia was one of the most remote places on earth and a place that few Europeans had visited in entire *centuries* of record keeping. It was Joanie who discovered the impossibly remote peoples of southern Ethiopia hidden in their thorn jungles.

After days in the library, Joanie had identified two tribes in southern Ethiopia as possible subjects of interest. They were the Galeb people on the Omo River and a tribe called the Hamar, who were barely mentioned and apparently evidenced only in rumor. As they were described, Joanie discovered this tribe as tantalizing unsubstantiated facts. Apparently, they dressed in skins and lived somewhere to the south of a town named Baco. Southern Ethiopia was, if Joanie's research was correct, less traveled than the most remote regions of Tibet. The Hamar occupied a difficult to enter and trackless area of jungle thorn.

A small sticking point to entering the areas occupied by these tribes was the impossible to obtain permission to enter much of Southern Ethiopia from the emperor. However, it seemed that thanks to our connections, we would obtain permission to enter any place in the country. That idea was about to be put to the test.

Armed with the little information he had from Joanie's weirdly productive library research, Robert asked for, and then received, an audience with Haile Selassie, the emperor.

What perhaps Joanie and I didn't appreciate while we waited for the day of Robert's audience was that southern Ethiopia was probably less traveled than even the regions of central Africa during the period of the grand explorations of Livingstone and Stanley in the nineteenth century.

In 1968, there were few dependable maps of Ethiopia. The roads in parts of the country existed only by hearsay, and they ranged from the passable to the nonexistent. What we learned in Addis Ababa was that few people knew anything about even the topography of southern Ethiopia or the districts of Ethiopia that abutted northern Kenya. One year earlier, Richard Leakey had gained permission from the emperor to enter the area of southern Ethiopia from Kenya, but apparently no one else had been allowed into the area.

The day of the emperor's audience came. Robert departed for it dressed in his almost ironed Abercrombie & Fitch explorer's bush jacket. During the audience, the emperor asked about Robert's trip into the center of the Danakil, and he then gave the Harvard–Smithsonian expedition additional permissions to enter southern Ethiopia. At the conclusion of the audience, Robert was allowed to have his photograph taken with the emperor and his heir apparent, the Duke of Wollo. Later, this photograph was to be of great help to our explorations.

***

For our journey off the macadam road grid into the unknown, we were equipped with two canvas Kenya-made ten-foot-by-eight-foot expedition tents. Robert slept in one. Joanie and I slept in the other. Each night, the expedition bedded down on the luxury of one inch-thick rubberized camping mats, and over the mats Joanie and I put our Indian-made cotton dhurrie rug that we'd bought in Rajasthan.

The domestic possessions of our journey were limited to the bare necessities.

Food on our expedition was supposed to originate either from "the bush," when we went out and shot our dinner, or from a stock of food brought with us into the bush: an ever-diminishing supply of what became badly dented tin cans.

We had a rickety hand-purifier pump for water that sometimes functioned, two shovels, four camp chairs, and a wobbly camp table. In our leader's Toyota, there was a refrigerator that somehow ran off the engine. In the refrigerator, the expedition kept its film supplies and, at my insistence, an antivenom snakebite kit.

Robert apparently didn't care whether he lived or died by a snakebite. We insisted on buying a snakebite kit. I worried that Robert's lack of fear of snakebites was an early warning sign of unspoken yearnings for ethnographic martyrdom. After the Danakil Desert, I shuddered at the thought.

I was learning in Ethiopia in a hard-won way that you never knew who someone was until you'd been with them in the bush for a month or two.

***

Southern Ethiopia, June 15, 1968

In her library research, there was a single additional story Joanie discovered. It was about to be tested, and it was a rumor that a north-to-south traverse of southern Ethiopia existed.

The road started at a place called Sodo. The road might or might not arrive at another place called Baco. This track was the sole, undefined, and seldom traveled traverse of the mountains of southern Ethiopia. It apparently offered the only way to get into the region.

As I read over Joanie's research, I was amazed that virtually nothing had ever been done in the way of documenting the tribes of southern Ethiopia. As far as the published record was concerned, her research confirmed this fact. So remote was southern Ethiopia from the world that it was a place both closed and virtually unknown.

Apparently, the last travelers to visit southern Ethiopia had attended the coronation ceremonies of Haile Selassie, who was crowned Emperor of Ethiopia in 1930. Two Dutchmen who attended the coronation later had visited the Konso people on the fringes of southern Ethiopia. They'd taken only a total of five photographs in an area that comprised 40 percent of the country.

That was it. Thirty-eight years before, five amateur snapshots had been taken of all the tribal people of southern Ethiopia.

A year earlier, members of the U.S. mapping personnel were thought to have made it into this area, but apparently no one knew if they were still in southern Ethiopia or if they'd been kidnapped by KGB operatives resident in Somaliland, then a Russian ally.

I thought about the disturbing idea that there was no way of knowing what awaited us in southern Ethiopia.

Competition for the most remote place on earth during the twentieth century was the Indian–Tibetan border region. Yet the arid regions of southern Ethiopia appeared to be even less accessible.

As we traveled down the macadam roads toward the south, it seemed to me that if the tantalizing rumors in Addis were true, in 1967 Richard Leakey had discovered the early fossils of *Homo sapiens* on the Ethiopian side of the Omo River in southern Ethiopia. It was a stunning find, and it would launch Leakey on a career that would surpass even the astonishing career of his father.

It was among strange coincidences that our own entrance into the remotest southern regions of the emperor's kingdom, at nearly the same moment, had been arranged only at the intercession of the emperor. If the dating of Leakey's fossils was correct, then in southern Ethiopia we might be able to reach, and then photograph, both a landscape and a people who still lived in the exact place where the first members of our species originated.

I thought about this heretofore utterly closed and inaccessible place.

With the road sinking down through highland geological formations, one bright morning, between rainstorms, we entered a countryside that was hotter and more humid.

Thanks to the rains, the whole countryside was now green. We headed toward the strangely named Lake Rudolf. Possessed of a strange 19th century association on the extreme southern border of Ethiopia, and the northern border of Kenya, the lake had been named in 1888 after Crown Prince Rudolf of Austria, by the Hungarian explorer Count Sámuel Teleki de Szék, the first

European to visit the lake. Later, Lake Rudolf was renamed Lake Turkana, after the Kenyan tribe on the southern side of the lake.

What one couldn't realize from the vantage point of Addis Ababa was the condition of the Italian-era roads in Ethiopia away from the large towns and cities. Few all-season roads existed in Ethiopia. Such roads that did exist were dirt tracks, usually ungraded, that were made impassible during the rainy season by the first stream, which the road met.

The problem was that if you wanted to get into southern Ethiopia, you had to come in overland from the north. Even though airstrips existed to supply both police posts and local imperial government functionaries, you couldn't fly into the area of southern Ethiopia. It was Hobson's choice. If you wanted to travel into the bush, you had to have vehicles. If you wanted to leave the airstrips and move both your supplies and equipment, the problem was that there were no wheeled vehicles to either buy or rent in southern Ethiopia.

In my first dawn in the humid lowlands, I wondered what was out there waiting for us on this traverse of southern Ethiopia that Joanie had discovered. The only person who probably knew the answer to that question was Richard Leakey.

During the last weeks, I'd speculated upon our presence in Addis Ababa and Ethiopia. There was one additional fact about Ethiopia and our work that, in retrospect, is important. But this information would not become public until thirty-seven years later, in 2005.

For decades it was reasoned that in southern Ethiopia, scientific enquiries would finally locate a site termed "the cradle of mankind." It was a near-mythical place where man's life on earth began. It was that place that answered every inquiry regarding where the germ plasmas of our species originated. The answer to this question was bound up by Richard Leakey's presence in southern Ethiopia and our own.

To give a precise idea of exactly how remote southern Ethiopia was from the world, during 1967 the noted paleoanthropologist and the father of Richard Leakey   Louis Leakey had met the emperor of Ethiopia, Haile Selassie, at an improbable luncheon at the Nairobi Club in Kenya. Sitting next to Leakey, the emperor had asked why all the fossils he was finding were in Kenya or on the Tanzanian border, and not in Ethiopia?

Leakey turned the emperor's question into a conversation about excavations in the Great Rift Valley, and finally into never-before-granted permissions to enter the previously closed southern regions of Ethiopia. He pointed out to the emperor that no one had looked for fossils in Ethiopia because no one was allowed to enter southern Ethiopia.

It was Leakey's idea to excavate the remotest regions of the Omo River and the drainage areas that emptied into Lake Rudolf. The emperor agreed to a Richard Leakey-mounted expedition, a first-ever effort.

Months later, on his first attempt to cross the Omo River from Kenya into Ethiopia, Richard Leakey and his expedition were almost devoured by astonishingly gigantic twenty-foot Nile crocodiles. The expedition members escaped alive, but the crocodiles succeeded in literally devouring the expedition's boat.

In a second attempt, now equipped with a metal boat to cross the formidable barrier of one of the most remote rivers on earth, Leakey, age 23, and his expedition managed to penetrate the formerly inaccessible landscape of southern Ethiopia.

In a few short weeks the excavations conducted by both Leakey, and the Kenyan ethnopalentologist Kamoya Kimeau, resulted spectacularly in the unearthing of the oldest fossilized *Homo sapiens* remains ever discovered. The definitive dating of these remains, even if they had been delayed by decades, are still extraordinary

"Fossil Reanalysis Pushes Back Origin of *Homo Sapiens*." *Scientific American,* Feb. 17, 2005. http://www.scientificamerican.com/article/fossil-reanalysis-pushes/

(Excerpt) "A new analysis of human remains first discovered in 1967 (in the Kibish formation on the Omo River by Richard Leakey and Kamoya Kimeu) suggests that they are in fact much older than previously believed.... researchers analyzed the volcanic ash layers above and below the river sediment that contained the fossils using argon dating.

They determined that the rock just below the fossils dated to 196,000 years ago. Because the layers of the Kibish Formation formed quickly during wet seasons that inundated the area with organic matter, the team posits that the bones are only slightly younger than this underlying layer".

Thirty years after the original finds, a detailed stratigraphic analysis of the area surrounding the fossils was carried out only after the great difficulties of actually getting to the site which included a revolution that closed Ethiopia to the rest of the world for twenty years, and the murder of the emperor.

If one then divides the age of a standard generation of man at thirty years by 195,000 years, 6,500 generations of mankind have continuously lived in southern Ethiopia. The article cited above has not been generally circulated. Have I been one of the few people living doing my long-division sums correctly?

During the last weeks since Joanie had turned in her research, I'd speculated about southern Ethiopia.

Data was perplexingly scarce about the region. It was a small detail to our own journey that our leader apparently didn't have any idea who the indigenous peoples of southern Ethiopia were. Nor what they looked like. Nor, actually, where they were.

The people who inhabited the Lake Rudolf region were the Oromotic tribes, who spoke ancient Cushitic, the second oldest language on earth. The areas adjacent to the lake were reported to be infested by outcast *shifta* bandits, or the Somali cousins of the Afar, who murdered their hapless captives in various unpleasant ways.

Did anyone know anything about the smaller groups of tribal people who lived in Ethiopia? No one had studied them. No one had photographed them. The deepest problem of all was quite simple: How did you discover whether these rumored tribes even existed?

For Joanie and me, the single hope I had was that a road existed between a place called Sodo and another place named Baco.

I hoped the light rains would not change to heavy rains. If we made it to Baco, we would then be faced with the next question: Did the Hamar exist? No one had photographed them. There was only a vague idea of where they were supposed to live.

Not well-prepared direction-wise, we left the last paved road and traveled into the regions of southern Ethiopia without even a map. A map of southern Ethiopia didn't exist.

***

A day later.

Ahead of us was a six-by-six U.S. Mapping Mission two-and-half-ton military truck with three axles and ten huge tires.

The truck was embedded crosswise, literally, in the middle of the narrow track.

Normally, the cab window of these huge trucks was six and a half feet above the road. The truck was stuck literally up to its door handles in concrete-hard dried mud.

Robert and I stood there. We looked down the track ahead. We looked back at the six-by-six truck. Wedged as it was into the mud, the truck was an awesome accident of travel.

I couldn't imagine Robert's feelings. This road was the latest beginning of a journey that was now years of travel. I took a deep breath.

Joanie came up. For a moment, she looked at the truck. Then she said a single word: "Heavens."

Beyond the six-by-six, the road seemed almost dried out. A quarter of a mile ahead of us down the track, the road disappeared around a bend.

Who knew when the rains would begin again? Staring at the huge truck, I couldn't imagine a vehicle this large, with ten tires for traction, becoming stuck like this.

We considered turning back. Instead, Robert and I walked the track together.

For half a mile we continued on, and the track looked perfectly fine. Our Land Cruisers had plenty of gas. We had come-alongs to which we could attach a six-foot length of cut-down steel railway track. With two sledgehammers, the idea was to pound our railway metal into the ground, then attach one end of the come-along to the railway steel while the other end could be attached to a Toyota.

Again we discussed the idea of returning to Addis. We could possibly fly into Baco. But then in Baco, how would we find transport into the areas we hoped would be inhabited by the Hamar?

We bypassed the six-by-six and got back onto the track.

That day, it was fine. We made a slow but steady ten miles or so. We made camp and celebrated by eating a can of Polish ham.

The next day, we hit the mud. Our plan had been to winch our vehicles forward out of door-deep mudholes with our come-alongs. Forward to Baco! Dream on. We were making a huge miscalculation of travel.

For the next eight days, as we winched our way forward down this terrible killing track, progress became a suppurating, bruised, and battered miasma.

I stopped counting the number of times we drove our six-foot piece of railway steel into the ground. From 7:00 a.m. until 9:00 p.m., we struggled forward down the road. On this entire journey, we didn't see another vehicle besides the abandoned six-by-six until our last day.

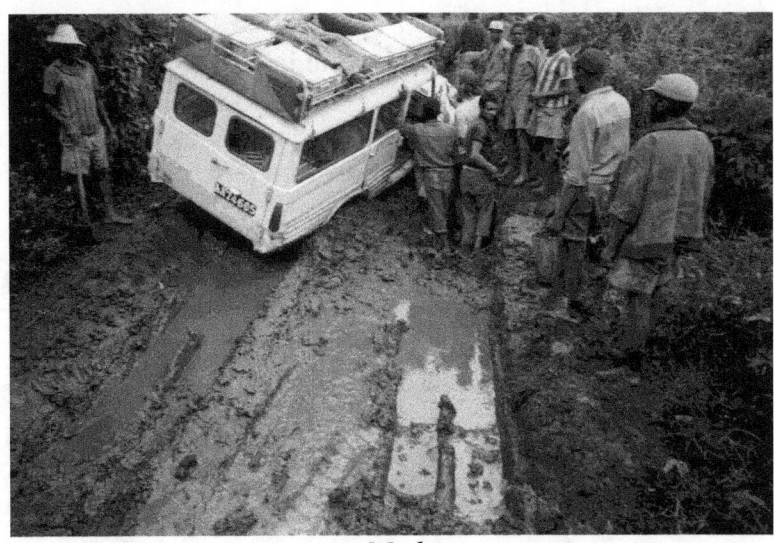

Mud

At the end of four days on the track, after fording the seventeenth, or the seventy-fifth, barely passable bog that the track had become, then climbing up and down nameless mountains, between the deep mudholes and the rain, our more or less workable Toyotas had been turned over, dented, broken, battered, and then crumpled into scrap heaps of junk metal.

On one horrendous day, after six hours under one of our Toyotas attempting repairs, we managed to thread one suspension bolt into one engine mount.

Bone-weary, covered in grease, and exhausted, I prayed that on one of the Toyotas, the engine would leap out of the engine compartment like Pegasus taking flight and destroy the radiator and fan assembly, and the Toyota would die a well-deserved, peaceful death. Then we could walk to Baco like Indian sadhus without possessions. Screw the cameras and Leni Riefenstahl's lenses.

On our eighth day of this horror journey, at the end of a final scarp of mountains, our Toyotas clawed their way up a boulder-pitted narrow track.

We were at the absolute limits of our endurance.

We managed to climb over an irregular-shaped four-foot-high boulder and reached the top of the last unnamed, ghastly mountain.

Ahead of us, the track suddenly moved across a wide, grassy plain.

Was this a final cruel joke?

We'd felt betrayed too often on this journey to think that it could ever end. Each of us on this journey to hell had given up hope.

I was beyond sure that the grassy plain would be another obstacle. Or that perhaps the road would do a vanishing act and simply disappear. One moment it would be there; the next, it would vanish and take any traveler caught on it to the center of the earth.

At the top of the mountain, I ate two heaping tablespoons of dehydrated coffee dry for a last jolt of instant caffeine energy enhancement. Our food was mostly gone. Our hands were cracked, and our fingers were bleeding from badly healed cuts.

Again we fired up our battered Toyotas. A half hour later, the road turned into a swamp.

Getting out of the Toyota, I stood there with Joanie at the edge of the swamp. In the heat, we sank down alongside some huge boulders to consider our position.

Robert was completely mute. He didn't say a word. He sat in the shade of another boulder. We were beyond weeping. It took too much effort, and we had no more tears.

***

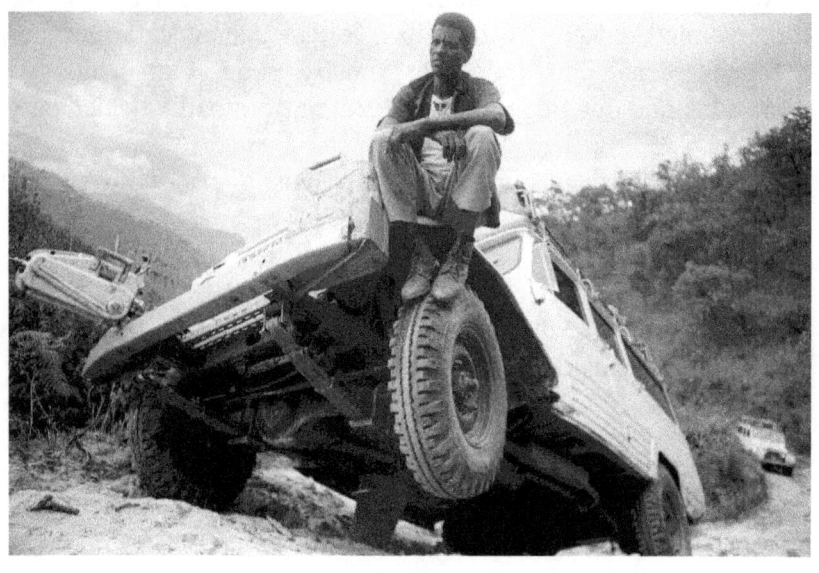

The Final Scarp, Tekle the Amhara

Southern Ethiopia, the Road to Baco, June 25, 1968

At the edge of the swamp, after half an hour of consideration, we laid out our options.

I wasn't happy about our choices. We needed two drivers of the Toyotas to get across the swamp that lay there in the heat, suppurating like a rotting soup, ahead of us. We decided that Abdullah and Joanie would go ahead on foot to Baco, which we calculated was somewhere seven to fifteen miles to the south.

Joanie agreed. She wasn't happy about this.

The plan was for Joanie and Abdullah to board a 1:00 p.m. biweekly airplane, which was supposed to fly out of Baco to connect to another transit airport.

From there, they would then board a bus to Addis. In Addis, Joanie was to obtain new parts for our shattered Toyotas. This included leaf springs, mangled and now taped together electrical parts, and carburetor solvents for melting the dirt and gum that clogged our fuel lines.

When Joanie and Abdullah reached Baco, but before they boarded the airplane for Addis, Abdullah would enlist a rescue party to return to where we'd gotten stuck in the swamp. In Ethiopia, the police in every moderate-sized town were equipped with Mercedes-Benz four-wheel-drive military Unimogs, which sometimes worked.

It was a lovely plan.

As Joanie and Abdullah circled away to the south, moving on foot along the verge of the steaming miasma of the swamp, I stood there, watching them disappear. They hugged a low line of hills, and then they were out of sight. This was something that East Coast ladies of a certain persuasion had never done.

I was already feeling guilty about sending Joanie off with Abdullah.

Perhaps the airplane wouldn't come that day? Perhaps we had the wrong day? Who even knew what might happen to Joanie on her journey to Addis, and who knew what greeted Joanie and Abdullah in Baco?

How could things have gotten this terrible? How could everything have gone this wrong?

Robert or I could have gone down that track to Baco just as well as Joanie.

I slumped down in the shade of some large rocks and waited for our rescue. Who knew how long we'd have to wait for the police and their Unimog from Baco? I sat there against the rocks, which grew hotter and hotter. I was filled with depression about the terrible road we'd come down and our situation. Very little had gone right for us in the last week.

Two hours later, in the distance I heard a noise. I couldn't quite define this noise. It somehow didn't fit into the silences of this remote place.

I stood up and looked toward the west.

The sound resolved itself into the rumbling of huge diesels. The sound seemed to be moving toward us, but we'd calculated that Baco was another direction, in the south. This sound was coming from the wrong direction.

Forty-five minutes later, out of a shimmering heat mirage hanging over the swamp, cresting a ridge to the west materialized the two most truly azure-blue Fiat trucks I'd ever seen.

These trucks were gigantic.

I'd heard talk of these sixteen-wheel rigs. They were operated by multi-tribal crews and owned by Lebanese or Greek traders. In the mid-1960s, these huge machines were the modern lifelines of the African bush.

Crossing entire mountain chains and deserts, these vehicles traveled in linked relays across the width of Africa to the Atlantic. Perhaps these trucks were on their way to Kenya or Somaliland?

The trucks had appeared out of the region of the Omo River, perhaps a hundred miles to the west.

Slowly, the trucks approached, and then they stopped in front of us.

Climbing down from their rigs, the truck crews gawked at us.

The top kick of these crews began bellowing in Amharic. He approached Tekle, our Amharic cook, and in a few moments, they were shouting at each other.

Their leader was a huge man with broken teeth and a bull neck. Tekle waved his arms and shouted. The top kick bellowed back. Then, after a couple of minutes of this strange conversation, they both broke into smiles. Something had been agreed.

Tekle approached Robert. He reported that we'd get a tow across the swamp. The crews of these trucks would see to it that we reached Baco.

The payoff was extortionate, however. Smiling at us, the huge man next to Tekle wanted our last case of beer and $150 in cash.

So much for foreign travel and a wider, happy knowledge of the world beyond Ethiopia.

Robert, a true parsimonious tightwad, sired by many generations of closefisted Boston merchants, was about to object. But he clenched his teeth and nodded. I wanted to see if he'd smile in relief at our salvation. He didn't.

The top kick screamed his orders to his troops in Swahili, mounted the lead truck, and shoved the driver out of the way. Inside five minutes, the truckers had attached both of our Toyotas to the rear of their two absolutely awesome trucks.

With the blast of a gigantic air horn, the huge man ripped the lead truck into gear.

Looking upward at the truck ahead of me, I felt I was a minnow about to be towed along by a whale.

Inside our Toyotas moments later, we were yanked forward then towed across what became two and half very long miles of swamp. We forged ahead, towed along a submerged and unseen track somewhere below us.

Within a minute, mud had coated our Toyotas, and we were turned into blinded, strangely life-size toy vehicles in comparison to the trucks ahead of us. We looked, I imagined, like we'd been dipped in chocolate from the action of the wildly spinning wheels ahead of us.

The trucks ahead of us were absolutely gigantic. All I could see, using my windshield wipers occasionally, were the spinning wheels of the truck in front of me. Looking at the backseat briefly, I wondered where Abdullah was at that moment? Usually, Abdullah rode behind Joanie on our ghastly journey of the last days.

***

Southern Ethiopia, Baco, June 25, 1968

Somehow, we made it to Baco. At 2:00 p.m., we reached the town.

The first thing Robert did was to go into a bar and order a beer. I was two steps behind him, and I slumped at a table next to Tekle, exhausted.

The lady who owned the bar watched Tekle from across the room. Tekle asked around if a white woman and her translator had taken the Baco-to-Addis airplane that departed that day?

The woman stared at Tekle. She then answered that the Somali Abdullah was in jail. She made a motion to her head holding a pistol; her index finger pulled the trigger.

We just stared at Tekle as he translated this information.

After both Robert and I had struggled across the eighth littoral of hell to get to Baco, we were in irritable, completely foul moods.

"Unbelievable." Robert finally managed to ask, "Is Joanie with him?"

Carefully, Tekle asked where the white woman was who had been with Abdullah? Was she in jail as well?

The owner of the bar smiled with a mouth full of gold teeth.

Tekle translated the woman's reply. "She says that the white woman passed out of sight on an airplane. She has left the town."

Robert rose from the table slowly. He walked back through the door of the bar.

I saw him through the window walking back to his Toyota, where he grabbed his briefcase from the backseat.

Slamming the door in white-hot anger, Robert stalked down the street toward the jail.

In the distance, down a long street, the captain of police stood there, watching us.

Clutching his briefcase, and ahead of Tekle and myself, down the dusty street Robert approached the captain of the police.

Politely, the police chief stepped aside and waved us into the jail ahead of him.

In the darkness of the little jail, the first thing we saw was Abdullah, who was in a dirty rear cell.

Abdullah was the worse for wear. He certainly hadn't left on the supposedly biweekly flight to Addis with Joanie. He looked like a man who knew that he'd be shot the next morning at dawn in a country where there existed a bare minimum of justice.

Without speaking, Robert made a remarkable show by first raising his battered briefcase, then slamming it down onto the captain's desk. All the buried frustrations of Ethiopia that Robert had gathered were now about to explode.

At the rear of the jail, Abdullah stared at us like a caged, terrified animal. His complexion was actually gray.

As I stood there watching Robert, I thought about us waiting for a police Unimog that had never been sent, and of Abdullah and his arrest.

With a theatrical gesture, Robert whipped open his briefcase. Wordlessly, he extracted a photograph.

I waited for Robert to do his bureaucratic juju.

Raising the photograph, he held it six inches in front of the police captain's face. It was a picture of himself with the Duke of Wollo, the emperor's son.

Robert stood there, shaking the photograph in front of the captain's face, and he shouted to Abdullah in his cell. "Translate this, please: 'Do you see this? Look carefully at this photograph. Do you see me and this man? Do you know who this man is?'"

Robert's voice was quaking with anger now. Behind the captain, at the rear of the jail, Abdullah fearfully translated.

It was now the Captain's turn to turn gray. The policeman looked at the photograph. He tried to speak, but nothing came out save a gurgle.

The Duke of Wollo ran much of Ethiopia, as well as the Ethiopian army and the Ethiopian police.

Next, Robert produced his trump card of an important Ethiopian photographic document.

He drove the picture down onto the desk in front of the captain with the slap of his palm.

As if his eyes were now reading his own death sentence, the chief of police's gaze moved to the desk. The photograph was a picture of the Emperor of Ethiopia, signed by the emperor himself. It showed Haile Selassie shaking hands with Robert.

I must say that at that moment, Robert looked very natty in his explorer's bush jacket, complete with his nifty bush belt tied carelessly, even rakishly.

I glanced over at the policeman. Was it possible that the captain might have a heart attack at that moment? He was clutching the middle left side of his chest and breathing huge, stentorian breaths.

The captain's hands literally shook as he picked up the emperor's picture. Then he bent forward and began kissing the picture. Behind him, a lieutenant and three policemen had appeared. With a movement that was almost devotional, the captain placed the picture on the desk carefully. He turned around, and in Amharic, the captain began shouting at these men, blaming everything on them.

Abdullah was released from his cell in great haste while Robert glared at the police captain.

There was a bruise on Abdullah's face. His clothes were rumpled. Were those gouges on his face? During the past few hours, Abdullah looked somehow as if he'd shrunken inward.

Abdullah didn't say goodbye to the captain but bolted out of the police station like a ravening pack of dogs was after him.

Gathering himself together, the captain offered his profuse and stuttered apologies. Next came his explanations suddenly in quite good English.

He described local conditions on the southern borders of Ethiopia and Somaliland next door. There was a war going on. He described Abdullah and the white woman's perplexing appearance in the town.

Evidently, there was little love lost between the emperor's Muslim subjects like Abdullah and his more numerous Christian subjects.

Beer was served.

The captain of police promised a feast tonight to make up for his minions' insensible mistakes. This was all a terrible mistake.

He explained that, as southern Ethiopia abutted the *shifta*-ridden areas of neighboring Somaliland, when these fell into the hands of the Christian Ethiopian police, they were taken into the thorn jungle. I think he described the process as "disappearing over the horizon."

For their part, the Somali *shifta* had a bad habit of summarily executing any Christian Ethiopian military personnel or police that fell into their hands.

Tit for tat. The police chief threw his arms wide and shrugged elaborately.

Because Abdullah had appeared with a white woman from the bush, of course he hadn't been taken to visit "the thorn jungle." Instead, he was being detained for careful examination.

According to the captain, Abdullah had some made-up story about white people appearing down a seldom-traveled road that was generally considered impassible at all times of the year except for the huge trading trucks from the Omo River regions and the west. No one had ever appeared on Baco Road during the rains. The police believed the road was impassible.

The name of the town was not Baco, by the way. It was Baco.

From time to time, the captain still glanced at Robert's picture of Robert with the emperor. No doubt the captain was considering his own possible encounter with the emperor's well-known and quick judicial impatience.

The dinner the captain put on for us was marvelous. The captain had learned his English at school in Addis. At the end of the dinner, he promised eternal service to our interests while we were in southern Ethiopia. He even promised a translator who spoke Hamar.

***

Southern Ethiopia, Baco, June, 27 1968

Two days later Joanie returned.

In Addis she had to charter an airplane, because Ethiopian Airlines was not scheduling any flights to the south until the rains broke. This was forecasted to be "An indeterminate period of time".

After a great struggle in assembling the Toyota parts we needed she found a charter pilot and an airplane. Aided by either great luck or perhaps magic she arrived at our camp outside Baco with three huge boxes of car parts.

Joanie looked tired, and battered as she climbed out of the airplane. "You have no idea how horrible my trip was," she said. "No. Idea."

"You have no idea how horrible our trip was either," I countered.

I'd come to hate the thought that the Captain would have murdered Abdullah, while we waited only a few miles away for the police who were supposedly reaching us with their Unimog.

In Baco we'd finally discovered the police Unimog behind a boarded up building.

It was resting upon four separate piles of bricks wedged under each empty wheel rim. The tires had been sold or stolen. The engine compartment had been gutted. The body was a rusted hulk.

Robert crossed to the boxes Joanie had brought without a single word of greeting. Perhaps he was fuming at the cost now of an air charter.

I watched him as I was now fuming at his rudeness to Joanie.

Joanie explained to Robert, "...the rains closed in on Addis. There were no flights back here so I had to do a charter. What was terrible was that the rains really locked down over the mountains when we were coming back down here."

Robert didn't answer. He opened one box and then the next.

"That pilot must be the most exceptional pilot on earth." Joanie paused. "There were mountains above us in the clouds. We had to fly down inside a river gorge *following a rushing river.*"

Robert stood there looking down at the boxes Joanie had brought.

Joanie continued her narrative, "... finally we flew out of the gorge, along caravan and camel tracks. The pilot had to use an Ethiopian road map at the end to get to Baco."

Robert stood five feet away.

He turned to Joanie. Slowly, he put his hands on his hips. The only thing he said was, "You know... I think you should know you brought the wrong parts."

Joanie simply looked at him. Tears filmed her eyes.

She turned, and slowly she retreated to our tent.

At our tent she looked back at me, then she pulled the tent flap down behind her.

Across the field the pilot took off. He and his airplane became just a speck against the mountains, then he was swallowed by the clouds.

I looked up at the towering thunderheads above the mountains in the distance.

I wondered how anyone could possibly have come down through those mountains and lived to tell the story. Madness. This whole journey had become complete madness.

I turned and stared at Robert.

 I didn't say anything. It took a huge amount out of me not to say anything. Instead I crossed to our tent.

Inside the tent Joanie sat there on our sleeping bags staring at her hands.

She looked up at me. Tears streaked her cheeks. I sat down next to her and hugged her.

"I'm sorry this whole thing has turned out so badly. I'm glad you're back." I was speaking about our whole trip to Ethiopia.

"I'm sorry. I'm so terribly sorry."

Joanie began to cry as I stoked her hair.

"It took me a day to get to Addis. I spent the whole first night in a terrible little hotel before I could get the bus to Addis. Drunks banged on the door all night long to get into my room. It was horrible."

Joanie paused.

"I finally managed to get the parts. I was then barely able to convince that poor pilot to make this trip back down here. Now this." She asked," What did I do wrong?"

"You are my fabulous darling," I said through my own tears now. "You're incredible," I whispered.

I'd deserted Joanie, again.

Before this I'd left her in Addis to do a shoot in the Danakil Desert with a hole in her head from an eye infection. I'd left her to go off on my own imagined professional duties to Robert Gardner.

Then, I dragged Joanie down the road to Baco or whatever this goddamn place was called. Finally, I was the one who'd asked her to go to Addis.

"How am I supposed to know what the right parts are?" Joanie asked. "How did I know these were the wrong parts? I gave the dealer in Addis the list of everything Robert gave me. I tried as very hard as I could."

Terrible. This was absolutely terrible.

At dinner that night no one spoke to each other.

Cambridge seemed a long way away. Everything in the whole world seemed astonishingly far away.

We managed to get through dinner. All of us. It was one of the greatest theatrical performance's I've ever seen at least Joanie's part and my own.

Five years later, at an eastside New York dinner party the subject of African bush pilots came up.

I mentioned Joanie's trip from the highlands of Ethiopia at the height of the rainy season to Baco.
The man next to me turned to me. He asked me the pilot's name. I told him.

The man stared at me for a long astonished moment.

"I've flown with this guy," he said. "That man is the greatest African bush pilot in east Africa."

The man paused as he looked at me. "I want to tell you that during the rains in those conditions flying into the Ethiopian highlands your lady is a very lucky person to still be alive. There is no reason why anyone has a right to, nor could anyone expect to survive that trip. "

The man looked at me. No doubt he was imagining his own horrors of flying into the Ethiopian highlands during the rains.

"I think that the African bush pilots as a group are the best pilots on earth. I've flown everywhere in the world where there are bush pilots but somehow your wife found the absolute best bush pilot on earth. That's his reputation."

I looked down at my hands. My knuckles were bone white.

***

The First Place, the Cradle of Mankind, late June–July 1968

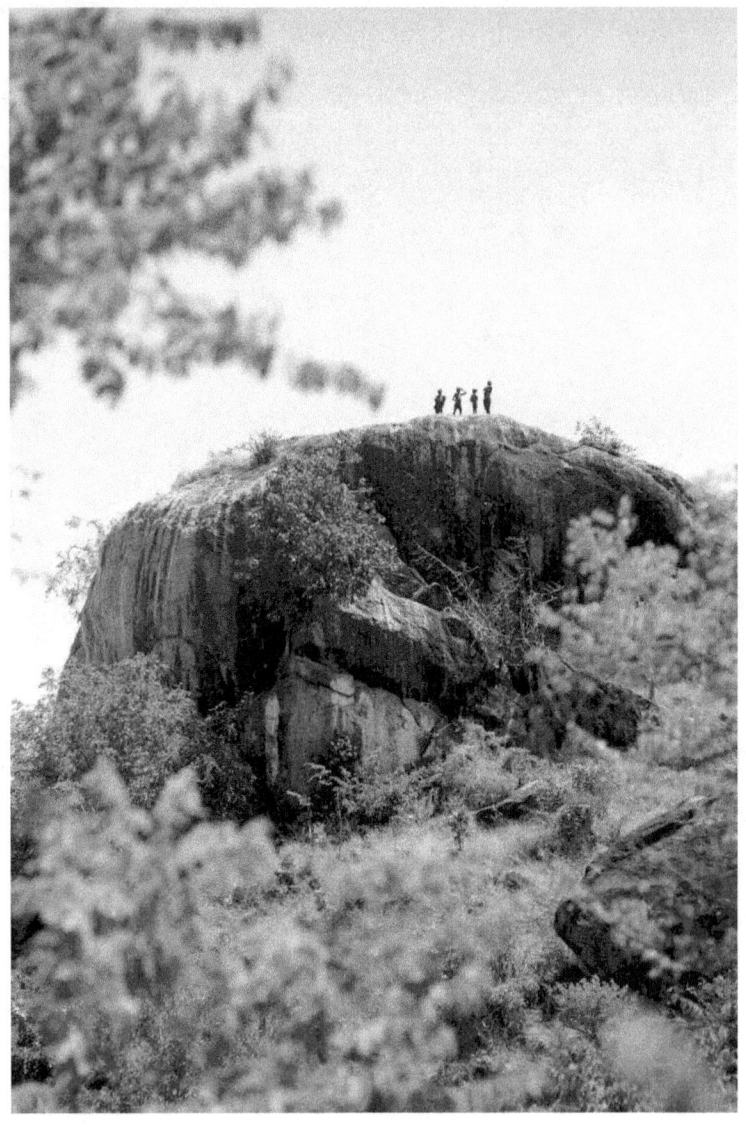

Southern Ethiopia, the Hamar People, Encounters

A month earlier, in Addis, Joanie had discovered the first hints of the Hamar in a two- paragraph text. No photographs of these people existed with this brief text. Apparently, they lived near a place called Turmi. In Addis, only a few people could even identify exactly where the Hamar lived. They were thought to live in the middle of a thorn jungle bisected by dry riverbeds of sand.

In Baco, Robert engaged the translator supplied by the police captain. Our translator explained carefully that the Hamar were a peaceful people. I wondered: Was he reassuring himself or us?

Beyond the town behind us, out the windows of our Land Cruisers, the topography was an immeasurable, featureless landscape. In the distance were the occasional ancient hills that time had worn away.

Approximately sixty miles down the track from Baco, we came to a sand river crossing the road.

Our guide motioned toward the right side of the road. We got out of the Toyotas and began to walk up the river of sand, ringed by thorns, in the direction that our guide pointed.

Near a place called Turmi we found the Hamar. They lived in an area occupied by mankind for uncounted millennia. I had the feeling we were walking back into time while immured in a trackless scrub of thorn jungle. According to the dating of the paleontological remains discovered by Richard Leakey, this is where our species began.

Twenty minutes later, around a bend in the empty sand river, we encountered two naked men.

Our guide approached them. They seemed to be anointing themselves with a white-colored mud. Later, we found out that their body decoration was in preparation for a ceremony that would take place later that day.

Our translator-interlocutor explained that we had come a long distance to visit this place. We asked if we could take pictures.

They seemed unsurprised by our appearance. The two men smiled broadly. Our guide made introductions for us.

We were perhaps the first Europeans to see these people. Neither man knew what cameras were or photography was.

Joanie and I began taking pictures....

In the next weeks, we filmed and took photographs of the Hamar tribe. They lived fifty miles north of Lake Rudolf. To the west, over another set of featureless hills, was the place where, the year before, Richard Leakey had discovered the earliest dated *Homo sapiens* remains. Both Leakey and we stood on the same earth inhabited by the earliest men.

Over the course of the next two months, we made the first films and the first photographs of the Hamar. We also ranged to the south toward Lake Rudolf and the Omo River.

No one I could discover, however, had ever ventured near the places we photographed above Lake Rudolf and below Baco. Possibly the person who came closest to this place was the young American photographer Peter Beard, who had photographed Lake Rudolf and the gigantic Nile crocodiles of the Omo River in 1965.

Since the Hamar didn't know what photography or film was, they were oblivious to the presence of cameras and what a camera recorded. Unaware of the social interactions of photography, they didn't interact with the camera.

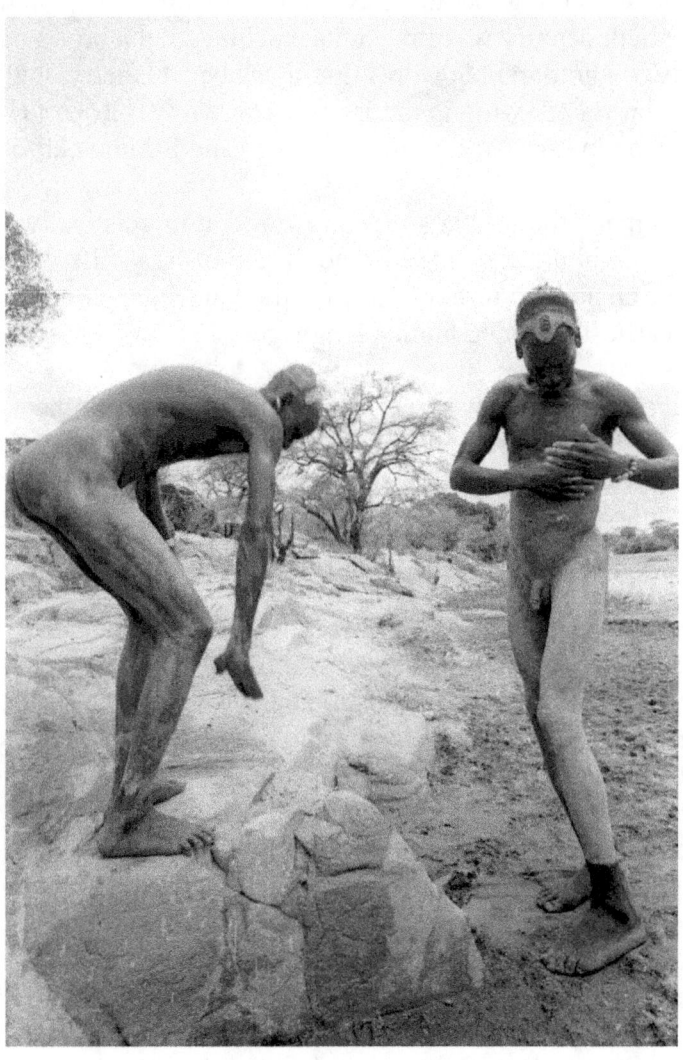

Two Hamar Men Painting Their Bodies, Joan Mitchell Worswick

In the world of ethnography, this rare state of being is called "first contact." In the world of photography, first contact was and is something like the holy grail. Only three times in the twentieth century was first contact achieved in a broad-based body of photographic work: first by Robert Flaherty, with the Hudson Bay Eskimo in the 1920s; then, on two Robert Gardner–led expeditions to New Guinea (1961) and Ethiopia (1968).

What made the Hamar so special was that linguistically, like their neighbors above Lake Rudolf in the Great Rift Valley, they spoke an archaic form of the Cushitic language, which is among the earliest recorded human languages.

Additionally, they were perhaps some of the last of the Paleolithic/ Neolithic people that then existed anywhere in 1968. What was particularly special about them, when we became better acquainted, was their attractive physical appearance and their accessible, easy, and open spirits.

In another place and in another time, the American artist Walker Evans described his own photographs and what he hoped for them, in the future, as "art documents." While we worked among the Hamar, both Joanie and myself tried to bring to our photographs the same artistically oriented but objectivist fact-filled viewpoint as the photographers of the nineteenth century and their twentieth-century equivalents, like August Sander, Walker Evans, and Henri Cartier-Bresson brought to their own work.

As we began to make an "art document" of the Hamar people in their spare and difficult environment, a remarkable idea occurred to me: the Hamar still lived as they had before the history of man was recorded.

They had very little in the way of domestic implements or objects or a material culture, which had evolved in the last twelve millennia elsewhere in the world.

We photographed hut exteriors made of pieces of scavenged wood, which appeared to be many hundreds of years old. We photographed the sparse domestic objects of the Hamar, which consisted of a few gourds and no pots.

Inside their huts, the Hamar women cooked on a ring of three or four ancient stones. The stones were three inches high and three inches broad. This was the extent of their domestic cooking artifacts: three or four rocks.

The tribe kept small herds of cattle and goats. They practiced rudimentary sorghum cultivation.

However, a small bit of the contemporary world had leaked into the lives of the Hamar. In order to protect themselves from continually predatory neighbors and wild animals, the men of the tribe had a few ancient rifles with a few rounds of ammunition.

Neither Joanie nor myself had rigid guidelines to follow in making our pictures of this place. In photography, if one considers the history of the medium, during the nineteenth and the early twentieth century's, the type of camera available dictated the kind of photographs that you created. In the past, both slow film emulsions and bulky glass-plate negatives required that subjects be posed rigidly, or they would blur.

With our own small, lightweight Leica and Nikon cameras, we were only limited by one fact: in making our pictures, by choice we only used available light.

Joanie's pictures were more "formalist" than my photographs. She used only one fixed 50mm lens to take pictures. The lens I preferred was a Nikkor 28mm lens on my Nikon F, which necessitated being three feet from your subject and letting your pictures seem to spread out around the subject.

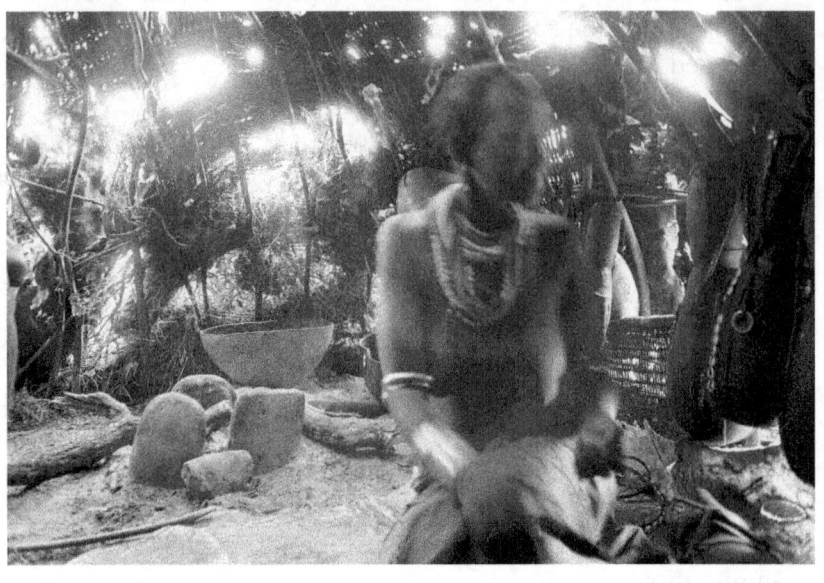

Interior, Woman and Four Cooking Stones, Joan Mitchell Worswick

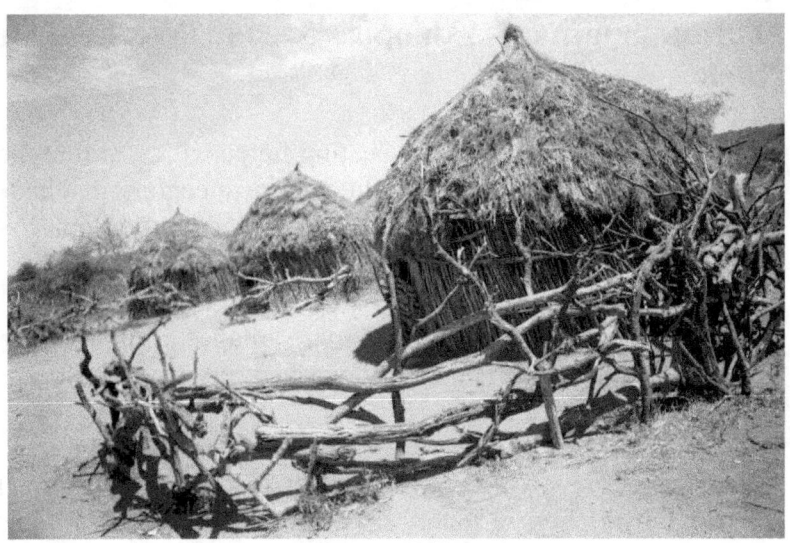

Hamar Village

Alternatively, with my own now much-abused Leica M2, I used a Summicron 35mm lens, which also created a style of wraparound wide-angle photography. Not limited by flash equipment or tripods, our pictures were defined only by our own personal style and outlook.

Each day, we photographed through midday and afternoon, until it became too dark to make more pictures.

To the Hamar, we brought a banquet of unexplainable objects that whirred and clacked. It was our ambition to make pictures of every observable activity of the Hamar. To their everlasting credit and patience, the Hamar put up with us week after week without complaint, demureness, or petulance.

***

Turmi, Southern Ethiopia, Second Week of July 1968

With the blinding sun and desiccating fierce winds, at first the only artifacts we discovered of the twentieth century that had leaked into this vastly remote place inhabited by the Hamar were a few old rifles and the metal bangles of the women.

As we worked among the Hamar villages, other castaway oddments appeared, apparently washed up from beyond the borders of the thorn jungle.

These were a few worn cotton T-shirts, two sets of leather rifle-cartridge bandoliers, a lonely set of pink Pop-It pearls, a pair of child's sunglasses, and a red bathrobe. All three of those items mysteriously appeared then disappeared. As we photographed the Hamar, I came to think these mysterious objects were beloved communal tribal property.

Among the men, the chief delights and activities of the Hamar seemed to consist of preening themselves and fashioning their elaborate mud-caked colored hairstyles. Occasionally, they'd strip off their earth-colored clothing, which covered their midsections, then decorate their bodies with different-hued clays.

Sometimes I observed these naked men, and they looked as though they'd been assaulted by a completely mad artist. With variegated muds, they'd turned themselves into objects of arrestingly elaborate body art, consisting of stripes, circles, twirls, whorls, rectangles, and streaks.

These painted body decorations appeared to be done in advance of elaborate dances held by the Hamar during the rainy season. In the dances, women would be on one side. Across from them, the men would stand in a long line next to one another. As one watched the dance unfold, one realized that each dance was an intricately choreographed millennial ritual. Next, jumping, singing, and clapping would begin.

The women of the tribe wore a single article of clothing: a leather skirt. It was a kind of smock that partially covered their breasts. As they walked their skirts jingled, and when they danced the tiny loops of metal edging attached to their leather skirts created rhythms as their feet struck the ground in synchronized pounding cadence.

As we photographed against a backdrop of lowering rainy-season skies, amid clouds of dust raised by wildly stamping feet, the pictures we made give some idea of the uncommon pageant of these people's existence that was so different from lives sustained by packaged foods and mass transit.

What is missing from our photographs are the sounds of women dancing and the chanting, the singing, and the clanking of the women's metal ankle decorations. Missing as well are the pageant and the delights of the men and boys dancing, jumping, shouting, and hooting in cadence.

What one misses in these pictures is the heat, the sudden storms, and then the lightning strikes with the crash of thunder during the rainy season.

Absent from these pages is also the physical presence of these splendid people.

Mankind had lived in this place forever. That was the miracle of the Hamar. Hidden in the thorn jungles was a moment when mankind began.

Somehow, astonishingly, we'd found this place from Joanie's chance reading of a few indefinite paragraphs in a book in Addis.

We'd stumbled into a period of man's history that came to life each morning when we took out our cameras.   But what cannot be captured in these pictures is the complete mystery of discovering the Hamar.

Our pictures became an evolving, ever-changing fantastical kaleidoscope of accident and exploration in a period when there were few more explorations left on our planet to be made.

***

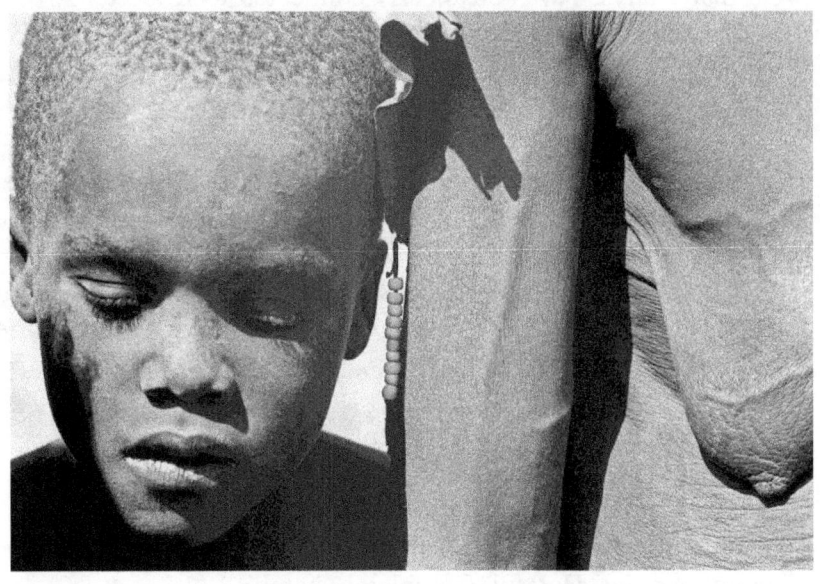

Boy and Grandmother, First People, Joan Mitchell Worswick

Turmi, July 18, 1968

On many days, I was physically connected to Robert's Arriflex sound-sync camera. My obligation in our filmmaking came from operating a heavy Swiss-made Nagra-brand tape recorder that I was physically attached to by a sync cable.

In order to shoot sound with the film, both Robert and I were hardwired together as we followed men hunting or trailed women going to the sand rivers for water. Chained to Robert, as we filmed and ducked between dancers, I sometimes choked on the dust raised by the groups of painted men, who cavorted wildly in and around us.

Invariably, if there was a track Robert followed, and he was behind a Hamar subject that he was filming, I'd be alongside him. Dragged through thickets of thorn, I'd desperately try to keep up with Robert. I'd get ripped to pieces carrying my Nagra sound recorder. Hateful. Completely hateful.

At best, the process of making films on tribal people is grueling. In a place like southern Ethiopia, a filmmaker pays for his every mistake. Each film pack that leaks light or is dropped inadvertently, and each damaged camera, is an irreversible tragedy. Where could we go to have our equipment repaired? Munich? The West 47th Street professional camera repair shop in Manhattan?

After working on films in many places, I came to the conclusion that a filmmaker has no friends whatsoever. When you make films, you have to be a kind of dictator more than a director.

After a film is finished, it always surprises me that anyone who worked on the film ever speaks to the director again. The filmmaker only has acquaintances, and these acquaintances might or might not still be speaking to a director even while a film is being made.

If Robert was difficult to deal with at times and massively self-centered, I understood that.

The whole exercise of making a documentary film is basically impossible. Such filmmaking in remote places is like a controlled accident, but more often it becomes an uncontrollable accident. What mad men would even undertake this work?

More than the technical problems of making a film is the greatest problem of such a life: every day, a filmmaker is bound into an iron straitjacket of his own making. Success is measured by how many rolls of film you've exposed that day, that week, that month. The smaller the pile, the greater the failure.
Each night after dinner, Robert wrote out his notes.

The worries, the constant frailties, and the unceasing unsolvable problems that a filmmaker has to face remain existentially unappeasable. No wonder Robert was preoccupied or sometimes out of sorts.

I often wondered what was in those notes he kept so assiduously writing. I wondred how I came out in these notes. The problem I had with the notes that I occasionally made was that a week later, or even a day later and probably as a good thing for our cooperative enterprise I couldn't read my own handwriting.

***

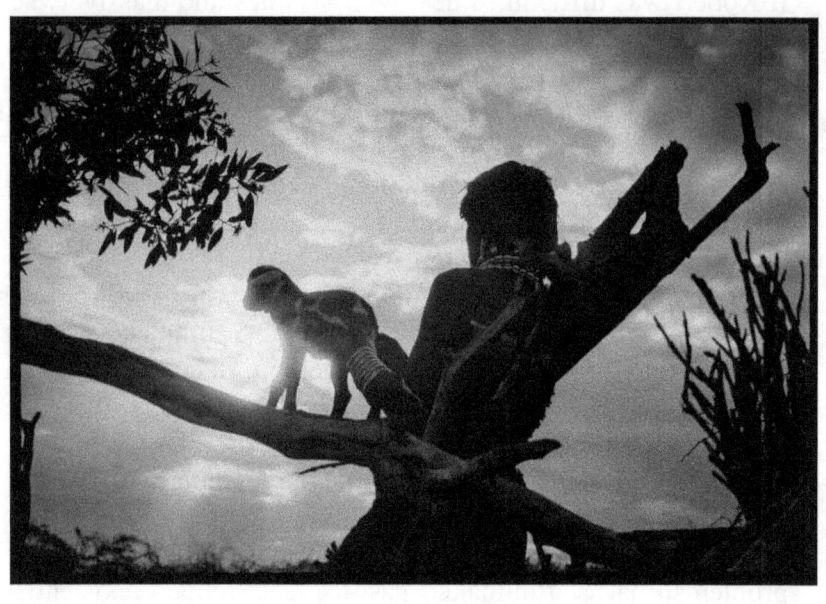

Sunset, Hamar, Woman with kid Joan Mitchell Worswick

Turmi, Southern Ethiopia, July 27, 1968

In the last days of July, Joanie was able to photograph a war party going out to raid a neighboring village for their cows. A few years after we left, we heard that half the men in a nearby village were killed on a similar raiding expedition.

It was a devastating loss of life to the village, and it would take a generation and a half to restore the physical ruin that these deaths meant to the work of the village. Children were without fathers. Women were without men. Life was massively interrupted. But life went on, and as it does, time swept over the village. Grief was buried deep inside the widows. It was the women who both created and preserved culture.

Protected by their barriers of thorn, the tribe had existed just as we found them in the Great Rift Valley from a period when scattered human groups first became village dwellers. In the world beyond the thorn jungle, and for the most part completely forgotten in modern urbanized society, are the roles which women played in this great civilizing of mankind.

It was the women who, in eons of matrilineal descent, transmitted and passed on the traditional values of the tribe. Finally, it was the women who bore the pains and the burdens of life. They became pregnant and often died giving birth. If mother and child survived the danger of birth, they went on to raise the children.

In the land of the Hamar, the women did the endless work of digging for water in the sand rivers and gathering firewood. They cooked and fed their families. But above all, it was the women that preserved the unique culture of this place by passing on the traditions of the Hamar from one generation to another.

In their difficult and unforgiving world, the Hamar women brought humanity and laughter to the life of their villages.

I learned that in both the villages of India and Africa, men don't know how to laugh as much, or as well as, women.

And then as everywhere on earth, and across all time, it is the women, finally, who mourn the dead after the battles and the wars created by men.

***

July merged into August of 1968. We logged our films; we took our photographs.

It is thought that in small communities like the Hamar, tribal people began to tend edible grasses or other plants in the period from 12,000 BCE to 8,000 BCE. This was when agriculture was born, and it was in this period that the long road was taken to civilization. Wedged somewhere between the Paleolithic and the Neolithic periods, the Hamar were survivors of an almost vanished period of our human history.

In the village one day, I photographed young girls engaged in body decorating and twittering to each other with birdlike chirps of laughter. Using butter caked onto their elaborately fashioned mud-coated hair, they created designs which were almost architectural. The attention given to constructing these hairstyles could have put many of the young women into the pages of fashion magazines and many of the beauty salons of the world out of business.

***

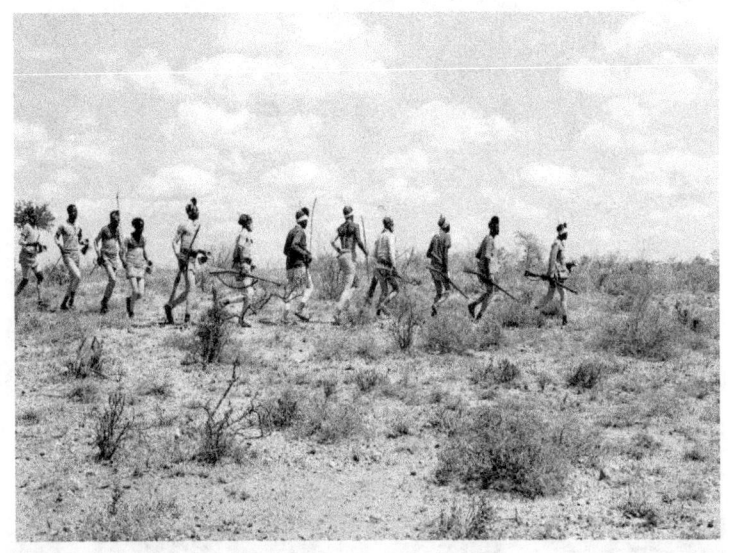

Hamar Raiding Party with Rifles, Joan Mitchell Worswick

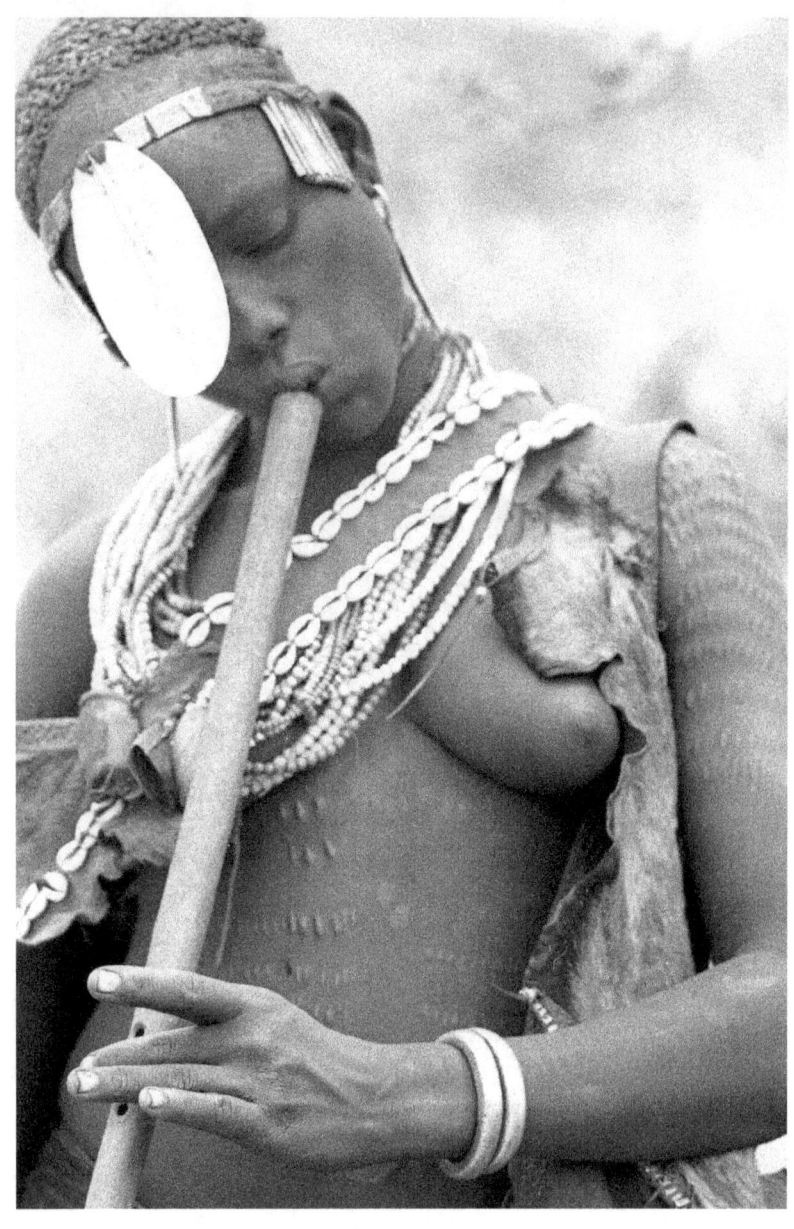

Young Hamar Woman,

Joan Mitchell Worswick

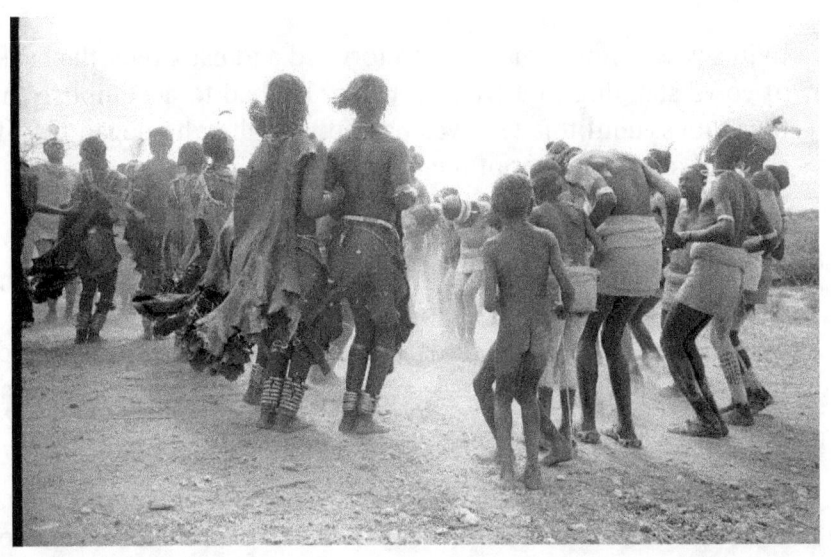

Dance of the Cattle-Jumping Ceremony, Hamar

The Last Week, Turmi, Southern Ethiopia, August 22, 1968

During late August, we spent a day photographing the Hamar cattle jumping. It was a final test for a young man, who needed to enter the tribal responsibilities of manhood.

In this rite, a young man leaped forward and back over the backs of cows standing in a fifty-foot line. He had to accomplish this four times, until this test was passed, and then he began his life as a full adult member of the tribe.

Before the cattle-jumping ceremony, the naked *meza* (priests) of the tribe smeared with blackened mud would whip the young women of the tribe with vicious cuts of willow like switches.
The women danced forward. Then the switches hit the women full force. They were struck across their backs, shoulders, and breasts. It was brutal.

Many of the Hamar women's rituals seemed to involve pain that established women's roles in the tribe. These rites established roles of submission and included decorative scarring and infibulation, which carved out a young girl's erotic desire.

***

Watching them, measuring the Hamar in some way, and taking photographs of the Hamar, I felt increasingly that it was an extraordinary experience.

It was strange to take pictures of a people who knew absolutely nothing about the processes, or even the world we came from. When we photographed the Hamar, I thought of the fragile evanescent moment in which they lived. It seemed to me that they were suspended for a brief moment of time, beyond and before our world. They could know nothing about us or photography.

Whenever you photographed people anywhere in the modern world, somehow they *knew* you were taking their picture. The Hamar would stare directly at the camera or away into another place. They looked completely through you with no knowledge of the camera and its purposes.

When you took their pictures they had no self-consciousness and no awareness of themselves.

When you looked at the Hamar, their faces were distinct and unlike any other face. Perhaps the Hamar tribe, inside its thorn jungle, was something like a DNA honey trap of all the people who had passed through East Africa over the uncounted millennia on their journey from the cradle of mankind to the rest of the world.

After the cattle jumping, Joanie and I went to one of the nearly dry sand rivers that passed through Hamar land.

In a large puddle left by the rains, we took a bath. Twice a week, we took a bath to try and remove the dust that coated us.

As I looked down into the puddle that day, I thought how strange it was that the only image the Hamar ever had of themselves during their lives came from their brief reflections in water. In this arid land, I wondered if a Hamar's vision of himself was affected by never actually seeing what he looked like. I wondered if, in their world, this was of any importance?

***

Finally, the day came when we left the Hamar. One day it was over, and our journey to this place came to an end.

Finding the Hamar, then photographing them, was perhaps chance and untoward great luck. We stepped out of our own time into the void of time occupied by the Hamar.

But that is not really quite what I mean. Rather, I think both Joanie and myself realized that nothing in our lives would ever be the same after photographing Ethiopia and the people there. I also thought that we'd never be able to explain this place, if we ever could, except through our photographs.

The Hamar were physically arresting, lovely, and surprising.I hoped that one day, our pictures would be a record of who the Hamar once were.

What I meant by stepping out of our own time was that in our increasingly crowded and modern world, I hoped our pictures could preserve what the Hamar had been before they discovered all the ills of modern man.

I thought then, as I think now, that the greatest gift we could give the Hamar was preserving a modest fragment of who they were.

***

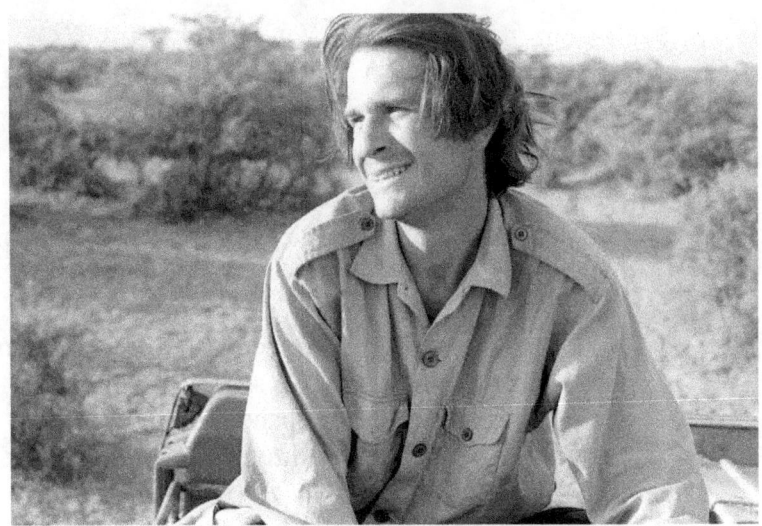

Clark Worswick, Ethiopia, 1968

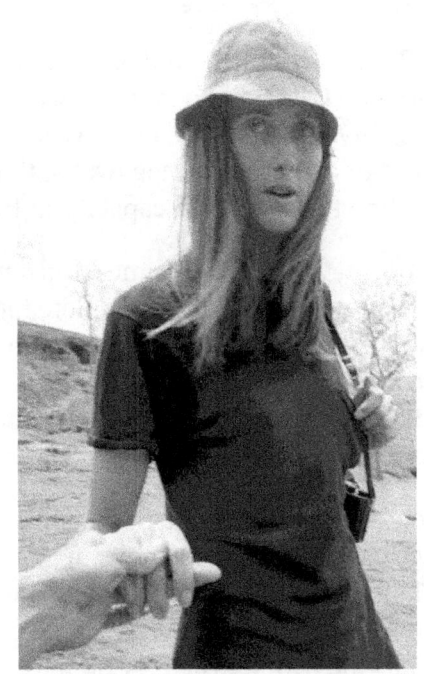

Joanie Mitchell Worswick, Ethiopia, 1968

Notes

1. During 1968, Joanie Mitchell and I spent six
months in Ethiopia. In that period, in what was
perhaps one of the longest ever purely photographic
expedition staged in Africa, we made 12,000
photographs. Decades later, due to a series of
bureaucratic, institutional, and university omissions,
forty-seven years later, not a single one of these
pictures has ever been published. In the years
between 1968 and 2015, thinking about these unseen
if not lost photographs, I often recalled the words of
William Butler Yeats, "Beware the fury of a patient
man."

2. Cf:
http://en.wikipedia.org/wiki/Gilgel_Gibe_III_Dam

"In 2015, it is projected that the 797-foot-tall, 2,000-
foot-wide Gilgel Gibe III Dam will be the second
largest hydroelectric plant in Africa with a power
output of about 1,870 megawatts, thus more than
doubling total installed capacity in Ethiopia.

In August 2010, then–Prime Minister of Ethiopia
Meles Zenawi vowed to complete the dam "at any
cost," telling critics, "They don't want to see
developed Africa. They want us to remain
undeveloped and backward to serve their tourists as a
museum."[

According to critics, the dam will be potentially
devastating to the indigenous population. The dam
will stop the seasonal flood, which will impact the
lower reach of the Omo River and Lake Turkana as
well as the people who rely on these ecosystems for
their livelihoods. According to Terri Hathaway,
director of International Rivers' Africa program, Gibe

III is 'the most destructive dam under construction in Africa.' The project would condemn 'half a million of the region's most vulnerable people to hunger and conflict.

Ethnic groups affected by the dam include eight distinct indigenous communities: the Mursi, Bodi (Mekan), Muguji (Kwegu), Kara (Karo), Hamar, Bashada, Nyangatom, and Daasanach.

Stephen Corry, director of the indigenous rights organization Survival International, said, 'The Gibe III dam will be a disaster of cataclysmic proportions for the tribes of the Omo Valley. Their land and livelihoods will be destroyed, yet few have any idea what lies ahead. The government has violated Ethiopia's constitution and international law in the procurement process. No respectable outside body should be funding this atrocious project.' Other sources note that, when interviewed, people in many villages have never even heard of the Gibe III dam, and many of them did not even know what a dam was.

The decreased water flow of the Omo River resulting from the Gibe III dam will have significant impacts on the ecosystems surrounding the river. The Omo River Basin is home to the only pristine riparian forest remaining in the drylands of sub-Saharan Africa. The survival of this forest is dependent upon the seasonal flooding of the Omo River, which will cease with construction of the dam. This may cause 290 square kilometers of forest to dry out from lack of water. The decreased water flow will also negatively impact, if not eliminate, all economic activities associated with the Omo River, such as farming, fishing, and tourism."

It should be pointed out, as well, that the earliest fossil record of our species *Homo sapiens*—which dated precisely 6,500 generations of man was found in the Omo River Valley.

Any further work extending Richard Leakey's earlier finds in the Omo area will be impossible in the foreseeable future under the waters of the huge Gilgel Gibe III Dam."

***

CHAPTER TWO

Travels, 1959–1964

Before Africa, before Ethiopia, before the counterculture, and before the Vietnam War, I'd been going in and out of India since 1959.

In another era, boats actually made journeys that lasted months. I'd approached India first westward, traveling through the Golden Gate of San Francisco Bay.

There was time to read long books and to wonder at the immensity of our world. On these journeys spanning the great oceans, you could go first class, second class, or third class. It took me three weeks to cross the nearly incomprehensible expanse of the Pacific.

Beyond Yokohama, Japan I booked my journey westward, traveling toward the setting sun, in fourth-class deck passage. This allowed me to sleep on the rotting planking of the ship's bare deck, as I crossed the South China Sea on warm nights that went on forever.

On subsequent journeys in the early 1960s, I traveled from Rotterdam, the Netherlands toward India.

I crossed Turkey and Anatolia under the shadows of Mount Ararat, where Noah was said to have survived the Great Flood and providentially enabled mankind's journey into the future. I crossed the Iranian border. I hitchhiked down through the mountains to Tabriz and to Tehran. From Tehran I had a choice. I could travel south toward Zahedan on the Pakistan border, or I could continue eastward toward the Iranian holy city of Mashhad before I crossed into Afghanistan and the desert city of Herat.

I discovered Afghanistan just after the French junkies discovered the cheap thrills of ten-cent heroin fixes in Kabul.

I discovered India five years before the hippies discovered the lotus position, hashish, and the dusty roads leading toward distant eastern sunrises.

For years, I devoted my life to collecting Indian art. Unfortunately, by 1964 I'd discovered that in both Europe and America, most people were indifferent to Indian classical art. I started collecting Indian art in 1959. By 1964, I had serious doubts that Indian classical art would be anything in the art market.

I'd taken a deep breath one day. The price for great Indian art, for half a decade, seemed to stagger sideways like a collapsed drunk trying to climb out of bed. In the coded world of European art dealers, I'd formed what was unhappily termed a "stranded art collection."

A senior art dealer in Paris told me in late 1963, "You have a marvelous collection. Be patient, dear man. You're still young. In three decades, Indian art will become the next big event in the international art market."

In India I'd spent way too much money on classical Indian art. Paintings I'd bought for five hundred dollars in Calcutta, or Jaipur, and Bombay, in the London market, started appearing for $150 dollars, then sinking below that.

I learnt the hardest possible way that the problem of entering an "emergent field of curatorial interest in the art world", when it is "emerging", is that this is a most dangerous endeavor. No matter how good your art might be, with a single bad guess in timing, you may wait a long time for your art to enter the mainstream.

I thought I should invent a whole new life for myself.

"Sic transit eternis"   So goes the glory of the world.

***

San Francisco, 1964

I was out of place.

 I think I had a mismatch with America. In California, the friends I'd grown up with were launched into lives I didn't much fit into.

I turned from art collecting to photography at a moment when few people took photography seriously. I wanted a settled, less complicated life. I wanted a life of clarity and a quiet life, free from confusion.

In India during 1960 I decided I wanted to do films and photography. In my reconstruction of myself, post my Indian art collecting, I moved to Los Angeles, but I couldn't find a job in the film world. The film industry was completely closed to outsiders. Three decades earlier, the Hollywood film unions had locked then barricaded, the entrance door to the film world.

Apparently, even a job sweeping up editing room floors was impossible to get. After a few months in a small apartment, where I wrote at night in a closet and took photographs during the day, I left Los Angeles. I went north, back to Berkeley, where I came from.

In San Francisco, help for me and my photography came from an extremely unlikely place.

I moved into a $10-a-month basement apartment in the city. After two months of living in this strange, wonderful place, I realized at last that, although I'd grown up across the bay, four miles away from San Francisco, the city was the refuge for people who didn't fit into the norms of American society.

In the red-baiting years of the late 1940s and 1950s, the Communists and the Socialists quietly populated the local institutions of learning in San Francisco. They'd also infested, like industrious burrowing insects, the San Francisco municipal government, as well as the San Francisco Longshoreman's Union. To the nest of left-leaning writers, folk singers, homosexuals, socialist "weirdo pinkos", and die-hard, unredeemed Communists, in the red baiting Joe McCarthy post World II period, San Francisco was heaven.

As part of making the world safe for the laboring class and the twisted, socially warped municipal ideas they espoused, the pinko, unionist-leaning city government of San Francisco set up a unique social institution in America: it was a completely equipped cooperative darkroom. Imagine free film-loading and film-developing rooms. Free enlargers. I even got free chemicals.

Nirvana. An Indian word.

The city-sponsored darkroom welcomed radical unionists, Communists, and even young artists like myself, as well as anyone who showed up with an interest in photography. Be they misfit, bisexual, anarchist, or cross-dresser, anyone could use the lavishly equipped San Francisco Recreation and Parks Department's photography laboratory free of charge.

The male and female employees of the municipal darkroom, presumably all of them progressively, politically-leaning to the core, were passionate and knowledgeable about photography. The darkroom foyer had a well-stocked library that held manuals and books on photography, as well as complete decadal runs of *US Camera Annuals*. The latter was then the only public annual periodical on photography in America. The issues dated from the late 1930s onward.

In these annuals, I found a virtual encyclopedia of the great artists of photography.

It fascinated me that such artists even existed, and it was in these annuals that I discovered the work of international practitioners of the art and science of photography, which at that point had already existed for 129 years. Who knew? No one seemed to be paying much attention to the medium, let alone its history.

Looking at these *US Camera Annuals* I realized that photography had a unique, and incredible history as an art all of its own.

How utterly strange, how completely, and fantastically strange that no one apparently appeared to know this. At this point, I had been taking photographs for almost five years.

During that time, I'd felt that the only way to learn photography was to make photographs. In India, I'd had all my darkroom work done by local Calcutta and Bombay photographers.

In San Francisco's municipal darkrooms, I learned how to develop my own films for the first time. Next, I learned how to print photographs with professional-grade equipment, rather than in my own transient self-invented San Francisco darkroom rigged to drain into the tub of my small apartment bathroom.

In order to save money, I now learned how to bulk-load Tri-X film from $5 spools of 35mm Eastman Kodak film. Previously, in camera shops, each cassette of film cost $1.50. This seemed a fixed cost, whether it was in Delhi, Tokyo, or Europe. From one $5 spool of Kodak 35mm film, in a miracle of economy, I could get twenty cassettes.

Bulk-loading was done inside something called a changing bag, and loading empty film cassettes with unexposed negative stock was a skill that I developed.

In the months that followed, by taking pictures of the growing interconnected scene in California, and then bringing my film into the cooperative darkrooms, I learned photography.

Under a dully glowing red lamp above a darkroom developing print tray, I discovered I could collect images of events and people in California and what was happening there.

Through my own printing, my images came to life. I became a collector, like a man who snags rare, fragile tropical moths in a net. It was like nothing I'd done before. It was total magic! Then I discovered, in these darkrooms, something even more exciting. Photography gave me a completely new way to see the world.

To begin any journey, all you have to do is take a first step.

I began a journey to a strange, changing place. With my photography, I was caught in a flood, a cataract of change.

The world I left in 1959 was becoming a very different world in the mid-1960s.

With my camera, I gathered images of an absolutely evanescent moment in time, after which nothing would be the same again, in either in America or in the world. I began a new kind of collecting.

***

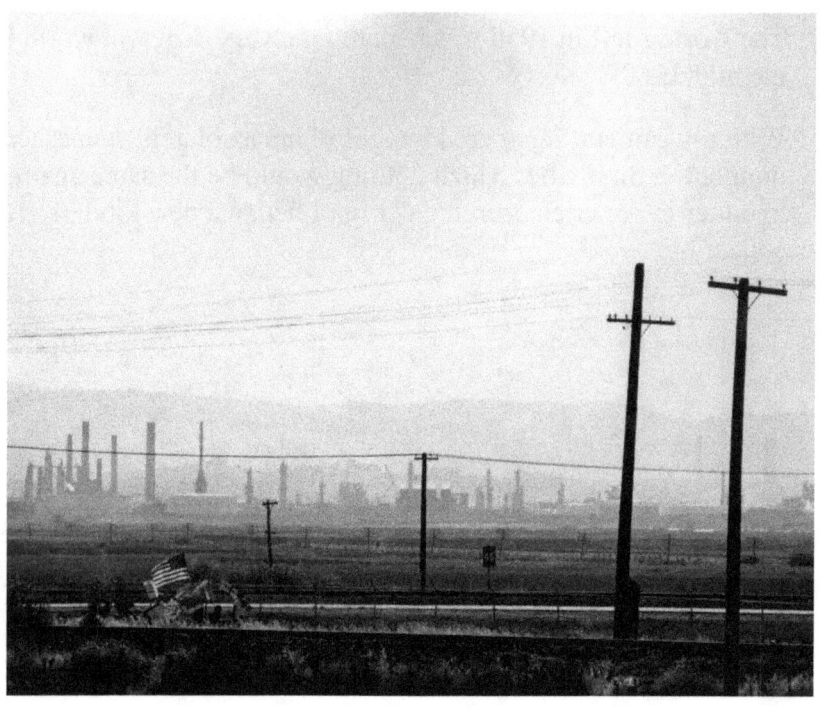

The years of Protest, California, the 1960's

The New Barbary Coast, San Francisco, 1964

In 1964, I was twenty-four years old. I moved out of my $10-a-month basement rental and began living in a seven-story mansion in San Francisco, which had been built by an enormously rich man in the era just after the Great Earthquake of 1906. That earthquake was for San Francisco the moment of Armageddon.

The city's gas mains burst, and much of the city was incinerated.

Built after the great fire, the house I now lived in was on the best street in San Francisco. It was so large, it had hidden back stairways and deep subterranean cellars with wines that had been put down in 1911. Inside its many stories, I gave up counting the numberless rooms of this house.

A friend of my parents had invited me to stay on the seventh floor of this house for as long as I wanted. The friend had married a General Motors heir named Freddie Higby. Freddie had a huge power yacht. He had a twin-engine Beechcraft Bonanza airplane. His colossal house had the best views of the San Francisco Bay, and now he had a glamorous wife to go with his huge house.

For a year and a half, I stayed on and off in this mansion. I came and went erratically. I was a sort of live-in artist-photographer–household ghost.

More than a century before, in the 1850s, San Francisco had a section of the city devoted to sin, eccentricity, red-light ladies, and gamblers. It was called the Barbary Coast.

By 1965, I seemed to be inventing a new version of the Barbary Coast all my own. I began to witness out-of-control events in the company of variegated people, all of whom were possessed at times by a questionable grip on their own sanity. The counterculture came into my life. LSD was still legal. There was free love. Then throw into this mix a rising number of increasingly unfriendly and virulent anti-Vietnam protests, along with a war that changed and defined a generation. Mind-bending.

Stir into this twisted stew of confusion a variety of strange Southern California Christian cults and Asian-related religions, then add rock and roll. The result was an entire state that was reforming and changing itself into a unfamiliar version of the future.

***

By 1965, the future seemed to be overwhelming San Francisco in new and unusual ways.

On one hand, I went to gatherings of Freddie Higby's people, with the definite well upholstered haves of society. I'd wander through these parties and through Freddie's house and its palatial rooms, each with panoramic vistas of San Francisco Bay. At Freddie's at-homes, the air was filled with the scent of Johnnie Walker Black Label, but the real men chugged down quantities of straight up Old Overholt. The people of Freddie's world, "Freddie's people" I came to call them, seemed exceptionally disconnected from what was occurring on their doorstep, while across the bay in Berkeley, life seemed laced with incense, Buddhist chants, and marijuana fumes cut with LSD.

Almost unnoticed at first in the mid-1960s, the new culture began to change and to reshape itself. Out there on the streets beyond Freddie's picture windows, I began to photograph the marginal countercultures of California.

What occurred was like a brush-fire blowup, when quite unexpectedly the once docile flames of a grass fire jump a fire line of smoke jumpers. It's at that moment that whole forests literally explode into flame.

In Northern California, drugs began to destabilize a generation. In Southern California, during one week in August 1965, a heat wave struck. The once peaceful citizenry of Los Angeles turned violent while Americans watched on TV.

During the period from August 11 to 17, the inhabitants of the predominantly black Los Angeles neighborhood of Watts burned down their own houses, as well as portions of the city at large. This conflagration of rage caused thirty-four deaths and 1,032 injuries and resulted in 3,438 arrests.

At one of Freddie's parties, I tried to explain this kind of social discontent to a few of the Republicans in the room. I told them what I was doing out on the streets with my photography. I told them I was documenting the hollowing out of California's landscape. I told them what was happening in Berkeley in the student protest movement.

The reaction was nervous laughter.

Freddie and his friends had stared at me with total bafflement. In Freddie's world, I'm sure, the name *Bob Dylan* sounded like a new brand of Highland single-malt Scotch. But then again, Freddie Higby's ideas about twentieth-century music probably stopped at Glenn Miller. I was afraid to ask him what he thought of Duke Ellington. Freddie and his friends probably thought LSD was an insect spray.

One day, I gave up trying to tell Freddie the texts of my life.

As 1965 aged, my life became a sort of underworld dance of music, drugs, social discontent, and war protests. At a meeting of students in Berkeley, one of the leaders of the protest movement, Stewart Alpert, had asked suspiciously the week before why I was taking photographs. I thought about this and said I was slowly preparing for an exhibition of photographs at the Museum of Modern Art in New York.

Bafflement surrounded me.

As the student protests about the war in Berkeley and San Francisco heated up, I remembered Saigon. I'd been in Saigon, Vietnam, in 1961.

How could I explain to anyone in America the treacheries Americans stepped into in Vietnam? How could you communicate to anyone in America the steaming landscapes lining the Mekong River?

I remembered another boat journey. I remembered another time....

The police who came to question me in my sweltering Saigon hotel were arrogant. They wanted to know what I did and why I was there. They wanted to know how much money I had.

One of them asked if I was a Socialist or a Communist. Was I an agitator?

In the Cholon section, I'd eaten in Chinese restaurants with low ceilings and dirty tables. The smoke-filled interiors of the restaurants smelled of burned cooking oil and despair. On the wide boulevards of Saigon, no one looked at you. Vietnamese would cross the street to get away from you.

Gorgeous women, distant wraiths dressed in flowing white ao dais, drifted past me as if I were invisible. There was apparently a long-standing no-fraternization policy between Europeans and the people of Vietnam. After my visit with the police, I abbreviated my trip and booked passage on the next ship leaving Saigon.

Six hours after departing Saigon and floating down the wide river toward the South China Sea, the tramp steamer I was on struck a mudbank. It was my going-away present from Vietnam—that, and the realization that this country was a quicksand of imperial Western ambitions.

We hung there on the mudbank for twelve hours being devoured by mosquitoes.

Lying in the shade of a bulkhead, I heard the sounds of explosions and detonations rocking up and then down the river. The deck made groaning noises from the heat.

In the silence that followed, a machine gun started up. The firing came closer. Bullets passed over the ship with the buzzing of wasps as we hunkered there, marooned on the mudbank. Bullets ricocheted off the bulkhead.

I didn't want to think of the future of this place. God alone knew what was happening in the countryside inside the low bushes that ringed the river.

I skittered sideways like a crab, then I threw myself down an open stairwell. The bulkhead behind which I was now hidden seemed to be made of thicker rusting plate steel.

In the late afternoon, the tide came up the river and floated us off the mudbank.

The last I saw of Saigon, it was a distant stain of dirty smoke against the horizon. My final parting gift from Vietnam was a fever that I'd contracted in the city.

In Singapore, I checked into a hotel and fought my fever poorly. I remember thinking that we'd fought a recent war in Korea. Wasn't one war per decade enough? It seemed to be that America was catching the habit of war, and as I slipped in and out of Vietnam, I saw a place of new American dreams and desolation. A memory of lovely women in their shimmering white ao dais floated through my fever.

***

San Francisco, 1965

To understand the 1960s in America, one had to understand the feelings of young men who were dragooned into the draft.

This was a new kind of war. It was a war first cooked up, and then baked, by the political class of Washington, D.C. It was a war abetted by professionals from the academic think-tank universe, by the military establishment, and by the armament and industrial manufacturers of America. This was a different kind of war for America. It was a war of apparently no beginning and no foreseeable end.

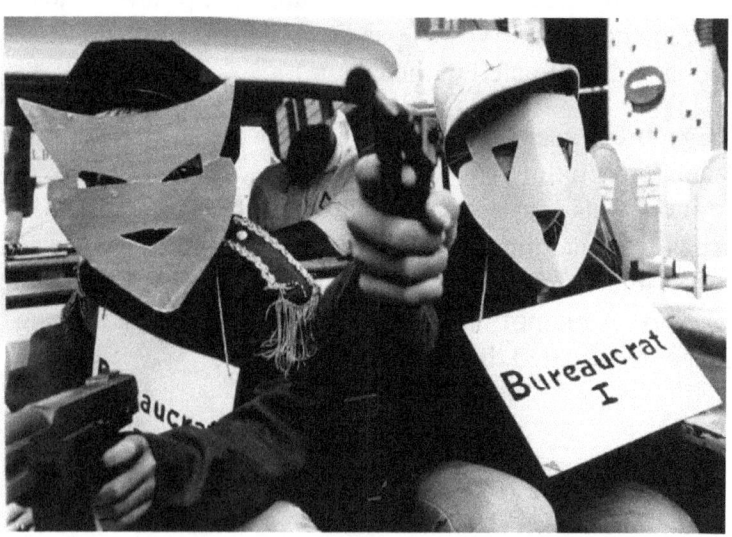

Young Boys, San Francisco, 1966

You were enrolled in the draft by being male and reaching the unfortunate age of eighteen. You were then automatically signed

up for the Vietnam War, whether you liked it or not, by
something called your local draft board.

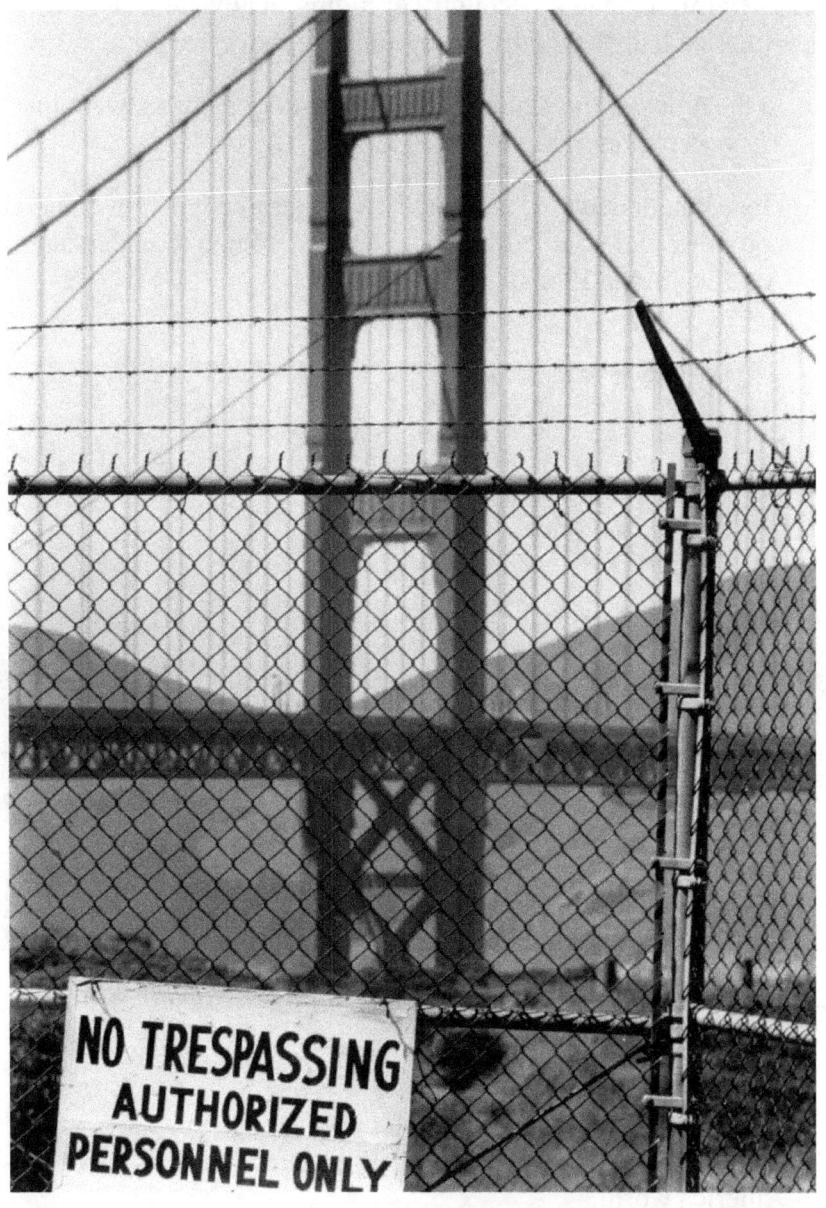

NO TRESPASSING
AUTHORIZED
PERSONNEL ONLY

The Golden Gate Bridge

In the minds of the people who created the Vietnam War, the Communists were everywhere. We'd fought them in Korea. They might be in any country or hiding in anyone's closet. America had to fight them anytime. Everywhere. Forever.

In the ethos of the United States, all America's wars were just. They were honorable.

Once you understood the epic U.S. government takeover by the corporate and political worlds, you could begin to understand America in the 1960s.

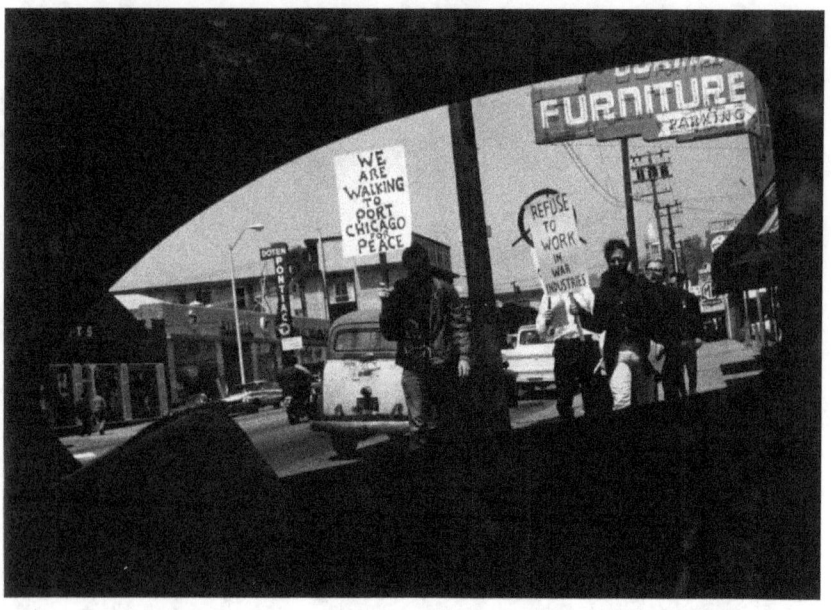

Port Chicago, Embarkation Point for Napalm, 1965

The new Washington congressional-military –industrial - academic class now danced cheek to cheek in a new made in America world.

They said: "Let's start a war that lasts forever. Let's start an unending series of wars."

And so America was signed up for Vietnam, the second paid-up installment of a generational series of wars that would come to consume the future.

In a counterpoint to this new version of America, to explain this vivacious moment in the 1960s, strange intellectual journeys tinged with ferocity came to describe a generation of young people who became progressively unmoored and unhinged.

These were my friends. The unmoored and the unhinged.

These were the people I hung out with and photographed on the streets and in their demonstrations. We'd been utterly betrayed by our political leaders.

In California, kept out of sight and away from the public and the media, the homecomings began at Port Chicago. Inside their aluminum coffins, a generation of young men started on their one-way journeys back home. They were returning from Vietnam.

I picked up my cameras, a Leica model M2, and a now-battered black-body Nikon model F. I started to take pictures of California and what was happening here.

I showed up at work.

***

But there was something else happening in California besides a protest movement. This something else seemed to grow and grow without people taking much notice of it. What was occurring in California was the gerrymandering of the American landscape, as month by month, California seemed to possess brand-spanking-new cities. In the state, whole cities seemed to spring up like mushrooms after a heavy rain.

As I thought about it, this was wholly new, manufactured place.

It was a place where everything was connected and everyone seemed to have been wedged into a new set of identities. It was a place upturned by a new system of roadways called freeways. In the process, California was riven, then carpeted, by urban and suburban sprawl.

In this new world, motivated consumers became highly urbanized millions. More importantly, these new consumers would soon represent billions of consumers.

As I photographed California, I began to believe that this late-twentieth-century version of America would take over the entire world. I'd take the bet that this new version of California just starting out would come to subsume the entire Earth. In time, the consumer would become the foot soldier of an increasingly wholly new manufactured world in which every place was the same.

Thinking back to the 1960s, and attempting to understand what was happening in America then, you had to first understand California. Next, you had to understand what this inundation represented.

In the 1960s, it was not just the war in Vietnam which unhinged America. Rather, it was a further insurgency, altogether created by untoward prosperity and people who loved to buy things.

Without anyone realizing it, California became the future, and the future arrived at its shopping destinations by automobile.

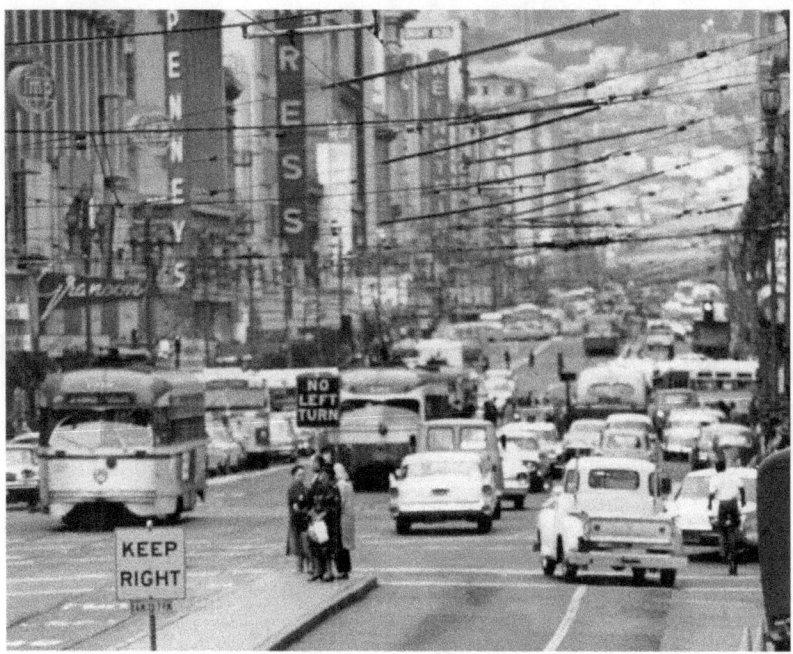

Market Street, San Francisco, 1965

As I photographed both Northern and Southern California, the state seemed to be changing along the deepest interior margins of itself.

California was inconveniently wedged along the 1,200 miles of its coastline on its western edges. As far as the eye could see, on the eastern boundaries of the state, the Sierra Nevada Mountains formed a stark barrier to the deserts which ringed the state.

I thought about this topographical and human sandwich. I next chose the most likely place to photograph this shifting, earthquake-talked place. It was Southern California.

Into my mix of documenting California and what was happening here, I added the emergence of a psychedelic dope culture, dynamitings, the destruction of the environment, and really quite splendid untested ideas of urban planning.

In a wild moment of hilarity on my growingly strange journey, I stopped in at the California Office of Planning and Research in Sacramento. As I exited the door of this place, I obtained a nearly demented urban footnote to what was happening to the state. It seemed to me that no one was ever going to step up to massively corrupt landgrabs of what had been formerly almost prodigally bountiful farmland, by a group of people who called themselves "developers".

I organized my own plan to photograph this place. In my photographs, I tried first to measure, and then to document, a startling juncture of history. In California, from the first moments I began to take photographs, I seemed caught in a cataract of change. I began to be a collector of a strange new sort. I collected time.

No one else seemed interested in a situation that was almost psychedelic.

***

Los Angeles, 1965

At the end of World War II, in 1945, Southern California had orange groves that stretched as far as the eye could see. It was a place lush with unpicked fruit, and with promises of the future.

In 1945, California was a landscape of almost breathless optimism.

From the farmland of Southern California, I moved on to the cities.

In 1965, as Hollywood's Technicolor inanities spun contentedly toward an eerily rosy fugue state that promised to go on forever, strange things began to happen in paradise. Two decades after 1945, at the front entrance of a thousand movie theaters spread across America, Doris Day and Rock Hudson were the idealized American movie couple. By means of a made-in-Hollywood movie-studio PR machine, images of Rock and Doris and their wholesomeness were omnipresent across America, but something else was happening in California.

Things were not shining and new everywhere in this place.

No one seemed to take pictures of the decaying social reality of Los Angeles, or Santa Monica, or Manhattan Beach, or even Hollywood itself.

Didn't anyone step through the entrance of Grauman's Chinese Theater on Hollywood Boulevard and wonder, What in God's name is this place? Is this a temple? Is it a giant outsize restaurant? Maybe it's actually a movie theater of some sort?

Is there anything sadder than a movie star fallen to earth waiting for a five-cent municipal bus ride? No one seemed to photograph a Hollywood populated by the sad and ancient human remains of the Silent Era, as they waited at a city bus stop for fans who'd forgotten them.

Where were the poets howling in the junkyards of this place? I felt like the only person documenting the stupendously vast auto graveyards that were filled with the rusted, failed journeys of Southern California.

In the Hollywood Hills and along Sunset Boulevard were the mansions and estates of the once internationally powerful movie moguls. The mansions moldered now in the heat with overgrown, out-of-control cancerous plantings run amok. As I took photographs, I seemed to float through a dream world where I made solitary pictures of the wreck of a once verdant civilization. Maybe I was making documents of something like the coming of the new Visigoths.

One month, boiling across never-ending stretches of softly undulating hills, the orange groves of Southern California seemed immutable. In the next month, as things quite literally went, an entire landscape was butchered and then hacked to pieces by the "developers."

As I watched, it was as if some gigantic new movie-produced monster, like Godzilla, had suddenly begun munching the entire Southern California landscape.

Who would have willingly voted for this future? The place was being divided up, shredded, and then mysteriously populated by cookie-cutter houses sited on quarter-acre lots.

I had a feeling of despair. Perhaps this was the same feeling that animals had when they sensed an oncoming earthquake of unfathomable power.

Around me, as I rode down the endless new freeways, I passed through a population that apparently believed that California was now succeeding in extraordinary ways.

As I took my photographs, I witnessed millions of acres of carefully nurtured agricultural land that had taken an entire century to nurture. It was first broken, then crushed, by the giant earth-eating machines.

I was born here. I knew California. I had to bear witness in my photographs to what was becoming a creeping millennial catastrophe.

Didn't anyone know the booms and busts of this place? Didn't anyone remember the Mexicans and the Spanish, who had stolen this place from the Native Americans? Didn't Americans themselves even remember stealing this place from the Mexicans? History in California was apparently unimportant to the new people who had arrived here from somewhere else.

As I stood out there beyond Indio, in the failed cities of the 1920s to the 1950s that were now subsumed by sand I stood on the borderlands of a new version of California. I wondered, "Didn't anyone remember what had happened in this place, again and again?"

At other moments, I came to accept the fact that, like it or not, month by month, California was being eaten by a vast army of ants and converted into a brand-new set of dreams.

***

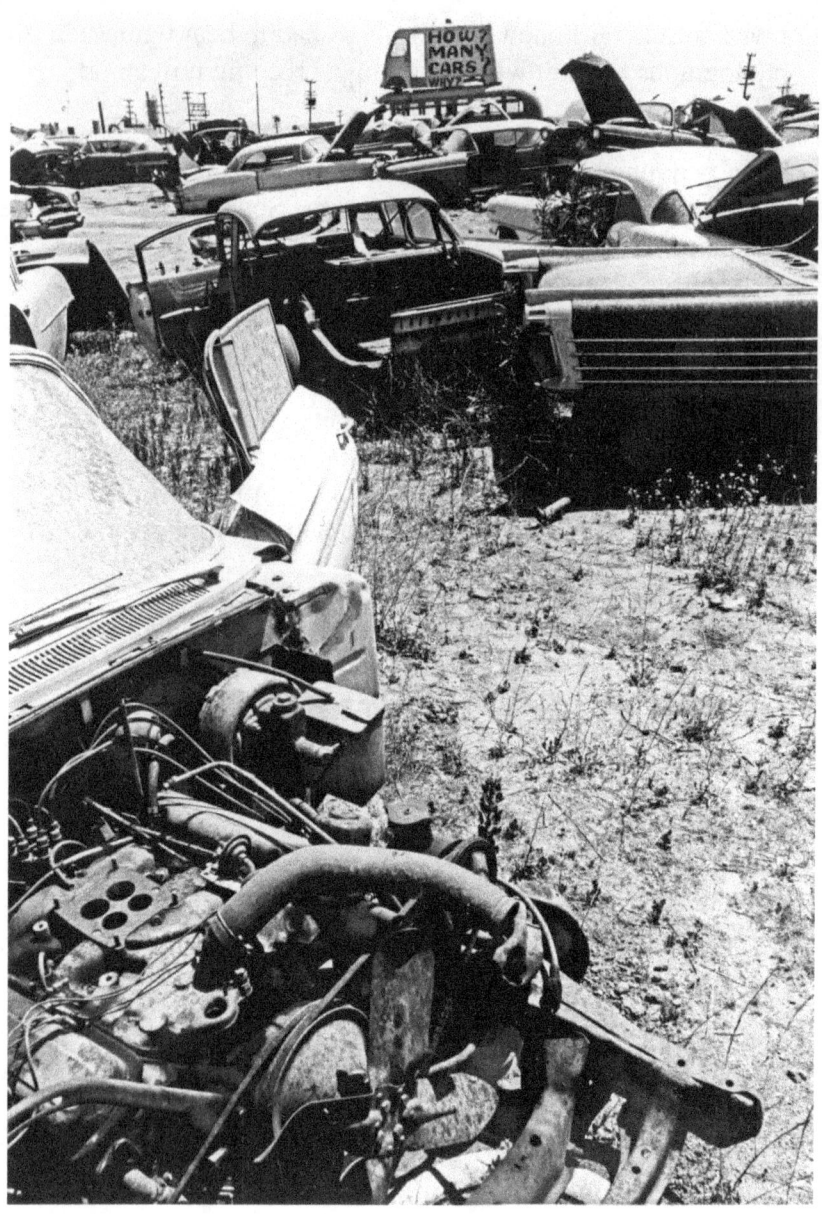

Auto Graveyard, Los Angeles, 1965

In Northern California, however, different things were going on.

During 1965, I suddenly felt I had company in San Francisco. The music scene and the protest scene began to *happen*.

Fueled by huge expense accounts from "back East," magazine photographers, passing as photojournalists, arrived to shoot the headlines. They were about to break the story, as they called it. *Life* and *Look* magazines had arrived, and now with national attention they were going to sing a siren song of flower power, free love, and what it was like to be young in the 1960s.

Perhaps only Lysergic Acid Diethylamide, more commonly known as LSD, was the sole substance that could describe the simultaneous destruction and discovery of the new "becoming" of California. Meanwhile, more photographers, some of them employed by local newspapers, and still others under contract to the FBI, kept copious records of the growing and massive student rallies and political protests which began to be centered on the Berkeley campus of the University of California.

There was actually a history to all this....

In May of 1960, when I'd briefly returned from India, I'd photographed an iconic moment in the American student-protest movement. A huge demonstration had gathered to object to the appearance of the House Un-American Activities Committee as a witch- and Commie-burning event that was being moved around America by the U.S. Congress, and for a moment had come to rest in San Francisco.

One day I photographed hundreds of students and citizens demonstrating outside of San Francisco City Hall. Mid-protest, I left for lunch. During my lunch break, the San Francisco Fire Department flushed scores of protestors down the grand staircases of City Hall with hard-to-escape high-pressure fire hoses.

At this event, the first protest event of the 1960s decade, a group of half-drowned protesters and students successfully objected to the odious Un-American Activities Committee, after a decade of grandstanding by Congress about who was and who wasn't American.

This moment also marked the beginning of the American student-protest movement.

The movement in Berkeley grew, and in the mid-1960s it was finally covered by the mainstream national media outlets.

Soon, people began arriving in California to share the pleasures of our unique state with its extraordinary new realities, and dream-like yearnings.

***

The topography of California seemed to create an altered state of expectation.

I thought about this state when nothing else could explain this place.

Normal people typically lived elsewhere. When they arrived in California, it was like a light switch was turned on; they changed. They had time to think deeper thoughts. Their language blurred. They seemed more deliberate and laid-back. They slowed down.

On the other hand, describing this place is possibly a wasted effort. Perhaps California during the mid-1960s was a place that could only be understood by acidheads or mystics. Once upon a time, the futurist Marc Reisner made an operatic grand stab at describing California. He called it "a theater of disaster."

Sited at the edge of the world's largest ocean, the entire state was physically situated atop one of the most active seismic regions on Earth. Geologically, California is constructed in the center of a slide zone.

In Southern California, backing the flatlands of Hollywood behind Sunset Boulevard, the entire city of Los Angeles is a built-out and built-up semi-desert.

Periodically, torrential, if infrequent, deluges of rain turn this desert to mud. Suddenly, entire hillsides slide downward in inconvenient landslips. Perhaps it is something not well known, but apart from occasional incontinent deluges of rain, Los Angeles itself is drier than Beirut. Dependent upon ever-diminishing water resources, Southern California is a chimera that exists in peril of constant drought.

In Northern California, the topographical facts are even more dire.

Although San Francisco's Golden Gate Park looks like a carefully tended miniature forest in places and the city appears to be green, when the Spaniards arrived in California in the eighteenth century, not a single tree grew in the San Francisco area.

The hills were too dry, and it was too windy.

San Francisco is another manufactured place. Without the water brought into the city from two hundred miles away through a huge tunnel in the Sierra Nevada Mountains, the city would die.

Similarly, in Southern California, the lawns of Santa Monica and Beverly Hills, as well as the turf of the Forest Lawn Cemetery, all live off the bounty of irrigation water quite literally stolen in the early twentieth century from the southern regions of the Sierra Nevada Mountains.

Everyone in California knows about the deserts that ring the state.

These deserts are far away. They are out near Palm Springs or Twentynine Palms. What people don't know is that California *is* a semi- desert, and what people have never been told is that the state is as dry as the southern regions of the Sahara.

California is always, always just a sip away from disaster.

I was born in Berkeley. I sometimes thought if I were ever to make a film about this place, it should be called *The Slide Zone.* Instead, when I made this film, I called it *California: Manufacturing the Future.*

In the mid-1960s, beyond the shimmering topographical realities of California, things in general were full of bountiful wonder.

Life in California was startling.

Things were new.

Suddenly, the whole American continent seemed bonded together in ways that had never been dreamed of before. For the first time in our history, new freeways united the entire nation. As my acid-dropping friend Larry Switzer once said to me, "Everything is now *so* connected, man."

He should know.

Larry's father had invented Day-Glo street signs, and Switzer signs in bright, glaring neon yellow now marked every single new freeway in America, north and south, east and west.

Ernest Lawrence, the father of another of my childhood friends, won a Nobel Prize for inventing the cyclotron, and much else. Little did Lawrence know, his invention would hurry the world along toward the atomic era and an uncertain, if potentially incandescently bright, future. Later on, perhaps sensing a lifetime of uncertain accomplishment, Lawrence then invented the earliest and best color TV. People in California liked to dream large, impractical dreams, but it was always those large, impractical dreams that worked out in this promised land of visionaries.

***

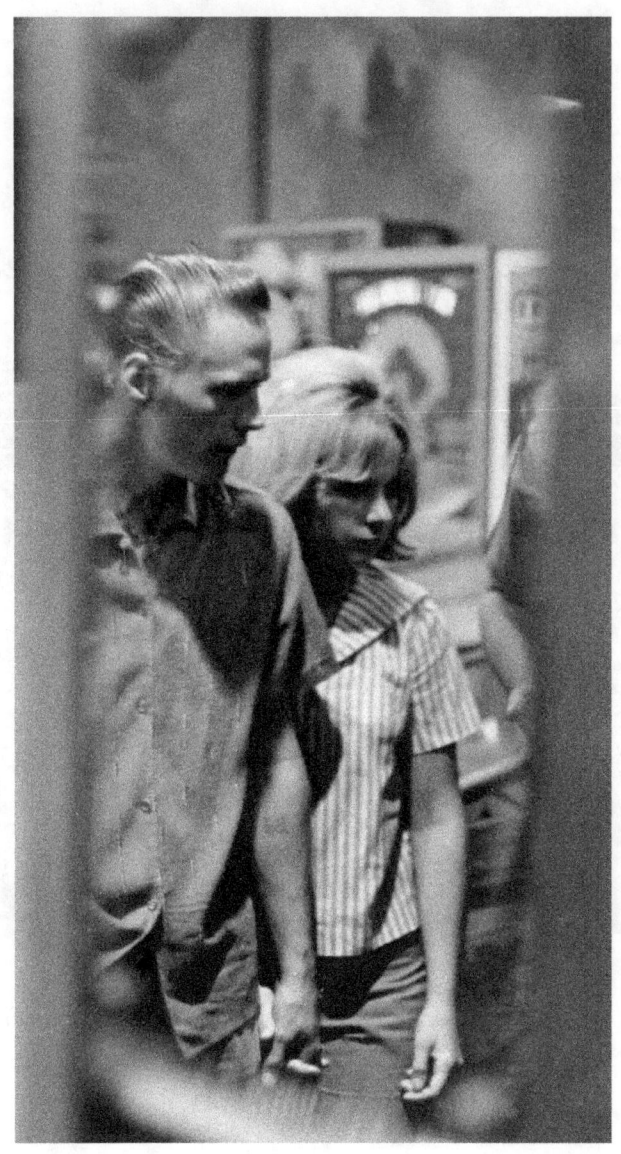

Couple, Arcade, Pismo Beach, California 1964

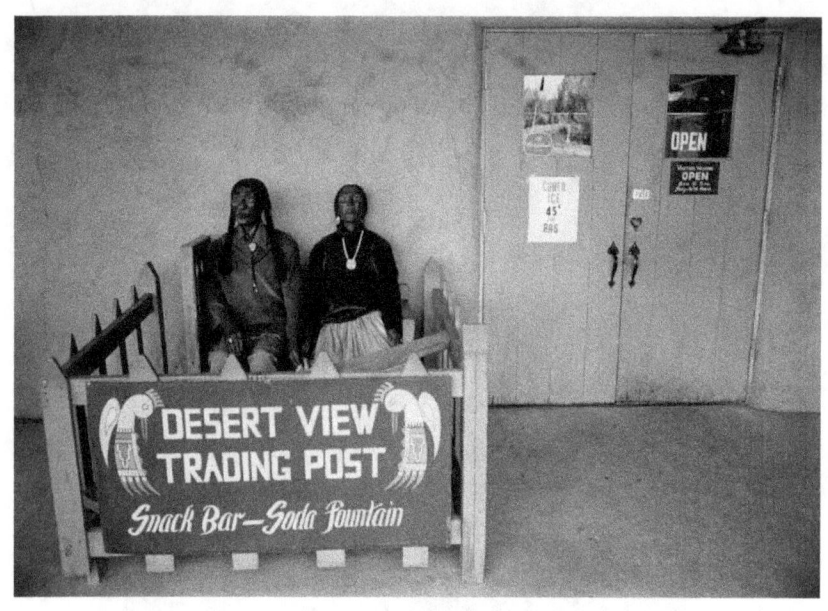

Captive Native Americans, Desert View Trading Post, 1965

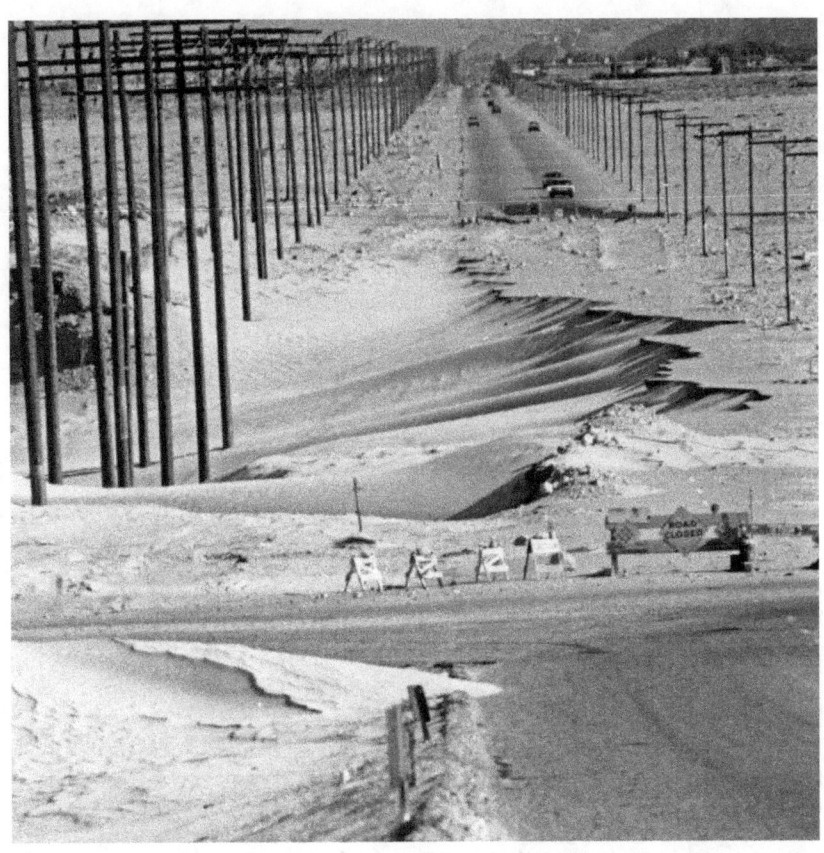

State Highway, once the Palm Springs Indian Reservation,1964

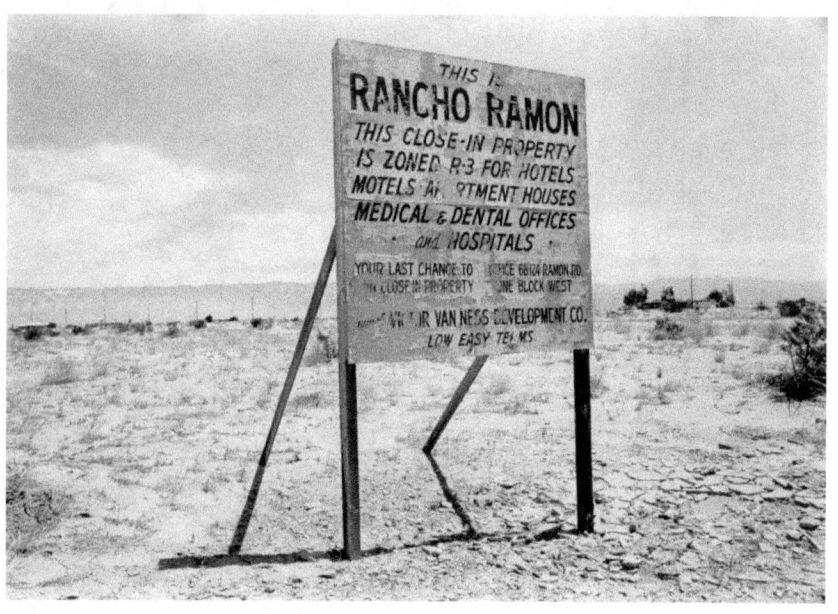

Failed Development Project, California and the Desert, 1965

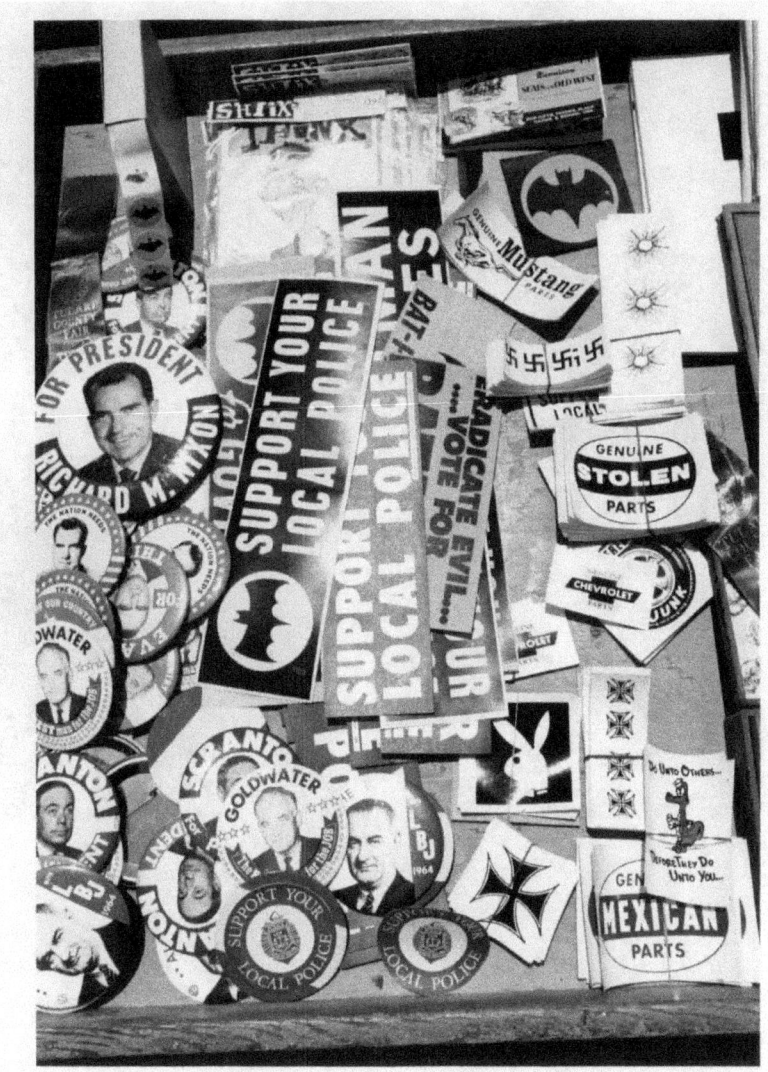

Election Choices, "Genuine Stolen Parts", 1966

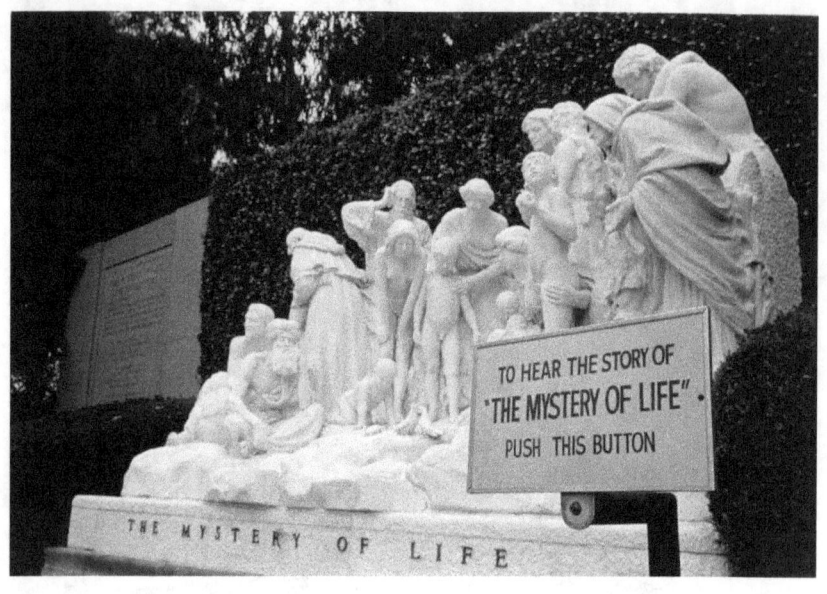

*Push This Button, the Mystery of Life, Forest Lawn Cemetery,
1966*

Hollywood, February 1966

I should point out as a preamble that in the whole state of California during the 1960s, there was only one sure way to become a huge success. Your success had to be extraordinary. It had to be off any measurable scale. You had to be a movie star!

It always seemed to me that the young Dennis Hopper summed up the California idea of great success in a wholly original manner.

Hopper's first decade and a half as a Hollywood actor was splattered across what seemed to be an extraordinarily long period. Hopper suffered neglect in his career so savage that his early struggles for stardom in Hollywood seem more like a slow-motion car wreck than a career. It included seven years, during which Hopper was blacklisted in Hollywood, and he'd been told he'd never work in movies again.

Originally from humble midwestern roots, Hopper first became a minor movie star, then *nada*. In the classic California rags-to-riches story of success, our hero was first a leper-like outcast in Tinseltown. Then, at age 33, Hopper finally had an off-the-charts mid-career success as a director–actor when he did *the* epic film of a generation, *Easy Rider*. Hopper had risen to the absolute pinnacle of the Hollywood heap, and he was a heartthrob actor, an emergent American icon of the counterculture, a movie star, and an A-list director. But Hopper's career had several different acts.

In the twists and turns of a complicated oeuvre, this led to something even grander in Hopper's life: a total crack-up!

If it was anything, in his post *Easy Rider* period, Hopper's crack-up was epic. He did drugs, he did a lot of drugs, and then more drugs. It left his brain frying like a Mexican pork rind, bubbling and spitting in a boiling vat of oil. With a career that was fatally damaged by this point, at the nadir of Hopper's disintegrating life, quite unbelievably (except in Hollywood) there was a happy ending.

Hopper found an understanding and caring fifth wife. He came into a lovely two-decade coda and final act, which entailed hitting the jackpot (again), with redemption (again) and, of course, since this is Hollywood, lots of cash.

With his new pile of dollars, as opposed to his diminished pile of old dollars (squandered on dope and a dissolute lifestyle), Hopper bought houses worth millions and filled them with expensive art.

Is any of this normal? No, but it's California. Boomland.

I knew Dennis. He was by turns brilliant, elusive, and wholly engaging. He was also his own worst enemy and his own best victim.

Of course, the acting parts Hopper played during the last two decades of his life were all men who were brilliant, ephemeral, and wholly engaging, that is, until they self- destructed. Only in Hollywood could you make a career like this.

Imagine creating an entirely new career out of disparate, legendary failures that made up the varied and weird narratives of your life, then channel them—with new-age emotive passion—into a wholly original and demented new artistic persona.

***

Hollywood first called to Dennis Hopper with its poisoned cup in 1955.

When he was nineteen years old, Hopper appeared in a film called *Rebel Without a Cause*. His appearance in this iconographic film was only a preamble to his vastly complex life.

In a twist of fate, everyone connected with *Rebel Without a Cause* seemed to be touched by tortured destinies. The director of the film, Nicholas Ray, witnessed his decadal career shrivel away to obscurity after making *Rebel Without a Cause*, while the other principal actors in the film, aside from Hopper, seemed doomed. James Dean was killed in a car crash shortly before the film was released; 21 years later Sal Mineo was murdered; and twenty six years later, in Catalina harbor, Natalie Wood drowned in suspicious circumstances.

Hopper's own misadventures in Hollywood began during the 1958 film production of *From Hell to Texas*, which was directed by the veteran director Henry Hathaway. As Hathaway narrated his encounter with Hopper, "I was the old Hollywood. He was the new Hollywood. I'd been making movies since 1930, but he figured that, because he'd appeared in *Rebel Without a Cause* with his buddy James Dean, he knew it all. [Hopper] figured he was the greatest young actor in the world."

"Well, he wasn't. He was a headstrong kid, full of dope and balls. He was a self-styled enfant terrible and a pain in the ass. I didn't like the way he was playing a scene, so I made him do it again...and again...and again. Take after take, from nine in the morning until ten at night. I did eighty separate long takes of this scene."

"Finally, he gave in, and I did the scene my way. But the studio dropped his contract like a hot tamale. He was on the fritz for a few years after that.... I think it taught him a lesson, but he never forgave me for driving him out of Hollywood." (Cf. "How did Hollywood hellraiser Dennis Hopper make it to the ripe age of 74?" Peter Evans for MailOnline 31 May 2010)

The "fritz" for Hopper, as Hathaway called it, lasted three-quarters of a decade. In Hollywood, that was a sentence of lifetime career termination.

I met Hopper in 1966. He lived in the Hollywood Hills with his wife, Brooke, and their young daughter, Marin.

The first time I met him, he told me about his seven-year hiatus from acting. It was something that ate away at him, and he never forgave Hollywood for neglecting him. During those seven years, unlike every other actor in Hollywood, he was determined to fashion a life for himself that was not dependent upon the film world. In our first meeting, he told me his life was centered on art and photography.

I'd been introduced to Hopper through Charles Cowles, who was then the publisher–owner of the young *Artforum* magazine, which later came to be the preeminent modern art magazine in the world. By 1966, Hopper collected both New York School painters and also what was known as Pop Art. He was very, very early into collecting '50s and '60s contemporary American art. There was a moment in the emergent art world of Los Angeles when you could buy an Andy Warhol soup can for $70.

I'd been told by Cowles that Hopper was one of the few contemporary photographers of California, in addition to being an art collector and actor.

Cowles said we should meet, as I was doing the same kind of photographic documentation of Southern California that Hopper was.

Hopper's house was on a tree-shaded street in the Hollywood Hills. It was a three-minute drive from the creeping seediness of what Hollywood Boulevard was becoming in the mid-1960s.

The movie people hated the dilapidation of what Hollywood now looked like. The Los Angeles artists, on the other hand, thought that the ongoing creep of Hollywood toward a tawdry kind of commercialized cinema-dream garbage dump was hugely entertaining. I drove past my own favorite building in Hollywood, Grauman's Chinese Theatre. It was the kind of building only a film-set designer would build, but only after a very bad night in an opium den in San Pedro.

As I began to climb into the Hollywood Hills, I found myself agreeing with the Los Angeles artists. Hollywood had reached a kind of uniquely recent perfection all its own. All of L.A. seemed to be on a tacky, vast downward slope, a two-story miasma of once-affordable housing gone to rot in the heat.

In the hills, I parked my car. I walked up to a modest house built in the 1930s. I knocked.

Dennis Hopper came to the door. He was of medium height. Cowles had phoned ahead and said that I was a friend of his and a photographer. Hopper smiled broadly. He had a kind of puckish glee to him as he waved me inside his house, as if the life he led in L.A. was constantly entertaining and amazing.

The inside of Hopper's smallish house was stuffed with the works of the pop artists on every surface. Other paintings of the slightly earlier New York School were overlapping each other and stacked three deep against the walls.

I'd only seen one single photograph of Hopper's. It had been taken in 1961. This photograph, in my opinion, was the greatest iconic Southern California photograph ever taken. It would never be equaled.

It was a photograph of two Standard Oil signs. It had been taken from inside a car, through the windshield. The picture marked where Santa Monica Boulevard, Melrose Avenue, and North Doheny Drive all met at the end of the most iconic road in America: Route 66. It was simultaneously about the past and the future of California.

Hopper settled into one of the two overstuffed chairs in his living room. I asked about his photographs. He said his work had been influenced by Los Angeles artists like Ed Kienholz and Ed Ruscha. He said he wanted to work in films but couldn't. "It is so frustrating, man," he said. "They slammed the door in my face. You have no fucking idea...."

He asked me what I was doing in L.A.

I said that when I was growing up in Berkeley, I'd once delivered newspapers to the iconic Farm Security Administration photographer Dorothea Lange. I'd been influenced by Lange's last grand idea before she died of cancer. Her idea was to create a document of California thirty-five years after the Great Depression. Its purpose was to recall when a select group of photographers at the Farm Security Administration (FSA) had documented America during the depths of the Depression.

"Damn. Absolutely wild," he mumbled.

I said I was working on this idea about what California had become in the generation after the FSA photographers.

Hopper told me that after his house and studio on Stone Canyon Road had burned in the 1961 Bel-Air Fire, there was nothing to keep him in L.A. He'd left Hollywood and gone to New York. In New York, he had studied acting with Lee Strasberg at the Actors Studio and gone to the exhibitions of the emergent young dealers who'd begun to show Pop Art.

Hopper had seen all the photography exhibitions put up at the Museum of Modern Art, and he hated the New York commercial worlds of fashion and advertising photography. He'd spent years in the city looking at exhibitions, buying art, and meeting artists.

We had tea.

When I asked what he was doing now, Hopper began to describe his own main discoveries in both photography and in art. "L.A. is the billboards, man. L.A. is the total, total automobile. Culture here never stops, night or day. In my own world, L.A. was movies and movie stars," he said. He paused, then described precisely what he was doing. "But then I saw what L.A. itself was. L.A. is what 'pop art' is about. That's why I collect all these paintings. L.A. is the future. This is the modern world. It's all these freeways. And I'm taking photographs of *everything*."

He waved around the room at his collection.

I looked around. I had to admit that if pop art ever went anywhere in the art world, Hopper would be a huge success with the art scattered around his modest house. But more important, perhaps, he was simply no longer an actor. He'd gone somewhere else. Hopper was living out his own creation, which was a kind of performance art. He loved it all. He was living out his own Hollywood dreams with a gorgeous wife, a crappy house in the Hollywood Hills, and an iconic yet failed career. In a way, I saw that by 1966, Hopper had succeeded in turning himself into his own movie.

"What I'm trying to do," Hopper said, "is explain what L.A. is. Maybe L.A. has always been this way.... It's just that no one's dealt with it before."

"You just can't believe the street culture of Los Angeles. It's so goddamn difficult to define, and it's so difficult to *get at* artistically. Think about it, man." Hopper paused, then he continued: "L.A. has this unique, consuming, fascinating, living and breathing culture. In L.A., you travel in order to buy things. Without a car, I'd be a dead man."

I thought about what he said. Perhaps the main new-world human artifact found in L.A. was a traffic light.

I'd now traveled 1,500 miles around L.A. trying to find people just to photograph them. Maybe Hopper and I crisscrossed L.A. and Hollywood using the same intersections. I didn't see how anyone driving through this place could avoid using the same cross streets. Maybe we'd staked out the same Vons Supermarket and the same exact Shakey's Pizza Parlor.

As documentary artists, every day of our lives we drove mile after mile through this consumer-obsessed miasma using the same lens. Dennis Hopper was the only other photographer I met during the 1960s in California who used a 28 mm lens to spread things to get to the center of pictures.

I left Hopper that afternoon with my head stuffed with a strange kind of revelation. We were both documenting L.A. and its totally new consumer-created landscape. We were both driving into our futures fixated on a version of America that was obsessed with buying things on sale and traveling vast distances to do so.

I saw Hopper one more time, when he invited me to his house because he wanted to see my pictures. I showed him some of my photographs of India, which I'd exhibited at the Santa Barbara Museum of Art, where they'd given me a whole gallery.

Then some of Hopper's friends arrived. In the general conversation that followed, we never spoke about photography again.

***

During a four-month period, I drove nearly 3,000 miles, moving through the gigantic urban sprawl of L.A.

But I wasn't driving around taking photographs of traffic lights and empty freeways. I was trying to find people to photograph.

I'd learned, in the hardest way possible, that people were nearly invisible in L.A. People didn't walk on the streets or gather in markets here. Perhaps they were all at home watching TV? In L.A., what you had was a curious connection between the invisibility of actual people to photograph on the streets and the astonishing public appearance of the suburban artifacts of a new type of American culture.

One of the observable, accessible places to make art documents of people were graveyards, places like Forest Lawn Cemetery. I was absolutely beset as well by the epic and magnificent auto graveyards of L.A.

As I worked around Forest Lawn over the weeks, I came to think of it as actually a kind of drive-in cemetery. You drove up, someone appeared with a hi-fi set, then the mourners arrived. For ten minutes, they listened to "Danny Boy" on hi-fi speakers. You parked the coffin by a hole. Friends and family cried, and then they left. Next, someone new appeared, and they buried the "client." Biff! Bam! Snap your fingers. In and out in fifteen minutes. Your time is over!

What always impressed me about Forest Lawn was that in the final inconvenient act of life, death was dealt with in such well-oiled expediency. This place was strange. Very strange. Some of the greatest names of Hollywood had taken up permanent residence here. Forest Lawn had invented a culture of no-fuss caring. After the mourners left the a grave, after the service I always marveled, that the turf fit just like a perfect, brand-new shirt. This was the new world, I supposed

For months, I photographed empty streets, gas stations, and broken people waiting at bus stops. I made documentary art out of a new period in American history.

***

Pacific Heights, San Francisco, 1966

I stepped back.

The answer of California's extraordinary indefinability became the great puzzles of my life.

How did one grapple with San Francisco and the whole state of California, both of which seemed to be evolving and disintegrating simultaneously, in some magnificent, incendiary, and karmic bundle?

Just as I wanted to photograph California, I also wanted to make a film on California.

From 1962 to 1965, I had made films on and off in India and America. It seemed to me, however, a film of California would be too random, too disparate. It had too many moving parts to it. As a practical matter, in Southern California at a place called Delano, you had the farmworkers agitating and organizing themselves. In time, the Delano Grape Strike and Boycott would become the emblematic moment of the entire Chicano community in America.

In parallel, Northern California and Southern California were two entirely separate "realities", both social and environmental, of what this state was and what it was becoming.

In addition, there were the other participants.

The Black Panthers were agitating for equality in Watts and East Oakland. There was the war in Vietnam, and the gigantic antiwar protests that had started in San Francisco five years before had travelled to Berkeley. Finally, there were the counterculture movements of a generation that was fighting its own battle for a different version of America.

The subject was too vast. It was too unwieldy. It was too huge.

I thought it through.

Narratively, a film on California and what was happening there was artistically impossible. It was an idea of too many levels. Then there was the expense involved. One could very easily expose 200,000 feet of 35 mm film on this subject and still not do it justice.

In the middle of a late night, I wondered if still photography didn't hold the answer to my problems of mental exhaustion, confusion, and a film that was so expensive to make, it was unaffordable.

I went for a walk in the fog-drenched streets of Pacific Heights in the early morning.

In the hours when opalescent fogs moved in over the Marin hills, then spilled silently across the bay toward San Francisco, I had an epiphany.

I knew of no one who had ever taken the approach of using solely photographs to make an entire documentary film. It hadn't happened because it was horrendously time-consuming.

You had to shoot hundreds upon thousands of photographs. Yet might it be possible to collapse time and create a filmed narrative of California with just photographs?

I wondered if filming my still photographs was the answer to my narrative problems.

It was an interesting thought.

Lately, there had even been new narrative additions to the creepy-crawly things that lived under the rocks of California.

California's suburbia seemed to have bred a brand-new group of Nazis. They had suddenly appeared like a flesh-eating social virus. Alternatively, what was occurring in the Haight-Ashbury district of San Francisco and on the Berkeley campus was also happening simultaneously in the tract houses of the Nazis in San Jose. These were things never seen before in America.

I remembered Dorothea Lange's idea of rephotographing both the locations and the people of the most important documentary project of the American 20th century.

 In the cold and fog of the early morning, I worried my narrative problem back and forth. I'd made films. I was a photographer. I thought of all the disparate strands that represented California in the mid-1960s.

At that moment, I realized I could animate all the narratives of this place with photographs. I could include blacks, Chicanos, American Nazis, and the psychedelic scene as well as the anti-Vietnam protests. I could also include an overlay of both the topography of Southern and Northern California. It would be in juxtaposition to an emerging suburban, mass-produced California and its new automobile culture.

I wanted to make a document of the greatest period I was living through.

It seemed to me that in this new kind of California we were looking at the future. It was a new kind of consumer culture—everywhere on Earth.

By the mid-1960s, California became the destination of an entire nation, which flocked to a state that offered seemingly never-ending prosperity.

But California, as the location for my film, had other things going for it that were equally important.

California was where a continent ended. It was also where the social bills that American society had run up were presented at the teller's office for payment.

Pry off the scabs of American racism and the iniquities faced by the American underclass, which included Native Americans, blacks, farmworkers, and the rural white poor, then whip up a cocktail of laboratory-produced psychedelic drugs, like LSD. The result was a new world.

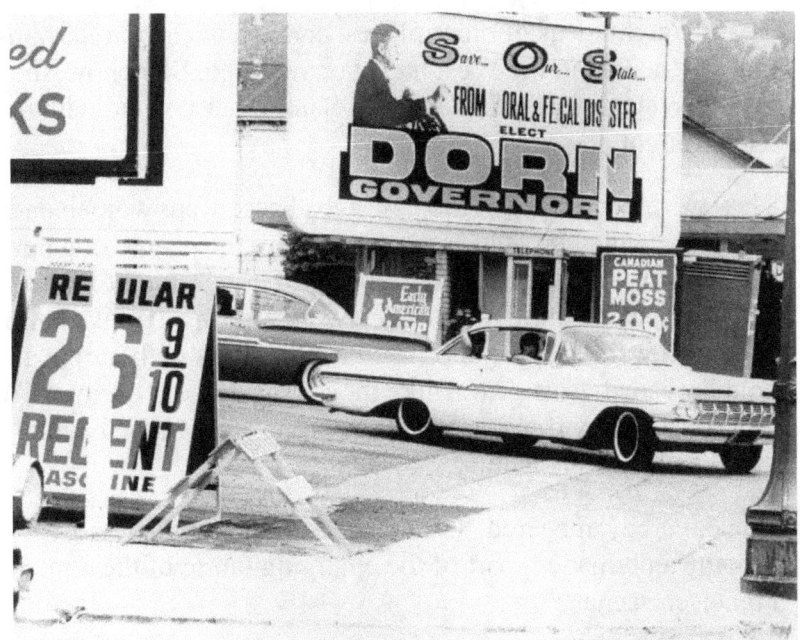

26 Cent Gas, Save Our State From Oral & Fecal Disaster, Los Angeles, 1966

In 1961, at the crossroads of the east in Kabul, I'd been out there. At the time, I'd wondered when the drug revolution would migrate from India and Afghanistan to America.

And then, as if by summoning up some brilliant flash of magic karma, to add something exotic and spicy to my film and its narrative, the most outrageous group on earth arrived in the Haight-Ashbury.

They were the people of the road.

They came from Kabul, Istanbul, Goa, North Africa, Kathmandu, and the Isla Mujeres. They were the variegated, tripped-out, international buccaneer brigands of the counterculture. Suddenly, they just appeared in San Francisco, and these were my sisters and brothers of the long, long Eastern road. (See: *The Orchid House: Art Smuggling and Appointments in India and Afghanistan,* Clark Worswick)

They brought ideas of other places, and of travels, into terrains that few people in the West had ever ventured. Somehow, they just *knew* what was going down in San Francisco, and with them they brought presents.

They were the people of the new age. These were women and men who had taken huge risks. They were the people of a new counterculture. Suddenly, they appeared in the Haight like smoke appears before a fire. They were wearing Turkish balloon pants and were dressed in ornate Pashtun coats with purple and gold brocaded vests; it was like they'd stepped out of time. They looked as if they'd just escaped the pirate coast at the beginning of the seventeenth century.

One day, they appeared. Then, at the end of 1965, they'd become a permanent part of the emerging fabric of the San Francisco scene.

It was then that I knew San Francisco would become the world center of the counterculture universe. The freaks had arrived.

I have no idea how they had reached America.

I also had no idea how anyone could get so much hashish into America.

Perhaps they'd just dropped down in San Francisco from Kabul through some unknown space-time continuum? Perhaps they'd discovered a path to higher consciousness and beamed themselves down here, along with their hashish? They came bearing tons, literally *tons,* of the best Waziristan hashish grown in the regions of the Tirah, from the inaccessible, unapproachable regions below the Khyber Pass, where a man could be killed for ten annas. (The anna is an old unit of Indian currency used under the British Raj, and one was equivalent to $0.75.)

What people in the West didn't yet realize was that these world travelers had established a five-year-old transnational movement of people that spanned the earth. These were people who had "dropped out" of Europe and America in the early 1960s.

In Kabul, in the Atlas Mountains of Morocco, on the beaches of the islands off the Yucatán Peninsula in Mexico, and on the burning *ghats* of Rajasthan, during the early 1960s, the freaks discovered that wherever you went in the world, you could carry your own space with you.

It was yours to define. Anywhere. Everywhere, to your individual detriment or your own benefit. The hippies, as they were mislabeled in San Francisco by the popular press, were the first Westerners who realized that all human interactions—yes, including commerce—first started inside one's own head.

I'd been in Kabul in 1961, when it began to happen. For me, it was like old-home week in San Francisco. My once lost, and now newly arrived sisters, and brothers of the endless roads of Asia dug in and changed the scene.

Living on a diet of naan, alkaloids, and pilaf on the streets of the Haight-Ashbury, they flowed past the local inhabitants as if they existed in their own temporal universe. In San Francisco, they began to thrive like the exotic, invasive, highly adaptable high-altitude plants they'd ingested in Southeast Asia, Java, Madagascar, and the beach towns of Kerala in India.

When I saw the first of them in San Francisco, somehow by Karmagram, they *knew*.

San Francisco was where it was *at*. They were the Swedes, the Germans, the Dutch, and the French. They were the British, as well as the Americans, the Italians, and, of course, the

Australians. First, small groups of them had appeared. Then came the deluge, and all of them together began to define San Francisco in a way no one had ever seen before.

***

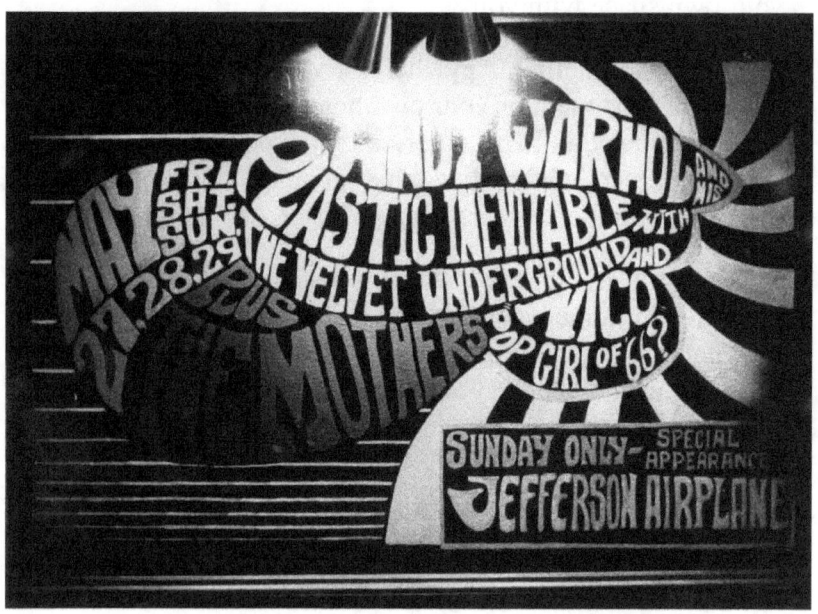

San Francisco /Fillmore Ballroom Poster,

May 27,1966

As the months went on, a kind of new San Francisco music *happened*. It was invented by groups like Big Brother and the Holding Company, Jefferson Airplane, and the Grateful Dead. Soon, even mainstream music in America would change. People began arriving in San Francisco from everywhere.

In the nights ahead, in places like the Avalon Ballroom and the Fillmore Auditorium, both music and the counterculture combined. This new coming together defined alternatives and different approaches, and changed people who wanted to live in a different world.

Whether they succeeded or failed was unimportant in the here and now. *It was happening.*

There would be concerts of increasingly important rock-and-roll musicians from all over the country, an, they too, came to San Francisco to see what was going down. Little did anyone know, this music, in a wail of guitars in the weeks, months, and years ahead, would provide a counterpoint to a war that was ripping America apart.

Frank Zappa appeared from Los Angeles. From New York came the Velvet Underground with Lou Reed, Nico, and Andy Warhol. From Chicago came the original King of Rock and Roll Ellas Otha Bates, better known as Bo Diddley, and he turned an insulting gig of doing a warm-up act for a local group into a moment that took rock and roll into a different place.

Coming on stage Mr.Diddley smiled hugely. After thousands of appearances over the decades in Chicago, Bo Diddley showed San Francisco where it was *at*. Looking offstage at Janice Joplin, and her group Big Brother and the Holding Company he ripped a hole through the center of the San Francisco music scene.

In a forty-minute set of the most tightly perfect, incendiary, unspooled, blast-the-top-of-your-head-off rock and roll I've ever heard in my life Bo Diddley tore the roof off the Avalon Ballroom that night. That night in the Avalon Ballroom San Francisco heard the music of the master.

***

In San Francisco, events were occurring that seemed to tumble over themselves into infinity.

It was barely possible to keep up.

Something was happening daily, even hourly.

You had to forget about wondering where it would go, then you had to forget to ask yourself whether this was good or malign. You had to forget everything you knew and simply go with it. You had the feeling that this was too good, too important, too astounding.

Making any sense of the things unfolding in slow motion in front of you was like trying to divine the progress of an otherworldly grand accident.

It was impossible. Something this remarkable could not last.

***

Newhall, California, February 1966

During late February, I decided, as a centerpiece to my work of documenting California, to photograph the final stages of the ruinous breakup of one of the greatest century-old landholdings still owned by a single California family.

The properties of the Newhall Land and Farming Company originally had been assembled by Henry Newhall, a California railway pioneer.

In the 1870s, Newhall had cannily purchased a checkerboard of truly gigantic eighteenth-century Mexican land grants. These blocks of land comprised a staggering 143,000 acres (579 square kilometers) of the state. They represented tracts of land up and down California, from Monterey to Los Angeles.

These holdings were so large, an entire oil field was discovered on one tract. On another tract, the publishing magnate William Randolph Hearst bought a chunk of California, upon which he built a castle complete with century-old furnishings ripped out of some of the great houses of Europe. Miles and miles of private Pacific coastline were sold by the Newhalls to Hearst, and they became the indispensably necessary baronial setting for Hearst's new castle. Even the U.S. government bought a parcel of Newhall land. It later formed one of the largest army bases in the United States Ford Ord.

A scant thirty miles north of Los Angeles, and with its still large remaining landholdings, the town of Newhall, California, was billed as the fastest-growing community in America in 1966.

For the Newhalls, there lay a narrative of what can happen to a great landholding family and its considerable estate when even the best-laid plans, made by some of the smartest people on earth over several generations, were ravaged by local politicians.

At the beginning of the twentieth century, the Newhall family, with great foresight, had invested heavily in planting huge orange groves to utilize the considerable resources of their land.

The idea was to create a new, sweeter orange. The Valencia groves of the Newhall family came to sweep across vast acreages in a gently rolling landscape. These ordered rows of orange trees, thick with fruit, seemed to stretch on forever.

In time, the orange groves of California became emblematic of a kinder, gentler place near the heart of the ever-shining sun of America.

The holdings of the Newhall Land and Farming Company started one valley north of downtown Los Angeles and Hollywood. During the 1960s, these landholdings became themselves too succulent to resist. For a new breed of California land developers, it was irresistible.

These developers first appeared in the state when new populations began to appear in California, during and after World War II. With the arrival of the 1950s, the developers had established relationships with adventurous marginal bankers, and a then-small group of potato politicians. In the decade and a half that followed, in an era of truly impressive state and municipal corruption, the developers' moment had arrived.

During the next forty years, this group would change the landscape of an entire continent. But nowhere was this viral infestation more pronounced than in California. To use a 1960s counterculture term to describe this devastation, it was a "happening" that remained in a league all its own.

In California, the developers went into hyperdrive. Impressively, they had one of the most advanced cases of American greed that was raised to astonishingly almost incandescent proportions.

Like some remarkable fruit-borer infestation, the developers ravaged the century-old California land-grant families, using their connections in the state capital of Sacramento, and with only a slight tweak in the rules governing property taxes.

No matter the land's present use; henceforth, land taxes would be levied on land at what its "best use" would be.

In the beginning of the 1960s, the "best use" of California agricultural land was considered to be taking thousands, even millions, of acres of dormant farmland, then planning and constructing uncountable numbers of suburban houses on this land. Terrifying.

The rape of California proceeded on a truly horrendous scale.

With a change of just two words in the statutes relating to land use, the huge agricultural landholdings of the Newhall family were doomed. The tax burden, which fell upon the Newhall Land and Farming Company and the other large land-grant holders, became overwhelming.

In answer to this onslaught, the family company evolved a master plan, which included the creation of new communities called Valencia and Newhall. But it also included the creation of what would become the prestigious California Institute of the Arts and a 256-acre amusement park called Magic Mountain.

From today's perspective, CalArts has become one of the most respected arts faculties in America. During 2013, Six Flags Magic Mountain amusement park saw more than two million eight hundred thousand visitors.

According to a statistic compiled from corporate records maintained byMagic Mountain itself, the park had a world record of eighteen roller coasters in operation.

The corporation announced "…the freefall drop attraction will be integrated into both sides of the park's 415-foot-tall tower structure. It will be called Superman: Escape from Krypton, and it will rank as the world's tallest drop tower."

***

In the early winter of 1966, I arrived in Newhall, California, in a beaten-up eight-year-old car with my cameras.

I had grown up with two of the Newhall boys. They were among my best friends. They were twins named Jon and Tony. Their father, Scott Newhall, was a buccaneering, larger-than-life figure that only occasionally occurs in the history of any family.

That morning, I'd passed through the waterless immediate valleys beyond the Hollywood Hills.

As I drove toward the town of Newhall, I moved across a battered landscape that was between nothing and more nothing. Beyond my car windows was a fantastical, barren world described topographically as a semidesert that cooked in the heat. It was a place that had been gouged. Riven.

Driving out of Los Angeles that morning, I saw what the developers had been doing. They seemed hard at work scooping and tearing up the landscape with an energetic and almost frantic energy against deadlines undreamed of.

As this depressing place scrolled past my car windows, the low scrublands on either side of the highway had been mutilated by huge bulldozers. The land had been ripped into a grid of newly laid-out roads. Surrealistically, the roads apparently led nowhere, and in this barren expanse, the roads headed toward a set of distant hills and then simply stopped at no apparent destination. The bleakness of this place was unrelieved. Perhaps these giant machines operated by manic-depressive optimists were creating a magnificent surrealistic earthwork in a brand new art form!

As I drove, a bright light had switched on. This was actually the landscape of nowhere. It was mile after mile of nowhere, stretching out endlessly on either side of the road leading into and out of Newhall, California.

When I reached Newhall, it seemed that the whole town was the sort of one-story place you used to see from one end of western America to the other. It was a place on the long highways you drove through. You dreaded stopping in any of those towns because they were all the same, and you thought you were in a fever dream from which you could never escape.

Newhall had a few two-story buildings. For the most part, the town was strung along a dusty, straight, sunblasted Southern California two-lane highway, and it seemed to have materialized here for no apparent reason.

My friend wasn't in. Jon was the editor of the family newspaper, *The Newhall Sentinel*. He would return shortly, I was told. I waited.

As I looked out the window in Jon's office, I realized that the only thing that seemed to happen at midday here was a dance of dust devils. Steep columns of wind whipped dirt and sand vertically into the sky. The dust devils swept slowly up and then down the main street. The wind blew fine sand into the office. It began to gum my eyes.

What a place to wind up! God.

I had the intuition that as large as California was, the state was running out of room. The future waited out there, and it had plans for Newhall. Perhaps this place was the new version of Hell?

The town didn't have the lush topographical abundance of California's rich agricultural central valley. It didn't look out on the elevations and opera of the Sierra Nevada Mountains. My friend Jon and his family seemed by some malign fate to occupy the soon-to-be subdivided dominions of their family's ancestral lands.

As I sat in this office, possibly suffering heatstroke, I had the happy intuition of being able to see California in a totally new light.

I imagined gainful work for an entire generation of seldom-employed people.

I imagined people who knew nothing except how to operate huge Caterpillar bulldozers at top speed. Somehow, the idea came to my possibly overheated mind that the chamber of commerce and the developers were intent on creating a wholly new Southern California landscape. It was a place where they expected millions of prospective inhabitants to materialize themselves from somewhere else.

Wasn't that how California had been first settled? People had just showed up?

I had lunch with Jon Newhall. I told him, quite happily, that I was in Newhall to document the changing future of California.

I wanted to document what was happening to the immediate landscape of Newhall. I thought the already-tilting sign at the entrance to town was both inspirational and, I trusted, prophetic. It read:

Welcome to Newhall, the fastest-growing community in America!

"Is that true?" I asked doubtfully. "Is this the fastest-growing community in America?"

"That was my brother Tony's idea," Jon said. "I think it stinks, but go look for yourself and report back."

He then added, with the typical candor that I always loved, "It's grotesque. I thought it was hysterical when they put up that sign."

Jon stared down at the sodden hamburger that had just been put on his plate. Then he lapsed into a deeply uncommunicative state. Perhaps he was studying his small, forlorn pile of incinerated French fries and wondering how he'd gotten here.

After lunch, I left Jon to his literary endeavors and retreated to my battered car. My interview with the oracle of Newhall hadn't gone well. At the end of our lunch, Jon was almost comatose.

***

Five or six miles away from Newhall, the paved roads that had been constructed out of the town veered off at right angles from the highway. If you made a violent right-hand turn across what seemed to be barren hillsides, after a mile or so you found a place where sewer culverts were sunk every hundred yards into the earth along the road. Then, in a triumphant clarion call of progress, through the afternoon glare, I saw that there already were street signs along this road.

I stopped my car and looked toward the west. In the blinding light, I could just imagine rows of houses that would ascend up the low hillsides. In the months and years ahead, modest two- and three-bedroom houses would rest peacefully on these gentle slopes under nighttime stars on clear desert nights. Twenty feet away was a street sign. It said *Orange Blossom Drive*. Ah, at last. Out there, another tilting sign almost collapsing in the heat, I saw the fine cynicism of the editor of *The Newhall Sentinel* that I knew. It was in full cry.

Orange Blossom Drive. Divine. At that moment, the landscape began to blow away in huge clouds of dust.

I couldn't imagine it becoming populated with tens of thousands of homes, created for the dreaming, teeming millions of California's new residents. With all that faith in a prosperous future, not even a single foundation had been put in. I gave up thinking practical thoughts like this and got into my car. I didn't take any photographs. There wasn't anything to take photographs of.

Farther down the road were small gaggles of half-built houses settled randomly over different sets of forlorn hills. Again, I tried to take photographs. But it was like making a corpse dance. I spent twenty frustrating minutes attempting to animate the inanimate.

Twelve miles away from Newhall, another proposed community sprouted in the distance.

As I drove closer, I discovered this new community was part of the empire of a Los Angeles developer who had connections with Bart Lytton, the sainted owner-entrepreneur of the Lytton Savings & Loan Association. Scores of houses had already been constructed. Others were near completion.

As I stood there squinting into the glare in a dazed state, many of these partially finished houses looked like tiny units of an unfinished children's school project. They seemed so flimsy and poorly constructed. I wondered, Could you actually poke your finger through one of the walls?

The cookie-cutter houses that had been finished were dwarfed by the immensity of the skies behind them.

I stood in front of a sign that advertised one of these new developments.

The words on the sign all came down on the side of a new kind of California-bred insanity.

After all, when I thought about it, weren't all the settlers of California in the 1850s and 1860s filled with a kind of heroic dementia, making nine-month treks across deserts, mountains, and interminable prairie grasslands? Hadn't the settlers who first reached California come to this place with only one thing in common? They were all broke.

The sign read:

$99 DOWN. 99 MORE PAYMENTS TO GO...FOR ONE OF THE FINEST RESIDENCES IN CALIFORNIA

A hundred yards further on there were two other signs parked out on the desert in the wind.

Spaced only feet apart the first, then the second read:

If you were home now, this would be your house!!

Your chance to own your piece of the future. $12,995 ONLY!

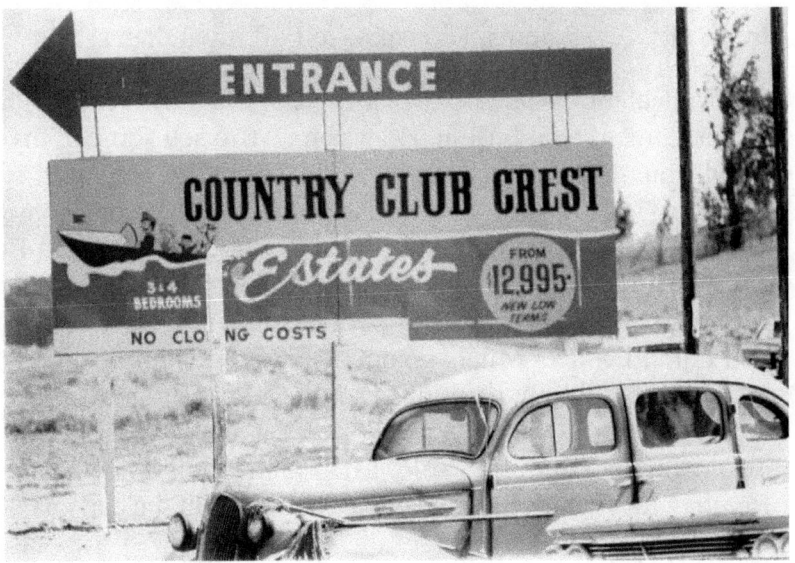

Country Club Crest, from $12,995, no closing costs, 1966

That night, I drove north to San Francisco.

When I considered it objectively, Southern California had entered a completely new era of inscrutability.

***

San Francisco, March 1966

In the past few months, I began to sell off my Indian art.

I had a dealer on Rodeo Drive in Beverly Hills with whom I had a consignment relationship. He was trying to sell some of my Gandharan third-century stucco Buddhas that I'd bought in Peshawar in 1961. In San Francisco, I had another consignment relationship with the Indian art dealer Ray Lewis, to whom I'd consigned hundreds of small Kishangarh paintings. He wanted paintings by the great Mughal-period court artist Baswant. I told him I didn't collect Mughal paintings. Ray settled for some incomparable Rajput paintings from the eighteenth century done in Rajasthan instead. The prices offered to me were $75 a picture, but not until they sold. I'd spent $500 in Calcutta and Bombay for Rajasthani Kishangarh paintings in the early 1960s.

Wipeout. Total art-collecting wipeout.

Perhaps someday, Indian paintings would be valued not only for their rarity, but also for their artistic importance. These Rajput works were some of the greatest paintings ever produced in India. But their time had not come, evidently—at least not yet.

I alternated my living quarters between Pacific Heights in San Francisco and the artist Arne Hiersoux's studio, just beyond the railway tracks in the vicinity of the Albany–Berkeley city line.

The studio was in a disused warehouse. On the right side of Arne's studio was another warehouse that contained the studio of Peter Voulkos. For months, I documented Voulkos and his work of casting his bronzes, which went on into the early mornings. Voulkos was a well-known sculptor and executed commissions at that moment for the municipal authorities of Fresno, California, his most important client .

On the left side of Arne's studio was yet another live-in warehouse. In this warehouse, a musician named Fred Marshall used his repurposed industrial space for improvisational jazz sessions with his friends. Fred's girlfriend was the diminutive Beverly Bivens, who had just had the number-one record in America with a group called the We Five. Their hit was called "You Were on My Mind."

It seemed to me that the most important preoccupation the inhabitants of these Berkeley warehouses had on their minds was living as cheaply as possible.

As Beverly Bivens struggled with fame—and now seemed to be melting away on a macrobiotic diet—in San Francisco, other musicians struggled with their music. These San Francisco musicians seemed to subsist on herbalist diets fueled by marijuana and LSD, and they had strange names like Jefferson Airplane, Big Brother and the Holding Company, or the Grateful Dead. Similar to those in the ratty warehouses of Berkeley, most of the San Francisco groups lived in run-down, post-earthquake, Edwardian houses in generally dilapidated, substandard conditions.

The small groups of people involved in "the scene" mostly knew one another in San Francisco, but this was a long, long way away from the New York media, recording, and art worlds. Although things were happening elsewhere, it was difficult to believe much would happen in San Francisco, or California as a whole. All my life, I'd heard that San Francisco would be the next great place from the people who lived there.

In the corner of Hiersoux's studio, I slept on a wooden bed platform with an inch-thick mattress. It was like living in Quetta, Pakistan, except for the cold of the Baluchistan Desert. The studio was full of Hiersoux's huge paintings, which were fourteen feet long and six feet high. I had a beaten-up German-made Opel sedan.

The Berkeley campus was ten minutes away. Much of what was happening in the protest movement these days in America was occurring at night on Telegraph Avenue.

On the streets of Berkeley, however, the anti-Vietnam protests were moving away from ordered reasoning about the war and toward argument, rancor, and violence.

Lately, the leaders of the protests had fallen to disagreeing with one another. You could tell who was winning these arguments by who got the most press coverage as a leader of the protests. I began to wonder why movements, that generated grand ideas eventually became controlled by people with the most rotten and controlling personalities.

According to the *San Francisco Chronicle*, a newspaper I occasionally took photographs for, there had been a "police riot" that I'd covered a few weeks before on Telegraph Avenue.

Police riot was a term I'd never heard until I read it in the *Chronicle*. What it referred to was the police losing control of themselves and going berserk.

Given the patriotic zeal of the average Berkeley policeman, of course, anything was possible. And since most police go around heavily armed, at some point they are going to make use of their weapons.

The scene: 9:30 p.m., Telegraph Avenue, Berkeley

Seven hundred marchers come up the avenue. They approach the Berkeley campus. The crowd surges forward. The campus gates are two blocks away.

Reverse angle: The Berkeley police are dressed in nonthreatening beige-colored riot helmets. They carry nightsticks, or blackjacks. The police move in from a side street where they've formed into tightly disciplined, uniformed squads, out of sight of the marchers.

Up the avenue, the protestors move toward the police.

The police have halted in the center of the street and block the protest's path.

I take photographs of the police. I am now inside a rapidly closing sandwich. I'm wedged between the police and the protestors.

I photograph one group, then I pivot and photograph the other group.

The protestors advance.

The idée fixe of the Berkeley police department was very simple. They are here to protect the treasures and intellectual riches held by the University of California's Berkeley campus. They are here to fend off the ungodly—the new barbarians.

The protestors wave their antiwar signs. Under the glare of the streetlights, they start chanting.

"One…two…three…four. We don't want another war. Five…six…seven…eight. We don't want a fascist state!"

The protestors halt in front of the police.

I run for my life, scuttling sideways through a row of angry protestors.

Close-up: A long line of rugged-looking but clean-cut Berkeley policemen grip their nightsticks as they hunch forward like grim, determined football linesmen about to charge the opposing team.

The linesmen set themselves…then, without a single word of command, the police charge the protestors.

It is fifty policemen against 700 protestors.

I'm about two seconds from becoming crushed. I flee for my life!

I turn and look at the policemen over my shoulder as I run.

Behind me, under the peculiar mercury-tinted glare of TV reporters' lights, is a symphony of chaos.

Young women have their heads split open.

Students go down, and they are trampled by the policemen's heavy boots.

Between Caffe Mediterraneum on one side of the street and Cody's Books on the other, the policemen run absolutely amok.

They wade into the center of the protestors, swinging their heavy batons like baseball bats.

The protestors try retreating, but there is nowhere to retreat to. Hundreds of protestors are now jammed into the narrow width of Telegraph Avenue.

For some reason, the policemen begin to realize they are about to be overwhelmed by the sheer number of protestors that they've taken on. They redouble their savagery.

Meanwhile, I'm photographing this monstrosity.

Putting my left arm up, I ward off a policeman who aims at my head with his baton. My arm gets totally whacked, and pain rockets up it. I shoot photographs with my right hand, advancing the film with my thumb. I wonder if my arm is broken.

At the same time, I'm moving to the side, away from the cop as he pivots from me and rams his nightstick point into the face of a young man next to me.

The protestor's nose cracks with a pop.

Blood spurts, splashing the policeman's face.

The police have gone absolutely insane.

On the protestors' part, given their wounds, the blood, and their broken faces, if one of them had at that moment punched a policeman in the face, that would have been the provocation that escalated this confrontation. In that case, I doubt seriously that some of the police would have survived being kicked to death.

There is no longer any room for the police to draw their guns, nor even raise their batons.

There is no escape for anyone. Four or five hundred people are now jammed into a space between buildings that is seventy-five feet wide by one hundred and fifty feet long.

Taking total, unremitting punishment, the young people are still gripping their signs, but slowly, ever so slowly, they are moving back the way they came, down the avenue.

The television crews were there from the local stations. The newspaper reporters were there. Every one of them saw what happened.

I grew up in Berkeley. In a few brief seconds, because of the absolute stupidity of the one police captain on duty that night, my respect for the Berkeley police department disappeared.

For another five minutes, Telegraph Avenue was a scene of prolonged, totally unnecessary brutality. Then, suddenly, it was over. The *San Francisco Chronicle* qualified this police action, in measured words, as a "protest riot".

The lieutenants and the captain who were there that night were never censured. Not a single policeman was ever charged in this outrage.

It was as if the protest and its aftermath had been a small municipal inconvenience, like chasing naughty chipmunks out of the local park.

***

The Music Scene, Los Angeles, April. 1966

As I photographed Berkeley and San Francisco, the musicians I once knew as normal people became celebrities after they'd touched the third rail of fame.

Perhaps those musicians, who had lived in ratty houses and dressed up in funny clothing, were just scalded by fame and not electrocuted. One can only hope. Whatever happened, it was a very odd transformation to watch.

In San Francisco and Berkeley, music groups never gave up their commitments to the community. In 1966 and '67, they were absolutely stalwart in their support of free music for the people.

The polar opposite were the musicians of Los Angeles. The L.A. groups seemed motivated only by cold, hard cash. Perhaps this was a central part of a new L.A. world that was coming for all of us. The Los Angeles music scene was typified by groups like the Beach Boys, who billed hundreds of thousands of dollars for their appearances, or the newly created psychedelic band ambiguously named the Seeds.

In L.A., world-class, eccentric, and marvelously strange things were happening to the rock-and-roll world.

In an almost perfect contrast to what was occurring in Northern California, the leader of the Seeds, Sky Saxon, began to have a nearly schizoid nervous breakdown. This was followed by collapse of the group.

Saxon suddenly quit and, in what might be thought of as a wildly-inspired lateral LA career move, joined the YaHoWha religious group.

YaHoWa? For the uninitiated, the YaHoWha was led by the venerated Father Yod.

Yod, formerly known as James Edward Baker, had been by turns a Marine, a Hollywood stuntman, and a jujitsu teacher, but then he turned into... you've probably already guessed it ... a Vedantic monk.

Spiritually, Father Yod's previous religious transformations had been influenced by his association with the Nature Boys. He was a vibrant, only-in-L.A. curriculum vitae.

In the Hollywood Hills the Nature Boys had practiced and lived close to the absolute spiritual center of the world while, according to nature's all-important laws, maintaining a balanced vegetarian diet.

Father Yod opened one of America's first health-food restaurants in the late 1960s. This restaurant was strategically located on the Sunset Strip, the semi crummy neon-lit cultural heart of West Hollywood.

Later, following his own spiritual "vibrations," Father Yod founded the Source Family, a spiritual commune located in a mansion in the Hollywood Hills.

Southern California. A garden of the spirit. A place of abundance, variety, vitality, and color. Sometimes it's very difficult to describe California to outsiders.

> **The Death of Yod** (Cf. Wikipedia) "At the end of 1974, the Source Family (headed by YaHoWa) sold their restaurant and moved to Hawaii. On August 25, 1975, despite having no previous hang-gliding experience, YaHoWha used a hang glider to leap off a 1300-foot cliff on the eastern shore of Oahu. He successfully flew his kite but crash-landed on the beach and died nine hours later. After three days of vigil, YaHoWha was cremated." http://en.wikipedia.org/wiki/Father_Yod - cite_note-LA-6)

***

The Music Scene, San Francisco, April 1966

What was unique about the musicians and their music in San Francisco, as opposed to L.A., was that the San Francisco groups seemed to be acting out wonderful, almost medieval, roles in the counterculture. Both photographically exotic, and spiritually distant from our time, they were riven by their tithing's to the community.

What also made San Francisco distinct from L.A. was that it was home to two quite unforgettable dance halls. Both the Avalon Ballroom, run by Chet Helms, and the Fillmore Auditorium, run by Bill Graham, were lodged in the most distressed and seedy commercial districts of the city. They were ground zero for a frantic, energized music scene. Both of these venues were marked, as well, by the singular personalities of their creators. Chet Helms had the highest regard for the community and for cooperative endeavors, while Bill Graham worshipped everything that money bought.

At least half of the credit for the music of the counterculture of San Francisco, as it came into its own in 1966, lay with Graham, a deeply repellent, grim, rumpled, physically dirty and mercenary creature. I personally despised Graham. He was neither a likable nor a kind person.

Born Wulf Wolodia Grajonca in Berlin, Graham grew up in an orphanage.

I am sure there are happy people born in Berlin. But Little Wulf was not one of them.

In the years I photographed him at the Fillmore, I don't remember Graham ever smiling once. He was Russian by ethnicity, and he carried the tragedies of Russia around with him like they were bonded to him in a dirty sack. If such a thing is possible, Graham's astoundingly nasty personality had a vileness that was almost epic.

It was Graham's policy to staff his auditorium with thug-like guards, because he didn't like nonpaying guests.

Given that Graham was running one of the greatest psychedelic emporiums in the world, he had an abiding paranoia about many of his guests' frequent use of mind-altering drugs. Over the years, Graham's chief fear was being closed down by "the Gestapo," as he called them.

In Graham's world, he imagined his enemies more or less constantly. Out there in the darkness, they were scheming to create a KGB-like "provocation" of inconvenient traces of marijuana backstage. They would plant bags full of glowing LSD dust during one of his musical evenings.

Without the Fillmore Auditorium, the scores, if not hundreds, of musicians that Graham booked, the music scene would never have developed the way it did in San Francisco. Without Graham, and his almost unappeasable ego seared by paranoia, would Lou Reed accompanied by Andy Warhol or Frank Zappa ever have appeared in San Francisco?

A crowd of 100,000 people turned out in Golden Gate Park to attend a free musical war-protest event. Outside the Fillmore, music groups played for little or no money to thousands, and then tens of thousands, of people.

***

Of all the things that came together in California during the 1960s, the year 1966 was the year when "it" happened in San Francisco and L.A.

"It" included the coming together of the drug scene, along with the invasion of California by the disenchanted, alienated suburban children of America. The year 1966 was also the moment when the California music scenes in both Los Angeles and San Francisco changed American popular culture, and the children of America flocked to California to be part of the scene.

Nineteen sixty-six became the year rock n'roll took over a whole country.

Chet Helms, an academic drifter, was the city's opposite of Bill Graham.

Helms first appeared in San Francisco from Texas during 1962. He was following the siren call of Jack Kerouac and the Beat generation, who, themselves, had heard the vibrations of this strange fogbound city.

In San Francisco, Helms put together a sort of life, squatting in other people's apartments and dealing marijuana. At one point, he moved into a low-rent boarding house in the Haight-Ashbury district, at 1090 Page Street. In this huge Edwardian-style, post-earthquake house, with its full-length basement, Helms began putting together jam sessions for local bands and musicians. In 1965, he started charging an admission fee of fifty cents.

Central to his future, and to the future of San Francisco music, Helms lured his friend Janis Joplin to the city from Texas. In company with Joplin, Helms formed a band called Big Brother and the Holding Company, with Joplin jamming in the Page Street district basement.

During this period, Helms also formed a loose connection with the Family Dog, a commune of hippies living at 2125 Pine Street in the Haight-Ashbury. By February 1966, Helms had moved into the Family Dog house and produced his first epic rock-and-roll concert at the San Francisco Longshoremen's Hall.

If the history of the music scene is ever written, it should include the moment that Ed Denson, the manager of another Bay Area group called Country Joe & the Fish, described the genesis of the Fish as a group. One can only think that the Surrealists in Paris during the 1920s should have founded a musical group to go along with their art movement. But then, they didn't have Day-Glo paint.

According to Denson, who wrote about the group's genesis in 1968:   http://www.well.com/~cjfish/begin.htm

> These were the days before the San Francisco dance halls.... That day we spent Day-Gloing our T-shirts with peace symbols and altering Barry's Beethoven sweatshirt to read *Marx*. The washtub [we played] was Day-Gloed psychedelic.

> That concert was a roaring success, halfway between a happening and a performance. We led off with antiwar songs mingled with the lyric pieces Joe [McDonald] was writing. We were not just the only antiwar band in the area, we were *the only* band in the area, and our daring was spectacular. We half expected to be arrested for singing our songs.

> Allen [Ginsberg] sat cross-legged on the chemistry workbench we were using for a stage, chanting and reading his poems, and then the Fugs [a New York group with poets Ed Sanders and Tuli Kupferberg, came on and finished off the evening. Their appearance was defiantly hippy, and to climax the evening's smashing of their instruments, their lead guitarist passed out and fell backward off the stage while they threw shredded IBM cards at the audience.

> That was our first public performance—an inchoate result of the spirit of the times[…]. The band members made $20 each, the audience was visibly shocked as it left, the poster appeared in various underground movies later. Of course we had no plans to appear again; our plans had gone no further than the day of the concert.

[…] Slowly, like an awakening dreamer
lost in time, the band formed during the
first months of 1966.

In early 1966, Helms formally founded Family Dog
Productions. With manic energy, he began promoting concerts
for the Fillmore Auditorium. However, after trying to deal with
Bill Graham, Helms's chief venue became the Avalon Ballroom
at 1268 Sutter Street.

The never-to-fail locomotive of Helms' wonderfully peculiar
empire henceforth became the Avalon.

Between April 1966 and November 1968, Helms and the
Avalon staged a series of legendary San Francisco concerts. To
promote these, Helms published Aubrey Beardsley–esque
psychedelic posters and handbills, which were created by a
group of San Francisco's off-the-grid artists, including Alton
Kelley, Stanley Mouse, Rick Griffin, Steve Renick and Victor
Moscoso. The posters were sold in local bookstores and at head
shops for $5 each. Today these posters, in their dual roles of art
and commerce, remain some of the few visible, world-class art
objects produced from the firmament that was San Francisco
during the mid-1960s.

When I first met Chet Helms, he'd adopted the costumes of the
1960's European vagabond travelers to Indian Asia circa 1961.
He looked like he'd migrated eastwards in a cloud of rich,
brown hashish fumes, a member of a Euro-Afghan dope
caravan.

At the Avalon Ballroom, it was Helms's style to promote
himself as well as his bands. In June 1966, Big Brother and the
Holding Company debuted at the Avalon, and the huge heroin-
laced career of Janis Joplin was born that night.

Helms had first met Janis in Texas years before and never
wavered in his support of her. The only time she ever failed him
was when he booked the most famous black rock-and-roll singer
in America, Bo Diddley, to appear on the same bill as his

protégé. That night, Diddley opened as a warm-up act ahead of Joplin. It was a choreographic mistake on the part of Helms, and Bo Diddley blew away the audience. When Joplin appeared in front of her greatest fans, she faded onstage like a damaged bird.

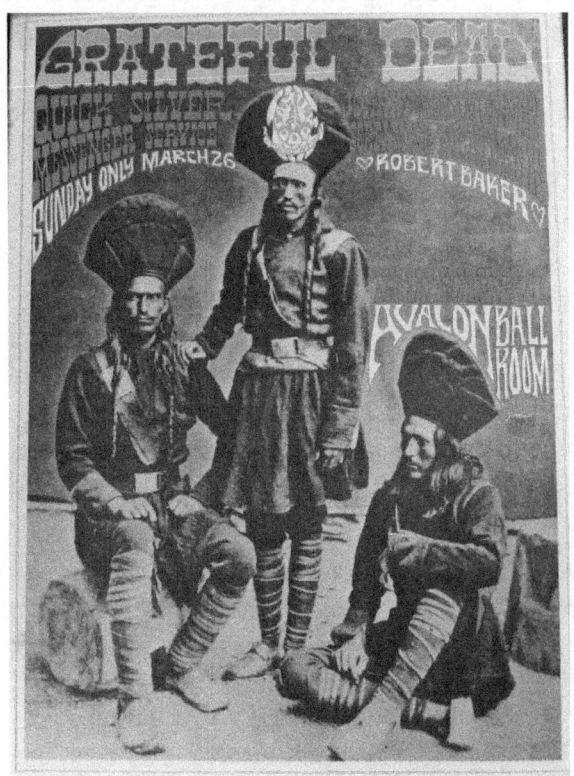

Avalon Ball Room Poster, March 26, 1966

In San Francisco during 1966, poets staged readings and impresarios created bands. Then, together, the bands and the impresarios created a different musical future. In the background, I carried my cameras back and forth across the San Francisco Bay Bridge from Berkeley, trying to photograph too many events and too many people.

During long nights at the Fillmore or the Avalon, another photographer named Jim Marshall and I seemed to be the only people documenting what was happening. Dennis Hopper was doing the work in L.A., and I was working in both places. Drugs were omnipresent, and they eventually dismantled both Marshall and Hopper. They were few of the afflicted that survived and beat their demons. Meanwhile, the terribly sad protests against the war went on and on. The Vietnam War had become a finely tuned killing machine with no end in sight.

Both Marshall and myself tried to hook up with magazines and newspapers that would print what we shot. I gave up. No one in the major media was interested. Instead, I kept shooting what I wanted to photograph. Twice a week at the San Francisco cooperative darkroom, I "souped" my negatives. I worked at exposing and printing my contact sheets. During the rest of my week, I documented an era that few people appeared to be interested in.

At the Avalon Ballroom Helms cast his music-promoter role aside and invited speakers onto the stage like the Zen-adept Alan Watts, Dr. Timothy Leary of Harvard, or the poet Allen Ginsberg. I photographed counterculture gurus like Claudio Naranjo, M.D., the Chilean psychiatrist, who had done work in the field of medical anthropology with a sidebar specialty in hallucinogens, psychedelics, dissociatives, and deliriants.

Somehow, political and literary theater magically merged, then became joined at the hip. Helms invited the premiere emergent musical groups of America to appear in San Francisco, and the list was endless.

***

The Delano March, California, 1966

The majority of Californians live and work amid the haze of smog-shrouded freeways, commuting through lives intent upon unsparing visions of prosperity.

Out there in the passing lane of economic prosperity, the Central Valley of California remains unknown and forgotten. Americans seem oblivious to where their fresh food comes from. The Central Valley feeds the entire state and nourishes much of America.

One hundred and ten miles north of Los Angeles is the town of Bakersfield, in Kern County. It is the fourth most productive agricultural county in America.

North of Bakersfield is the town of Delano, where in 1965, farmworkers staged an epic protest that was to last five long years. The protest centered upon an event that became known as the Delano March. In a state synonymous with unending prosperity and opportunity, the protests of the farmworkers were the last great American labor actions of the twentieth century.

By 1966, the predominantly Mexican-American National Farm Workers Association, in company with their fellow Filipino workers, began a grassroots effort using the tactics of nonviolent resistance to bring national awareness of their cause.

At first, the protests had no wide credibility. In the opinion of the New York–dominated national media, their cause would never gain traction in the public mind.

At the epicenter of the workers' movement, an unusual labor organizer named Cesar Chavez emerged. When Chavez was eleven years old, his family was so

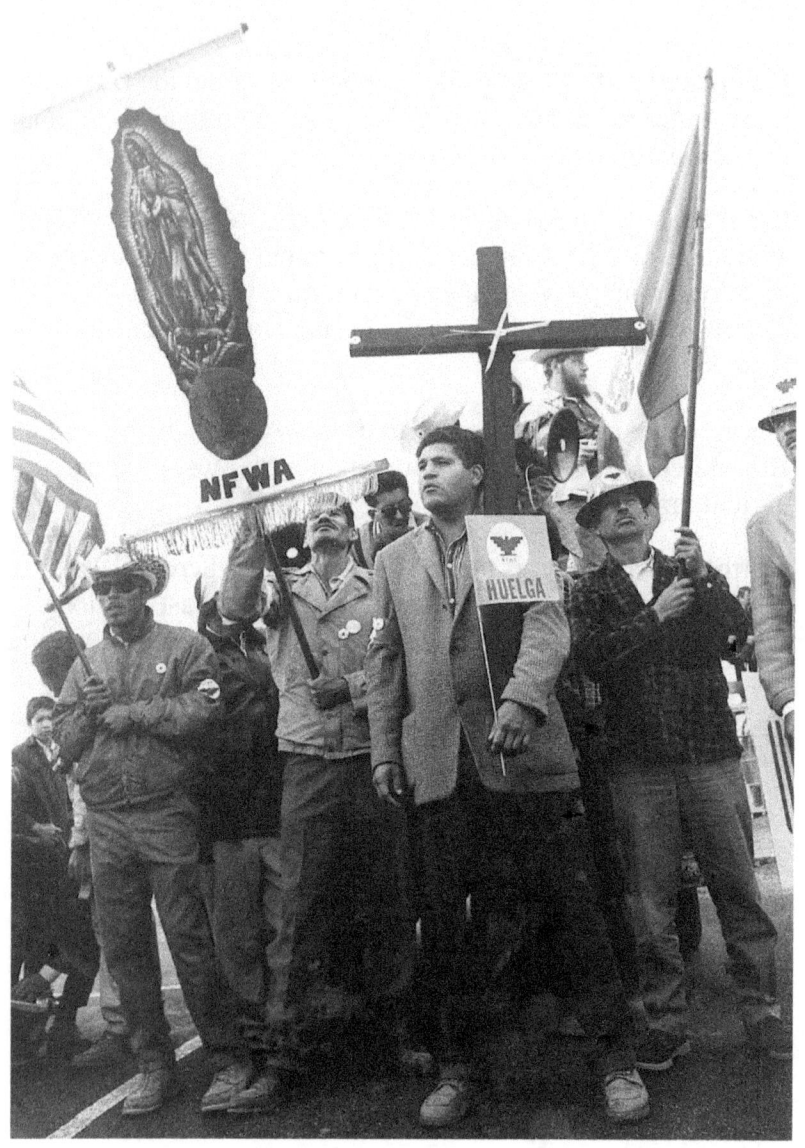

The Delano March, 1966

impoverished that he had to walk to school barefoot. In 1966, the federal poverty level was defined at an aggregate family income of $3,100 a year. His family subsisted on far less.

It was Chavez who began to employ the tactics of peaceful passive resistance, coupled with highly public protests. These tactics had been used earlier in the century by Mohandas K. Gandhi in both South Africa and India to startling effect.

In standing up and becoming the public face of a forgotten people, it was Chavez who became the moral center of the oppressed American farmworker community. He said, "The plight of the farmworkers in this country is a moral cause worthy of your support. It is deserving of nationwide support."

The Delano march grew out of the boycott against the table grape growers, and grew to included issues and conditions under which laborers worked.

Raising the cry of "Huelga!" the Spanish word for "strike," on March 17, 1966, the farmworkers and Chavez walked out of the fields of the Central Valley. They embarked upon a march that came to resemble a pilgrimage from Delano, California, to the state's capital in Sacramento.

It was during this march that Chavez became, like Dr. Martin Luther King Jr., one of two men in twentieth-century America who were lifted into the pantheon of a nation's conscience.

***

At the beginning of the march, only sixty-seven people followed Chavez out of the fields and into an uncertain future.

The marchers did not know if they would ever again be employed as farm laborers, due to the universal hostility of the growers against them. With temperatures hovering around one hundred degrees, day in and day out, Sacramento was a distant 340 miles away.

For many of the marchers, their most pressing problem was where their next meal would come from. Each day they carried the Virgin of Guadalupe, el Nuestra Señora de Guadalupe.

Along the cracked rural roads, they continued north.

What few people beyond the Central Valley knew was that these were the poorest of the poor in America. What they did was grueling, unrewarding, and physically emptying work.

Three years before, in the Alexander Valley, north of Napa, I'd tried picking grapes.

I lasted forty-five minutes in the sun. I lifted a seventy-five-pound wooden box of grapes I'd picked and carried it for a third of a mile over steeply plowed, unstable furrows.

One journey along the furrows was difficult, but my second was impossible, and I barely made it to the truck parked at the edge of the fields.

I imagined doing this work for a shift of eight hours under the broiling sun. It was somewhere beyond terrible. But the farmworkers did this work day after day, year after year.

***

In the first weeks of the Delano march, despite the *huelguistas* harvesting some of the most productive farmland in America, their protest attracted little notice. Even the governor of California, Pat Brown, seemed oblivious to their cause.

To the American media establishment, it was as if the march didn't exist. Then, something touched America in spite of the media. Suddenly people began to notice what was occurring in the Central Valley. As the march drew closer to Sacramento, it seemed to take on a life of its own in the public mind.

Each day, scores of people—and then hundreds—joined the march. Finally, two or three days from Sacramento, the numbers had reached thousands who walked in solidarity with the farmworkers.

What the Delano marchers and Chavez wanted to accomplish was to tell America they existed, that they too had a place in the country. They wanted fair pay for their labors, and asked only a ten-cent raise from $1.20 to $1.30 an hour.

There were no sit-ins or provocations of the law. Their protest didn't involve civil disobedience.

Before Sacramento, I joined the marchers.

What struck me most about them was their humility. They were immensely grateful that notice had been taken of their plight.

They usually worked until they dropped. They worked until they were too old or too broken to continue on in the fields. Then, they were thrown onto the junk heap of America, where many lived out the rest of their lives in shantytowns and skid rows.

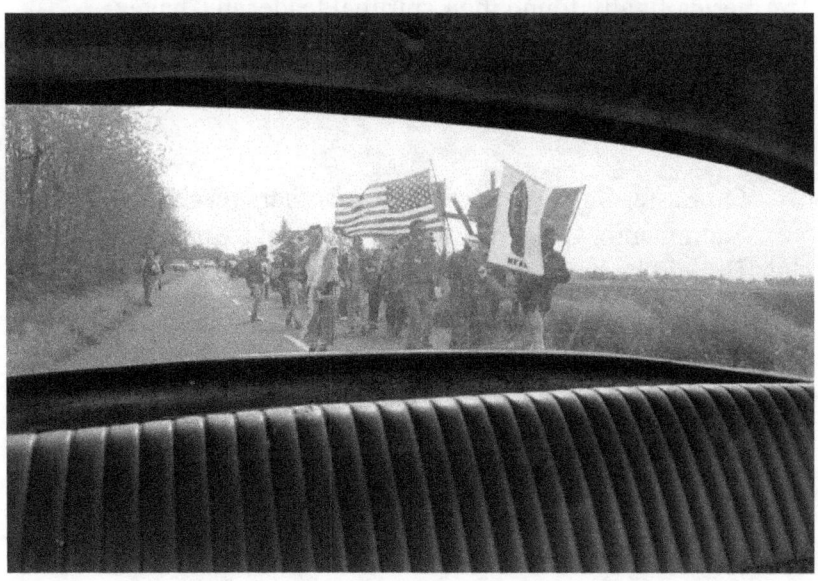

Delano March, 1966

They had no unemployment insurance and no health care. They had no Social Security to look forward to. They were the poorest hourly-paid people in America.

In the last days of the march, they were finally noticed. Guadalupe had seen them through.

When the marchers arrived in the state capital, a tidal wave of people joined them to carry *la huelga* into the city. Their faces in my pictures were radiant, beatific. They were unbelievably strong.

To me, their march had become a rite of religion. It was an unforgettable triumph, what Chavez and the farmworkers had achieved in the blistering heat .

To be part of this march was extraordinary. I saw these people finally gain a sense of self-worth and importance about who they were. It was a rare transformational moment.

After being dispossessed of the states of Arizona, New Mexico, Texas, and California, the voiceless, faceless Chicanos of America finally found their spiritual leader in Chavez.

****

Postscript

On Easter Sunday, the day the marchers reached Sacramento, Governor Brown declined to meet with them. He said he had a previous appointment to spend the holiday with his family.

As author John Gregory Dunne reported in his remarkable book *Delano: The Story of the California Grape Strike,* "With ill-concealed delight, the National Farm Workers Association announced that the setting for the governor's family holiday was the Palm Springs home of Frank Sinatra."

Allen Ginsberg and San Francisco: A Layered, Complex Exchange, May 1966

"Howl" was a glorious, and outraged poem that changed the generation that came of age in the mid-1960s. It had been written in 1955 by Allen Ginsberg.

The opening lines of "Howl," Ginsberg's most famous poem, went:

> I saw the best minds of my generation destroyed by madness,
> starving hysterical
> > naked,
> dragging themselves through the negro streets at dawn
> looking for an angry fix

An anthem of disgust, Ginsberg's poem was an intemperate, impassioned call for freedom.

When one looks at the extraordinary career of Allen Ginsberg, he was arguably the great American poet of the twentieth century. What most people have forgotten, or never knew, about Ginsberg was that he had literally walked away and abandoned San Francisco in disgust during the mid-1950s. Odd as it seems today, a decade later, Ginsberg emerged as the unsung spiritual father of everything that happened in San Francisco during the 1960s.

By 1966, Ginsberg was a legend, and in the history of America, a place of uncommon firsts, he was possibly the first American narrative poet to be publicly accused and prosecuted in the headlines of a large metropolitan newspaper. The city fathers were disgusted and outraged by "Howl." The prosecutor for the city of San Francisco called for jail time.

For Ginsberg, the rewards and punishments of free expression in America apparently entailed considerable personal battering along the way.

During a groundbreaking obscenity trial in 1957, the prosecutor argued that "Howl" contained "filthy, vulgar, obscene, and disgusting language."

And so began Ginsberg's earliest battering by the laws of the land and a lifetime of battering from the judicial establishment.

At the end of the trial the court held a different opinion than the prosecutor, and Ginsberg's epic poem was declared by Judge Clayton W. Horn to possess redeeming artistic value.

For those who knew Ginsberg, he was a rare, unique spirit. He was a man wrapped in contradictions, and his fulminating furies caused him untold delight.

Ginsberg's various dislikes centered at one time or another on political parties, academies, income tax, the army, homophobes, the navy, American antidrug laws, the Vietnam War, and, as the overarching credo of his life, any limits whatsoever on personal freedoms. From the late 1940s until his death in 1997, Ginsberg's life centered upon his decision to defy each and every social system of control, day and night, decade in and decade out. In a lifetime of protest, he faced down any limits which society placed upon individual freedoms.

I first became aware of "Howl" because it was the only major literary work I knew of that had ever been written in Berkeley. It was written at the Caffe Mediterraneum on Telegraph Avenue, two miles from where I grew up.

I read *Howl and Other Poems* when it was first published by Lawrence Ferlinghetti at City Lights Press. Ferlinghetti's bookstore in San Francisco's North Beach neighborhood was the spiritual home of the Beats.

Once his obscenity trial was over in 1957, Ginsberg departed San Francisco for Morocco and Paris. After the way municipal authorities had mugged him, no one believed he'd return, or even in his wildest imagination would he ever want to return to San Francisco.

With his lover, Peter Orlovsky, Ginsberg traveled to India. From 1962 to 1963, they lived primarily in Calcutta, on the Kalighat burning grounds along the Hooghly River.

In Calcutta, both the poet and his companion spent much of their time investigating and smoking India's holy alkaloid products.

For recreation, they shot up friendly easily available morphine, which was used originally to cure one of Ginsberg's colds, and for his on-and-off attacks of jaundice. Like the sadhus they'd come to admire so much in Kalighat, both Orlovsky and Ginsberg wandered naked on the smoky, orange-tinted dawn-lit burning ghats.

A few months after the poet appeared in Calcutta, a friend of mine there, who was walking the midnight streets of Calcutta, heard chanting on the apparently deserted street in front of him. He couldn't exactly place where the raucous chanting was coming from.

Moving cautiously down the street, my friend passed Ginsberg. The poet was lying on his back in the gutter and seemed to be staring up at the stars. In a booming, stentorian voice, Ginsberg was reciting his version of the Indian epic poem "The Mahabharata."

It would be nine years before Ginsberg would return to San Francisco after his near-incarceration in the 1950s.

I first met Ginsberg at poet Michael McClure's house in San Francisco in May of 1966. McClure and fellow poet Gary Snyder had been performers at "Howl"'s first reading, eleven years before at the Six Gallery.

Ginsberg had returned to San Francisco in disguise. Instead of the Indian sadhu I expected to see, he wore a white shirt, dress pants, and a suit jacket.

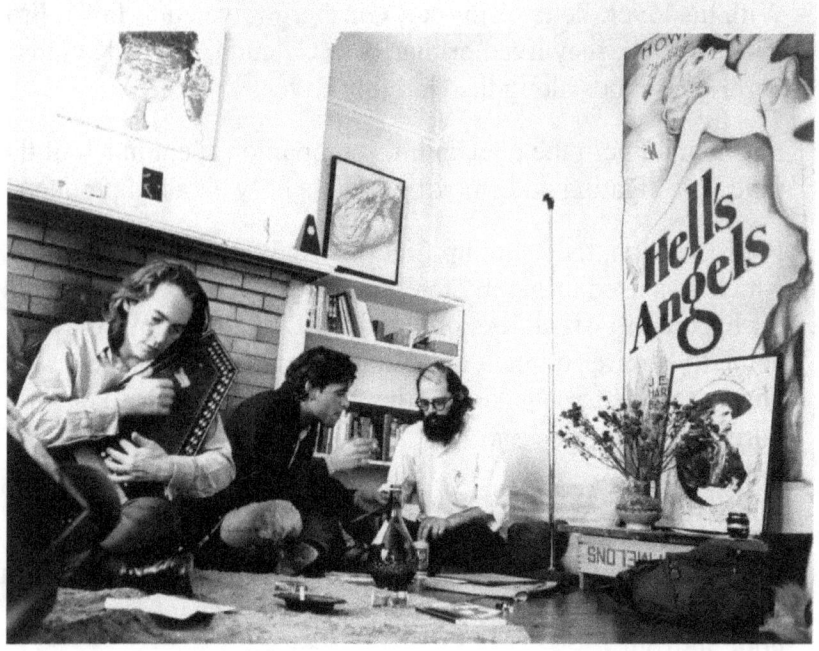

Michael McClure's Living Room, San Francisco, 1966

As I began to set up my photographs, staring at Ginsberg from behind my Leica, I had the thought that I was photographing the kind of American literary icon who appears perhaps once in a century. But the man in front of my camera, with his large, black plastic–framed glasses, looked like a mid-Atlantic, nondescript college academic, inhabiting a rumpled shirt.

According to my friend McClure, reception to Ginsberg's poem was the clarion call of the last half of the twentieth century, against the mechanics of the American machine.

"A barrier had been broken, and a human voice and body had been hurled against the harsh wall of America and its supporting armies and navies and academies and institutions and ownership systems and power-support bases." (Cf. *Scratching the Beat Surface*, Michael McClure, Penguin Books, 1982)

I began to take pictures.

In person, Ginsberg seemed distant and uncommunicative. Almost immediately, he retreated behind his owlish glasses.

After ten minutes, he picked up an auto harp and began to fashion a sort of strange melody in time to what I thought was his faux Indian chanting.

Across the room, McClure picked up the autoharp after Ginsberg put it down. Under an original 1930 movie poster for *The Hell's Angels*, McClure began to accompany Ginsberg's chanting. Visually perfect. Great pictures, but much too theatrical, I thought.

***

Under very different circumstances, a month later I met Ginsberg again.

It was at a benefit reading for the defense fund of Timothy Leary, who was just then facing several federal and city indictments for LSD possession.

At that moment, the power centers of the city were divided between the conservative, right-wing Republicans of local power politics, made up of people like Freddie Higby, the owner of the house where I was still living off and on. Against the Republicans was everyone else who lived in San Francisco.

In tandem with his LSD charges, Leary was also being tried by the inaptly named U.S. Justice Department. His crimes were aiding and abetting the psychedelic revolution, of which he had certainly been a founding member. Leary's useful work in the creation of the revolution had occurred while he had been on the faculty of Harvard University.

Poised at that moment against the same Republican establishment that ten years before had driven him from the city, Ginsberg rose to the occasion with a vehemence I never suspected.

In a spirited reading, Ginsberg called out to the doctors, scientists, lawyers, bankers, publishers, entrepreneurs, writers, and the entire leftist union establishment of San Francisco to form ranks against the stupid, regressive Republican establishment of the city. At this reading, somehow a crowd of San Francisco's new power people had appeared. They cheered Ginsberg's poem.

I'm sure Freddie Higby would have been baffled by Ginsberg's poem, but I am more certain that he would have been even more baffled by the professionals of the city who had suddenly risen to oppose the Republican establishment.

**

The third time I met Ginsberg, he was sitting alone at a table in a coffeehouse in North Beach. Invariably, he was writing in one of the notebooks he carried.

I've never liked celebrities. They're fun to photograph, but they are always a disappointment when you talk to them. I didn't want to be another person in the world of very long lines of people who wanted to have a conversation with Ginsberg. I stood there in the coffeehouse, wondering if I should bother him or pass on down the street.

Ginsberg looked up from his notebook and stared at me.

There was no expression on his face. It was unnerving. "What is the most interesting thing you ever did in your life?" he asked suddenly.

I stood there.

Behind me, the traffic was accelerating loudly up the street toward a tunnel, which had been cut through one of San Francisco's steep hills. The question, I learned in the next few minutes, was a typical Ginsberg interrogation–have a nice day–good-bye question. It was off-center. It was unanswerable without the recipient having minutes, rather than seconds, to think.

For a long moment, I stared at Ginsberg. Then I answered his question.

"When I was eighteen years old, I traveled deck passage from Yokohama to Bombay."

As I thought about this journey, I continued: "I think that the most interesting thing I ever did in my life was go to India in 1959 when I was eighteen. After that, I spent four to five years of my life learning to survive India. That's the most interesting thing I've ever done."

Ginsberg made an *O* shape with his lips, and a "Wooooo" sound came out.

He thought about what I'd said a bit more. He then asked suddenly, "Not too many people have done that, have they? How did you live?"

Barging onward, he next asked, "Where did you find the cash to live? Or are you a trust baby? Always follow the money, right? Then you get the quick answer about who people really are."

"Did you ever meet a trust baby in India?" I asked. "And when I think about that, I don't think in all the years I lived in India that I ever met one trust baby."

Ginsberg didn't answer.

"I lived for years on really horrible Indian food. Really awful, terrible stuff, and I collected great art no one else wanted. That's what I did. I collected art. I smuggled art."

Across the table, Ginsberg was looking at me more closely now.

"And what is the most interesting thing you have ever done in your life?" I asked pleasantly in reply. "I don't think your question was very friendly, quite apart from its arrogance."

Ginsberg gathered up his drink, then his notebook. He looked at me, then pointed to inside the café away from the noise of the traffic.

In the darkness of the café, Ginsberg moved away from the other patrons and the street. I followed him as he selected a table at the rear.

With a flowing two-handed gesture, he pointed me to a chair opposite him. "This needful pause gives me a chance to think about your question, doesn't it?" he asked cheerfully.

He gave me a big, glowing, gleaming smile.

I took a chair. A waiter approached; I ordered an espresso.

In the semidarkness, Ginsberg leaned back against the wall. "I survived India. That's my answer. I'm *amazed* that I survived India. I think certainly that this is the most interesting thing I've ever done in my life."

Ginsberg stared into the darkness at the rear of the restaurant, then he began to talk quietly.

"I gave up everything I ever knew in order to survive India," he began. For a long moment, Ginsberg was lost in thought, then he continued: "Most people have never done anything interesting. Hardly anyone ever answers that question I asked you. You know, I ask people this sort of trick question, and what I've found out is that most people don't have any imagination, or they've never done anything. I don't know what's worse. That's pretty crappy, isn't it? I have to tell you, also, that nobody has ever asked that same question back. It says something about timidity, about the unwavering sameness of people during our period, doesn't it?"

I thought about that.

Slowly, I raised my Leica and took a picture of Ginsberg. It seemed to unnerve him. I ventured an opinion. "In America and in Europe, people are much too busy elbowing each other aside so they can stand in the exact same place as the person next to them."

"Holy cow, as they'd say in India." Ginsberg laughed at his terrible joke.

In the darkness, the poet looked far older than thirty-nine. My espresso came. I sipped slowly.

As the afternoon went on, Ginsberg tried to unravel why he went to India. I took pictures. I listened.

"I spent weeks, then months on the burning ghats," he said. "I tried to learn chakras and to collect energy. I realized instead of spiritual energy, I was trying to locate all I was accomplishing. I was developing a huge, consuming fondness for ganja. After that, I gave up searching for meanings and things like that. I just sort of jumped into the flow, and I learned to swim in new ways."

Ginsberg beamed at me.

For a minute, he was lost in silence. Then he asked in an almost bemused way, "You don't look over twenty years old. What I'd like to know is what happened inside *your* head in India?"

I smiled. "I look young, and I'm not a dope addict like you are. I disappeared into the flow of India without ganja."

Across from me, Ginsberg put his head in his hands. He began shaking his head. "God. I'm humbled. He has an answer for everything."

He looked up, and then in a canny way, he asked, "What did you do with the art you acquired? Do you have a lot of art?"

"I had tons and tons of Shivas," I answered. "And Ganeshas. And Gandharan Buddhist sculpture. I then switched over from sculpture to Indian painting, because an Indian miniature painting weighs what, an ounce and half?"

Ginsberg spread his hands like he didn't know.

"I collected very good Indian paintings, but honestly I was way too early getting into Indian classical art. I've sold most of it."

"Too early? What does that mean?" he asked.

"That means that in Bombay," I explained, "around 1963, it would cost you $500 for a great Indian painting. If you try to sell this same painting in London in 1965, what you found out was that Indian art is difficult if not impossible to sell. By today, a $500 Indian masterpiece you bought in Bombay will get you $75 in San Francisco."

"Kaboom. Wipeout," Ginsberg said. He made an exploding noise.

I sighed and nodded my head. "I had the greatest Indian art collection it was possible to buy. But there's no real market, or even a single museum today in the West that would take my collection. It's quite sad. That's what being 'in too early' means."

I removed the exposed film from my camera after I rewound it. From my army surplus jacket, I slipped another cassette of Tri-X into the back of my Leica. I closed the hinged back and replaced the bottom cover of the camera.

"I've been totally mauled in the art world," I said. "You never ever want to be in the position that you have to sell your art in a market that isn't strong. Believe me."

Then I laughed. "It's very Indian, isn't it? Shedding your possessions."

He didn't answer.

Ginsberg paid for our coffee. He waved me after him. I followed.

We crossed the street against the traffic, dodging cars.

We climbed a few blocks toward Coit Tower, and then we climbed a set of stairs into an apartment building. Then more stairs.

Finally, we entered the apartment of one of his friends.

In the apartment, Ginsberg closed the door. I sat on the couch and switched cameras to my Nikon.

"Do you ever think back to Calcutta, or about the Himalayas?" Ginsberg asked. "I could never get into the Himalayas like I wanted to."

He was sitting on the couch next to me. He put his finger on the bridge of his nose and pushed back his heavy glasses. He then got up and crossed the room to the kitchen.

I thought about the question and didn't answer. Questions about the Himalayas always baffled me because they were unanswerable.

You reached the summit of a mountain in the Himalayas, and you stood there. You stared at the next mountain, then the next mountain beyond that, each with a successive fifty-degree gradient.

What I had found out in the mountains beyond Darjeeling was that it was not about a destination that you had planned. It was about the next ascent you had to make. It was about climbing the next terrible mountain trail where you thought you'd die of fatigue and exhaustion and never escape this awful place.

In the kitchen, Ginsberg nodded. "You were so goddamned young to find out about the beauty and the mysteries of the Himalayas," he said. "It must have been a big price you paid."

A few moments later, I watched Ginsberg move out of the kitchen and cross the room. "Didn't you pay a price?" he asked.

"How old were you when you wrote 'Howl'?" I asked suddenly. I wanted to stop this dreary conversation about Indian mountains.

Ginsberg pointed at my camera. I handed it up to him to look at. He held the Leica in front of him, then he looked through the viewfinder.

"I do photography. Did you know that?" he asked. "I was twenty-eight when I wrote 'Howl.' I thought it was very good, and then I got buried by fame." He giggled.

"You have to advance the film." I pointed at a lever on the top right-hand side of the Leica.

Ginsberg pushed the lever forward and started taking pictures of me.

I'd taken pictures of him. Now he took pictures of me. *Click. Click.* Ginsberg smiled shyly.

I was beginning to feel very insecure.

He moved in front of me in a semicircle.

In all the time I'd taken photographs, no one had ever taken one of my cameras and started taking pictures of me. I was somehow being seduced by means of my own art. It was unnerving.

Ginsberg took perhaps six pictures of me, and then he said, "You know. You are very handsome."

I nodded my head, but not in agreement.

If you looked the way I did, you couldn't live in Asia for years and not have men beating on your door at night. Certain types of men always seemed to want to put you into their own movies.

It went on from there into lands too well-known, unfortunately. In these private journeys, people of a certain persuasion started out by telling you that you were handsome.

"Oh. Goddamn it," I whispered.

I got up suddenly. "I want my camera back. I think I have to go. Definitely."

Ginsberg no longer looked shy. He looked angry.

The seventh unlucky picture. *Click.*

I put out my hand, and Ginsberg slowly handed me my Leica.

He took a deep breath, then he silently went to the door and opened it. With an elaborate gesture, he waved me out the door with two hands and a bow.

I passed through the door. I didn't look back.

On the sidewalk, I put my head back against one of the walls of the apartment building. I let out a long breath. I said. "Goddamn it. Christ!"

***

Two weeks later, at the Cow Palace, during a rock-n'-roll concert in front of 10,000 people, into the almost bottomless rapt silence of the converted, Allen Ginsberg chanted Buddhist prayers for peace.

A month later, Ginsberg and the writer Ken Kesey decided they had to diffuse a dangerous confrontation that was looming between the Hell's Angels and 5,000 anti–Vietnam War peace demonstrators poised to march up Telegraph Avenue onto the Berkeley campus the next day.

Together, Kesey and Ginsberg decided they would visit the Hell's Angels in their clubhouse.

The day before, a skirmish had occurred between peace marchers and the Angels. There were broken heads and broken bones. The Angels had blocked that march with their motorcycles, and the police had stood by as the Hell's Angels knocked some of the marchers onto the ground and then stomped them with their motorcycle boots.

In this melee, the rest of the Angels had jumped off their bikes, screaming "Go back to Russia, you fucking Communists!" as they rushed the peace marchers.

Before the next day's march, Ginsberg and Kesey appeared at the Hell's Angels house.

Sonny Barger, then the leader of the club, appeared in his colors at the door. When the two writers showed up, Barger was on the telephone calling the Hell's Angels Northern California chapters to set up the next day's stomp-fest.

It was rumored that to join the Hell's Angels, applicants had to be white males with a legal driver's license and a motorcycle. But prospective members also had to "have the right combination of unique personal qualities... [and not be] seeking to become police or prison guards."

At the door, after a few difficult moments, both Kesey and Ginsberg explained to Barger why peace marchers should be supported and not beaten up.

Kesey had worked in a mental hospital, where he had previously met some of the Hell's Angels as patients who had been badly in need of help. He'd come as a friend of the Angels. He was now also a famous writer who had published the wildly popular novel *One Flew Over the Cuckoo's Nest.* It was set in the Hell's Angels happy home away from home—a psychiatric hospital.

Ginsberg, all five-foot-seven of him, reportedly seized Barger, who was much larger than he was, in a friendly bear hug full of prana. Presumably, he then shot chakras full of spiritual energy into Barger.

In Barger's ensuing confusion, Kesey began to talk, and talk, and talk.

The march went ahead the next day without problems from the Hell's Angels.

***

In the years ahead, Allen Ginsberg would become the most famous poet in America. In the decades that followed, Ginsberg increasingly felt assaulted by the growing plague of worldwide government totalitarianism.

He believed in a guarantee at birth of every human being's inalienable right to express his or her sexuality.

To his last breath, Ginsberg dedicated his life and his work to the unswerving beacon of free expression.

***

America, The Road, August 1966

In the 1960s, the way you crossed America on a budget was something called a "driveaway car."

On both coasts of the country were agencies that transported automobiles from one coast to another, across the expanse of the continent, through a sort of employment exchange. For the car owners who didn't want to drive that distance, these exchanges hired people to transport driveaway cars across the continent.

For the driver, the deal was this: "We supply the car and pay the insurance. You provide your own gas to drive across the country. You also make a deposit for the car, which is paid to us against an insurance deductible of $100, in case you damage the car. No bumps, dings, wrecks. You deliver the car to the other side of America, and you get your deposit back."

The economics of a driveaway car were wonderful, assuming you didn't get into an accident. For a journey of 3,200 miles when I drove a car across America, I used 160 gallons of gas. Gas was about $0.27 a gallon in 1966. Hamburgers along the way were $0.15 to $0.25 each. If you slept in your car, it cost you only $43 to get from one side of America to the other, including food and gas on the three- or four-day journey.

In late 1966, I'd reached a point where I had to generate some cash in order to live. My Indian art collection was selling poorly, and my once large pile of cash had diminished to nothing because of ill-timed art purchases and filmmaking. By 1966, my thoughts of traveling across the Middle East to India again were on hold. The Indian government didn't want to give me a visa; I'd been blacklisted for the film I made there. The Indian Criminal Investigation Department didn't like me either, due to my previous career of Indian-art collecting and export.

I decided I could make some money shooting record covers. I knew an art designer at Capitol Records, but I had to get to New York to talk to this designer. I'd then return to California and go back to work on my California documentation project.

Two days out of San Francisco, the driveaway Corvair I was driving, a kind of General Motors rear-engine, air-cooled imitation of the Volkswagen, that seemed to have been made from cardboard, began wheezing. In the baking heat of a September heat wave, I pulled into a garage in a small Midwestern town. I explained that my problem seemed to be overheating. After ten minutes of rummaging around his garage, the mechanic appeared with a water pump in his hand.

As tactfully as I could, I explained that the Corvair had an air-cooled engine. It didn't have a radiator. Unpromisingly, the mechanic and I then went over the instruction manual manifest and examined this miracle of American technology. I didn't dare mention that Volkswagen had been using air-cooled engines since 1938. Eventually, we found a mouse nest inside the lungs of the Corvair. I went on my way across the rolling immensity of America, eating a hamburger every four hours to keep my strength up.

***

In Somerville, Massachusetts, I delivered the abominably uncomfortable and weird American-made vehicle. I collected my deposit, and I took a bus to Harvard Square three miles away.

At Harvard, I crossed the yard and stood in front of the building that I'd come here to visit. I stared upward.

In front of me was something sculpted into right angles. It was a four-story, plain gray concrete building. The middle of the structure was pierced with a ramp that ran up and then through the building.

I remembered reading about this building the year before. It was the only building ever built in America by the French architect Charles-Édouard Jeanneret, also known as Le Corbusier, who had died ten months earlier, in August of 1965.

One hundred feet away from the Corbusier building was the Fogg Museum of Art. I wondered what it would be like to work in buildings like this at a university like Harvard. The life I'd lived was so distant from this place. I felt like a visitor from some faraway asteroid. The Fogg was the greatest university art museum in America.

As I walked toward the front door of the Corbusier building, I asked a maintenance man if this was the Carpenter Center. The man pointed inside the building, then, wordlessly, he disappeared around the back.

Inside, beyond an exhibition area, was an office forty feet away.

I approached the office. Inside were two administrative assistants talking to one another. I asked where the Harvard film department was and if they knew a filmmaker named Robert Gardner.

One of the assistants stood up. She motioned me to follow her.

Wordlessly, she crossed the exhibition area and pointed down a set of wide concrete stairs that led down to the basement.

In front of me, my guide turned. Then, without speaking a word, she abandoned me on the stairs. I wondered if any of the people at Harvard actually had the power of speech. Strange. No one had yet spoken to me.

In the basement, I entered another office. A secretary looked up at me questioningly.

I smiled tightly.

The secretary didn't ask what I wanted; she didn't appear to be able to speak, either. Were all these people mutes? Or was this a larger New England problem?

"Robert Gardner asked me to see him if I was ever in Cambridge," I said. "I'm only here for fifteen minutes, before I have an appointment at the Fogg."

In a plumy British voice, the secretary asked, "And you are?"

I told her my name. The woman looked up at me.

Rising from her desk, she walked to another door. She knocked, then without waiting for a reply, she disappeared into the room beyond the door.

The first time I ever saw Robert Gardner, he was wearing a Spanish hand-tailored light brown corduroy suit. He wore handmade suede Peel shoes.

He walked through the door, smiled at me, and stuck out his hand in a friendly handshake. "You came. I hoped you'd come by someday. I was very impressed with your attempt," he said.

He stood aside and waved me ahead of him into his small office.

Two years earlier, I'd applied for a grant-in-aid to complete my India film. I'd neglected to get permission from the government of India to make a film there, and I was still trying to get completion money to finish my film.

In his office, Gardner waved me into a chair. I knew nothing about him except that he'd said he was an ethnographic filmmaker. My India film had yielded an invitation to visit him at Harvard if I ever came east. At that moment, there were perhaps five ethnographic filmmakers in the entire U.S.

Gardner asked how long I'd been on the East Coast. I told him about two days.

He asked if I was staying long in Cambridge. I said I was on my way to New York, and that I was thinking I'd like to go back to India. I neglected to mention I was on the Indian blacklist.

Gardner asked what happened to my film. I told him I was still trying to find money to finish it and do the final edits.

He nodded, and he seemed preoccupied.

Gardner was between thirty-five and forty years old. He had a fine face. He was over six feet tall. He carried himself stiffly erect. Coffee was brought in by his distant, unfriendly British secretary. Her name was Serina, and Serina was instructed to close the door.

I asked Gardner if he'd been doing films on tribal people for a long time.

He replied that he'd first done a film called *Blunden Harbor*, on Northwest Coast Americans, in the late 1950s. He'd also done another film on the Dani tribe in the central highlands of New Guinea, which was titled *Dead Birds*.

I thought about that. We finished our coffee. Who hadn't heard of *Dead Birds?* I hadn't realized that Gardner had made *Dead Birds*.

After Robert Flaherty's early 1920s film, *Nanook of the North,* done on the Inuit Eskimo, Gardner's film was the second most important ethnographic film ever made. It was a tour de force that featured warring Paleolithic tribes only recently discovered in the Dutch New Guinea highlands.

Gardner's film was probably the most important film that would ever be made on the almost vanished Paleolithic period of human history. By reputation, his film was incredible both in ambition and scope.

I explained that I'd missed the Sturm und Drang of Gardner's success. Because I'd been in Kabul, and then in western India, I hadn't been able to read much cultural news when the film appeared.

Then I remembered the story of Michael Rockefeller.

As a terrible coda to *Dead Birds*, one of the Harvard students working on the film had died. This occurred after the main personnel of the expedition had left New Guinea. Rockefeller stayed behind in order to collect art objects in the Sepik River region. His death had been an irreparable blow not only to his family, but also to future philanthropic sponsorship of ethnographic film and studies in America.

Gardner seemed bemused by the fact that I hadn't until just then connected *Dead Birds* to its maker.

He apologized that he was busy with faculty meetings all afternoon.

We made an appointment for the next day, when he wanted to show me the studios that Harvard had given him to make films. From the bottom of the stairs, he watched me climb upward back into the real world. I wondered what it would be like to be at a place like Harvard making films. My life, by comparison, seemed fragmentary and recklessly untenable.

***

I left the Corbusier building and walked toward the Fogg Museum next door, to my nonexistent appointment. To stay on for my appointment tomorrow, I'd have to find a cheap hotel somewhere, perhaps in downtown Boston.

At the reception desk of the Fogg, I asked for Professor John Rosenfield. At that time, Rosenfield was at the American center of the Indian art–studies world. The receptionist lifted a phone to ask if Professor Rosenfield was free.

I was directed toward the back of the museum, into an interior courtyard, and finally up a set of stairs.

Rosenfield's office was to the left, at the top of the stairs, then down toward the back of the building. Such was the obscurity of both film studies and art history in America that I could meet the two most important academics in their respective fields simply by showing up, unannounced, at Harvard.

In the darkness at the rear of the Fogg's second floor stood a small man dressed like a bank clerk. He wore an ill-fitting suit and tie. We shook hands in a formal way. I introduced myself. Rosenfield seemed a bit taken aback by being presented with a thin young man wearing an Indian tie-dye shirt and with long hair.

With misgivings, he stepped aside and ushered me toward his office.

Once inside, he settled behind his desk. I sat in front of his desk, and he stared back at me, blinking through his dark 1950s-style glasses, with those heavy, black-plastic frames. Stacks of papers and journals were dumped at random on the cluttered desk in front of him.

"I'm a photographer," I said without preamble. "I've been working on a project list I once made of the 210 most important Indian monuments. I began documenting monuments on this list in 1959, with a basic first set of photographs of Islamic and Buddhist sites."

Rosenfield stared at me, as if a maniac had just stepped into his life. "I see," he said cautiously.

"In India and Pakistan, so far I've visited about sixty of these monuments," I added.

"Could you tell me where you started?" he asked.

"Let's see. First, I did the Bengali terra-cotta temples. Then I photographed most of the cave temples in eastern India at Udayagiri and Khandagiri. I then crossed the continent and photographed most of the cave temples in western India."

I paused, then continued: "…To my knowledge, no one has ever photographed the cave temples of western India, apart from Major Gill's work at Ajanta in the early 1850s."

Rosenfield looked stunned. He sat there as if at a loss for words. I don't think he knew who Major Gill was, or that his photographs had been destroyed in a great fire during the 1850s.

Then, I charged forward. "To the reasons I've come here…In my own mind, both Professor Benjamin Rowland and yourself are currently the most important art historians in America. I'd like to ask you if you'd buy copies of some of my pictures to put into your archives, so that students can see the extraordinary classic architectural art of India. This is the first time I think they've been documented in color."

Both Rowland and Rosenfield were Harvard professors at the Fogg. I knew they had many black-and-white prints of the art and architecture of the subcontinent, from the Victorian period onward, but I doubted they had color photographs of any of the greatest monuments of India.

Rosenfield seemed bemused. Then he replied, "This is all irregular. You're quite young to do all this work. Why did you start this strange project? What did you say your name was?" he asked. He paused, adding quickly,"Of course, we must buy these pictures. Of course. We must, I think...."

I repeated my name again. I told Rosenfield I'd like to show him my work.

Rosenfield stood up abruptly. "You look hungry," he said.

He invited me to lunch at Iruna, which served Spanish food just off Harvard Square.

Rosenfield asked me again why I began my photography. I told him of my trips into Balochistan, Iran, Afghanistan, and Pakistan. I told him about my trips to India, and from India to Europe. I said I was returning to India at some point to take more pictures of Indian architectural monuments. I didn't bring up my current visa problems.

We finished the dessert. A cherubic man with a florid bow tie had entered the restaurant. He stood at the door looking around, then he approached our table and Rosenfield stood up abruptly, like a man jerking to attention.

Dressed in a style affected by the dons of both Cambridge and Oxford, the man was in his late thirties. He looked like a typical member of the British upper class, and he wore a tailored suit. It was fashioned from those sturdy British woolen fabrics that seemed to last not just decades but forever, and it looked like a suit that fit its wearer poorly.

I stood up. Formally, we shook hands.

The man carefully selected a chair from a nearby unoccupied table. Clutching a four-inch-thick Louis Vuitton briefcase in his hand, he sank into his chair, then dropped the briefcase next to him on the floor with a heavy clunk.

Still standing, Rosenfield introduced the man. "Cary Welch. Honorary assistant keeper of Islamic art at the Fogg Museum."

I stared at Cary Welch. I simply stared. For years, I'd heard about this man in India. He was a legend, and in the Indian-art-collecting field, this man was semidivine.

It had been five or six years prior when the great Bombay Indian art dealer, Essagee, first told me about Welch. It was Essagee's opinion that Cary Welch had perfect taste. He was also possessed of the most finely developed sense of connoisseurship that Essagee had ever seen in the field of classical Indian painting.

According to Essagee, it was Welch's penchant to go through a three-foot-tall stack of eighteenth-century Indian paintings in a period of fifteen minutes. During this operation, the pile of ordinary paintings grew into a stack on the left side, while the masterpieces went into a much smaller pile on the right. If anyone in the Indian-art world besides Essagee had told me this, I wouldn't have listened.

But Essagee went even further. "He has flawless taste, sir. He sees perfection."

In my mind, I'd always thought of Cary Welch as ninety years old.

If there was a single man in the Indian-art field whom I'd never dreamed of meeting, it was this man. I imagined him immured in a British country house, hidden behind the barbed wire and protocols of the British upper class. I imagined him to be an impossible to reach, hoary ex–Indian civil servant who, for the most part, despised Americans.

"So? And who are you in the company of our august Professor Rosenfield?" Welch asked.

Welch's accent was generic East Coast American establishment. He had a receding hairline. He wore an emblematic bow tie, left over from another era, but affected today by the über-Wasp.

I told Cary Welch my name. Then I told him what I'd been doing lately. "This morning, for example, I delivered a broken-down, sorely used Chevrolet Corvair in Somerville. I drove it across America from San Francisco. Also this morning, I met someone named Robert Gardner. We talked about a film I made on the Bhils of central India. And who am I? I'm just a twenty-five year old who's been sleeping on people's floors for the last seven years. between here and Asia—ever since I first went to Bombay in 1959."

Welch stood. He reached out over the table. Next, he wrung my hand in a hearty handshake. It was very odd indeed.

"Amazing. Incredible," he said. "You were with the Bhils outside of Baroda? Near Chhota Udaipur? Who else has ever gone there, let alone survived the heat? My god...."

With a sour look, Rosenfield stared at Welch.

There's something going on, I thought. One of these men, with just his momentary glance, did not very much esteem the other. Definitely, an elephant turd lay on the jungle pathway here between these two.

Ah, the sad narratives of college life, the poorly paid academic. And another man who evidently didn't much worry about his art-collecting expenses.

I smiled at both of them.

"Well, happy to meet both of you," I said. "A pleasure to meet such distinguished men. I actually come from Berkeley, which is a place very much like Cambridge, with all its happy collegial ties."

I beamed. Both Cary Welch and John Rosenfield took deep breaths and didn't reply.

***

The next day, Robert Gardner invited me to come and work at Harvard.

He offered to produce my film on the Bhil tribe to completion, and he said Harvard would pay for release prints.

I was almost undone. In my life, I did the work but received scant support or encouragement. I practically wept. Gardner's offers of support were too uncommonly generous. I said, however, I'd like to think about this. I was exhausted by men of a certain preference making me offers.

Gardner said I could think about his offer as long as I wanted. His offer was completely open-ended. He liked my work. He did like my work, he repeated.

But things just got better at Harvard, as it turned out. They became better and better.

The next afternoon, Rosenfield bought 200 of my pictures of Indian Buddhist and Islamic cultural monuments. He suggested, as well, that he'd like me to photograph the Fogg's unbelievable collection of Chinese Northern Wei bronzes. I could then sell these pictures to other institutions and keep whatever money I made, with no royalties required by the Fogg Museum. Would that help me with my work?

The following day, I had another lunch. I ate at Iruna without Rosenfield but again with Cary Welch. The restaurant seemed a kind of social club for the faculty of the Fogg Museum.

Welch asked where I'd been in India. I told him about my travels, then, in vague, general terms, I told him about my collecting. I then asked what, exactly, he did at Harvard.

Welch replied that he taught a sort of seminar for graduate students at the Fogg in their Ph.D. program. He was also an adjunct curator for the Asia Society in New York, where he'd curated the first classical Indian painting exhibition in the United States. At that moment, the Asia Society, a Rockefeller-supported cultural organization, was *the* great exhibition space for Asian art in the world! What an amazing résumé Cary Welch had. Staggering.

"I've been wondering," I said tentatively. I'd been puzzling over this question for the last two days, since I'd first met Welch. It had been nagging at me. "How long have you been collecting Indian art?"

Welch thought about the question. "I've been collecting Asian art since I was in boarding school. Perhaps since I was thirteen years old. For the last decade and a half, I've been putting together a collection of Indian paintings. I buy in London, in India."

He paused. "I think that if you want to get a good collection in any art field, you've got to be in early. But if you want a great collection, you have to be the first into a collecting field. I think I was early in. I first went to India in 1957, when I began to collect Indian art. "

I thought about that. We were almost contemporaries in the Indian-art scene in Bombay.

Welch sipped a glass of water and smiled. "What I do at the Fogg is completely wonderful. They leave me alone. In turn, I teach a single course on aesthetics for them. I also give my students career advice."

"Advice?"

"Well, perhaps not advice. I should explain this better. What I do in my course is test how good one's eye is. Then I push people toward the absolutes of art."

I was totally puzzled. "How did the Fogg ever take up teaching this kind of course?"

Welch thought about my question. "In another generation, my position was created by the ever-practical men of the Boston establishment. They wanted to keep art in the family, I suppose. In this case, they wanted to make Harvard the center of the art-collecting world in America. For example, in 1911, a former banker at Goldman Sachs left the world of commerce and came to the Fogg to teach. As a rising young collector, one Paul J. Sachs gave a museum studies course at the Fogg on Fridays."

Welch paused. "The course actually trained many of the greatest generation of American museum directors from the 1920s to the 1950s. Sachs gave his seminars at his own house in Cambridge, and upon his sainted Fridays, he gave his course to his class at the museum."

In a thoughtful way, Welch continued, "In his course, Sachs laid out in deliberate and considered detail the meaning of the holy grail in art."

"And what's the holy grail in art?" I asked.

"It is connoisseurship! Don't you agree that connoisseurship is everything in art?" he asked abruptly.

Dodging his question, I asked, "What exactly is an honorary assistant keeper of Islamic art at the Fogg Museum?" To me, connoisseurship was a very private matter. It was me and my eye against the whole world. You either had an eye, or you didn't.

"An honorary assistant keeper of Islamic art at the Fogg Museum means," Welch paused, then chuckled. "That from Harvard, I'm paid a salary of $1 per year. It also means the trustees of my inheritance see that I'm gainfully employed by a reputable institution like Harvard."

For a long moment, Welch studied me, after we'd ordered. "You've been all over India. What do you collect?"

I stared at him. There is a kind of dance between collectors I didn't play. It's like two alpha dogs sniffing each other's coats when they first meet. I ran my finger around the top of my water glass. "Things. A bit here. A bit there," I admitted.

"What do you collect?" Welch pressed. Not many people collected classsical Indian art. This was turning into a very high level conversation of some importance, and he wanted to know the answer.

"Essagee in Bombay was the first person to tell me about you."

I paused, and then I continued. "I collect the same things you collect, more or less. But then, since I've read everything you've ever written, I'd have to say that your collections are probably much more finely tuned than my own. By their nature, art collectors are opportunists, aren't they?"

"On the other hand, perhaps you've been learning quite a bit from my mistakes?" Welch asked.

A canny question, certainly. This conversation was becoming dangerous. I answered most cautiously. "I don't think that's a given, do you? I've collected what I've found. I began to collect in Bombay. It was incredible what you could find during 1959 in India, wasn't it?"

"Actually," I continued, "It was unbelievable. If you had an eye, and you knew what great art was, things were all over, but then we were in first, weren't we?"

Across the table, Welch stared at me for a long time. A very long time.

"I think we'll be friends," he said finally. Then he burst into a huge laugh.

Evidently, I'd just navigated the water jump in the mud-spattered steeplechase. I can't say that I remembered anyone in the East Coast establishment who laughed like this, and this man whooped with laughter. I didn't think I'd ever met a member of the East Coast Wasp establishment who admitted to much humility, either.

Remarkable, I thought.

Our lunch went on for three hours and late into the afternoon. We both talked about our collections. Across the table, I told Welch everywhere I'd been on the subcontinent and in Afghanistan.

About two hours into this lunch, I realized a startling fact about all my conversations at Harvard. Each one had only taken place because I'd driven a beaten-up Chevrolet across the United States. Could anything be weirder?

Somehow, by some strange happenstance, I found where I wanted to be in the world. I realized how tired I was of California. No one in California supported artists. The 1960s in the California art world was a desert, as far as artists finding local support for their art. I did the work and hoped people would catch up with it. I realized how tired I was explaining what I did in photography.

Despite having been born and having lived much of my life in Berkeley, which currently had thirteen Nobel Prize winners on the University of California's faculty, neither it, nor any other university in the world, had a photography course.

I wondered about finding support at Harvard. No university in America possessed the horsepower that Harvard currently had. Right then, in the mid-1960s, Cambridge, Massachusetts, was the intellectual center of America. Quite by happenstance, it appeared I'd wandered into the center of the American intellectual academic establishment.

After three days in Cambridge in 1966, I was stunned that men like Robert Gardner and Cary Welch even existed.

At the end of our lunch,, Welch asked, "Will you ever come back here?"

"Hard to tell where I'll be," I answered.

"If you do come back, stay at my house. With my wife and family."

It was an invitation to return.

I smiled at Welch. I felt a lump in my throat. It had been so long I belonged anywhere. It would be so good to belong somewhere. "That is very uncommonly generous. That would be very kind of you both," I said. I wiped at my eyes, which filmed with water. "I want you both to know that's a reason for me to come back. I thank you very much for this."

I looked at Welch, and then I told him my feelings about connoisseurship in art.

We agreed completely. We both agreed with everything each said to the other. What we said was bedrock. It was absolutely everything in art.

I would return. I had to return to Cambridge. First, I had to go to New York. Then, I had to go back to California to finish what I'd begun. Next, somehow I'd go back India. Then in another year, in Cambridge I could show Welch what was happening in California through my photographs. I could introduce him to the future.

***

New York, August 1966

If you wanted to get ready for a grueling foreign journey, the Valencia Hotel on the Bowery in New York City was a good place to do a warm-up for a trip to hell. The Valencia Hotel was where I always tried to start my journeys towards the rotting boundaries of the earth.

From New York Rotterdam on the Holland America Line was a five- to seven-day ocean voyage that cost $145. The rest of the world wasn't so far away from Rotterdam. If you wanted to go to India, from there it was another journey of a month. Meals, buses, and railway journeys overland included, it was $150 to the edge of the world and Calcutta.

There were general cleanliness and operating problems with the Valencia Hotel. The walking dead navigated the poorly lit corridors on their long journeys to nowhere. The toilets looked like they'd survived temporary, impossible problems you didn't want to think about, while each floor of the hotel was equipped with only a single forty-watt lightbulb. I always seemed to be the only paying guest who stayed at the Valencia overnight: the hotel had a special short-stay rate. Even though it was only $3 a day, most guests pursued their interests by the hour.

The first floor of the hotel was occupied by the historic Five Spot Café. It was one of the great New York jazz meeting places, where Ornette Coleman, Thelonious Monk, Miles Davis, and John Coltrane had all played within the last decade.

I spent the next week photographing my neighbors who lived an open-air life on the Bowery.

I photographed pushcarts. I shot the hard, mean, brick-lined streets of the Lower East Side and the bums. I photographed East Eighth Street, which was somehow beginning to look like Kabul in 1962. Each shop on East Eighth had Afghan Pashtun sheepskin coats. There were hubble-bubble water pipes. For that friendly pick-me-up hit of hashish, there were even hand-carved *chara* holders. The railroad apartments of the Lower East Side had been repurposed into hippie heaven.

I thought that the very moment I headed down East Eighth Street from Astor Place, there must be hugely laden Mercedes diesel trucks filled with trippy junk from Chicken Street in Kabul headed this way. I wondered who the hell were these enterprising entrepreneur freaks on Manhattan's Lower East Side carting all this junk out of Afghanistan? Probably new loads were on the way, just then crossing the Dashti Margo, the Afghan "desert of death."

Did I ever think the Kabul of 1960 would end up this way? When I walked down East Eighth Street, everyone who passed me looked like a land pirate of Kabul. The whole Lower East Side looked sunken into the latest weird fashion statement out of Afghanistan.

However, if you looked again, the people who filled the sidewalks were suburban-sourced teenagers from New Jersey and Connecticut, with pimply chests and podgy bodies going to fat from too many carbs. They had fresh, unlined faces undented by pain. They were all so young. Their newly bought land-pirate clothes looked carefully rumpled and untidy. The knees on every set of Levi's had been carefully worn. I missed the gaunt, howling end-of-the-road desperation that you saw in the people who first inhabited Kabul in the '60s. I even missed the real life tribulations of the ravaged junkies of Kabul.

After five days in the Valencia, I took my last pictures of this strange version of another place and time. I didn't have much hope for my pictures. Everyone looked as if they were dressing up.

I took one last turn around the old neighborhood.

I supposed that San Francisco, and what was happening there, simply found its alter ego on East Eighth Street. If you dressed the part, you became the part. The new world. Afghanistan and its freaks had now entered the land of secondhand experience, where nothing was real and everything was quantifiable and for sale. Soon models in *Vogue* and *Harper's Bazaar* would be dressed like freaks, if they weren't already. Soon there would be movies on the freaks. I couldn't wait; it was so deliciously weird.

***

At a New York pay phone, slipping in my quarters one by one, I phoned Cambridge. In my first conversation, I told Robert Gardner that I was returning to California to finish a film that I was working on, and I'd be in touch. I thanked him for his offer of sponsorship.

My second telephone call was to Cary Welch. I told him I had decided, definitely, that I'd come back to Cambridge and take him up on his offer of a place to stay. I said I'd write him the details of what I was doing when I got to San Francisco. I thanked him for his support. I told him I had to finish shooting a film that I was working on in California.

I hung up the telephone receiver. Who knew if I'd ever be able to go back to India?

My contact at the record company petered out, as such people do, in a cloud of vagueness. The man couldn't decide what he wanted. He wanted me to shoot the old Metropolitan Opera House, then he remembered it had just been torn down. Could anyone become more vague than that?

I snagged another driveaway car back to San Francisco.

Driving a Cadillac Seville cross-country was not nearly as exciting as driving a broken-down Chevrolet Corvair. Five days after I left New York, I drove onto the San Francisco Bay Bridge. I paid my toll of $0.25, and a half hour later I turned in the Cadillac at the driveaway agency and retrieved my $100 deposit.

On Market Street, I caught a San Francisco transit bus to a stop near Freddie Higby's house in Pacific Heights.

I entered the house just in time for one of his elaborate cocktail parties. No one noticed I hadn't been there, so no one asked where I'd been. My trip had been very strange. In the company of Freddie's guests, my trip had a sort of out-of-body unreality to it.

My memory of my dinner that night was ham-and-asparagus canapés. After the party wound down, I climbed up to my top-floor room.

I lay on the bed. I wondered at the strange course my life kept taking. It was as if I'd never left San Francisco, and I considered that I'd hallucinated Cary Welch and Robert Gardner after bingeing on driveaway cars.

Cambridge. Harvard. The Bowery. New York. It seemed all a blur. But for the first time in years, my life seemed totally contented.

All this adventure. "Amazing," I said to myself quietly.

***

San Francisco, October 15, 1966

I think my patience is ending.

At the entrance to the Berkeley campus at the end of Telegraph Avenue, I watch a group of American Nazis. They are putting their propaganda booklets out on card tables. They unfurl their flags decorated with swastikas.

In the last two weeks, I feel like I've been attacked by the asylum inmates.

Lately, both the drug scene and the music scene have reached the same destination in differing ways. They seem to be headed toward the barricades.

In this land of golden tomorrows, some of the people I've photographed recently have become very tense. Unnervingly tense.

Like a member of an unholy tag team of monsters, a man who reminds me of Robespierre during the excesses of the French Revolution has emerged from the protest movements centered on Berkeley. In the local political world of the anti-Vietnam protests, Jerry Rubin has made a pact of solidarity with a group of unstable student dreamers on the Berkeley campus. In the last few months, he has created ownership positions of control of the scene.

My own immediate problem with made-in-California control freaks was there in front of me. It was a group of rightist rompers who were just then passing out kindly, uplifting giveaway magazines on Telegraph Avenue. Titled promisingly *The Storm Trooper*, the magazine they passed around was produced by the American Nazi Party.

Unfortunately for me, I'd made the mistake of photographing this group one too many times.

I was wary of these people. I used to be concerned about Jerry Rubin and his group of increasingly hard-line antiwar protestors. Now I worried much more about the American Nazis.

At first, months ago, they seemed to regard me as a sort of acquaintance, who occasionally photographed them as people abused them verbally. Lately, they had been counting on me as a fellow provocateur, while recasting themselves as a local, legitimate, happily optimistic and ordinary political party.

They'd even engaged a public-relations hack. He advised them to replace their hail-fellow-well-met greeting of "Sieg Heil!" with the more measured and musical sort of salutation, "White Power for All!" Can we call this social progress?

When he spoke, he covered his mouth with his hand in case the FBI or the CIA was trying to lip-read his invitation from a hidden-camera position.

"Next Friday," he whispered. "Just one week now. We're gonna flame out those niggers down in San Jose."

The lieutenant paused, then continued, "We're gonna put a goddamned fifteen-foot burning cross on these son-of-a-bitch fucker's lawns. That'll give 'em a hint they ought to go back to Birmingham, or wherever the hell they come from. Those niggers. I need some photographs of this beautiful event and this magnificent cross burning. It's our message that they leave the immediate neighborhood. Are you a patriot or not? Got me?" he asked.

This wasn't an invitation I heard every day. I managed to say something like "Smashing."

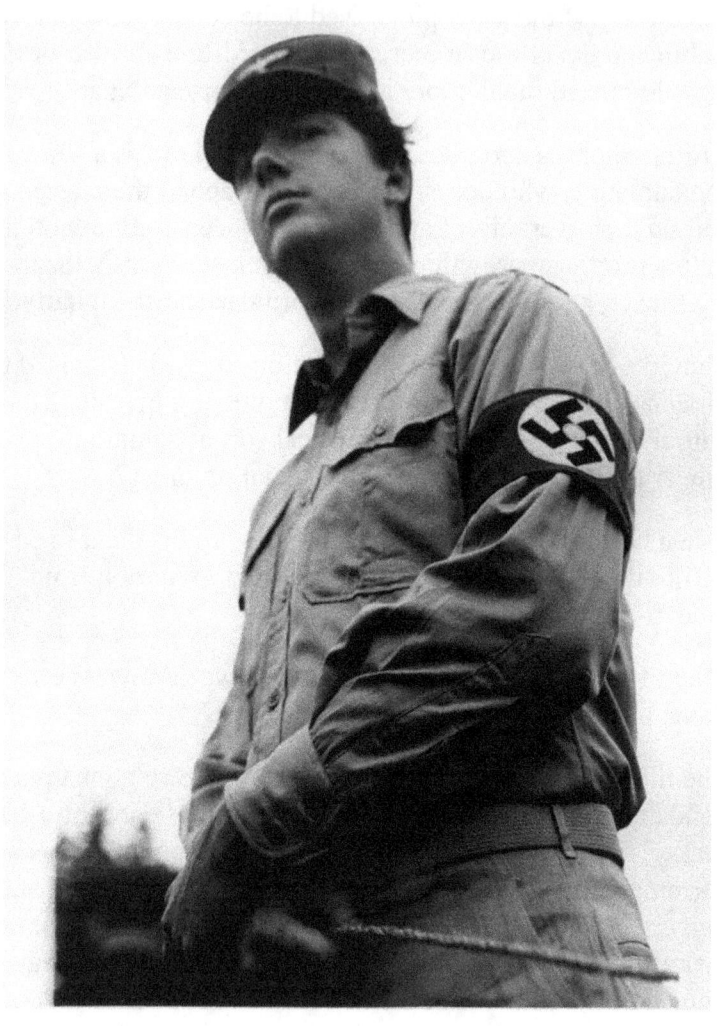

American Nazi, 1966

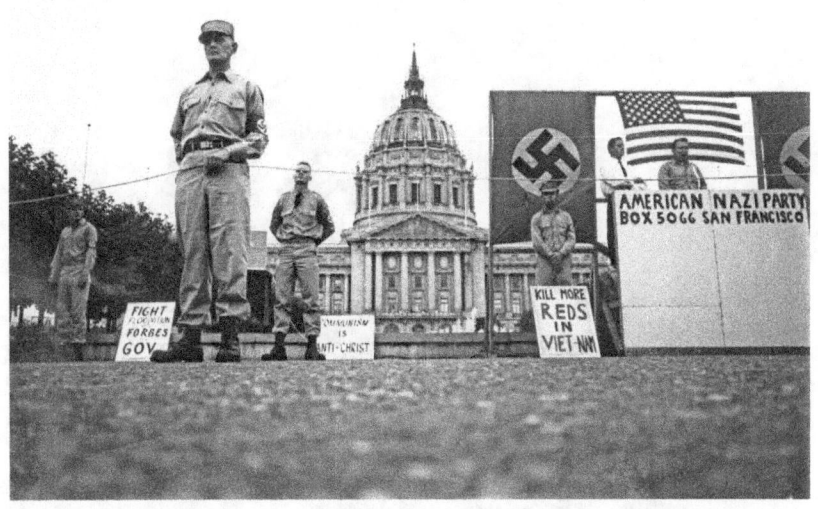

Fight Fluoridation, Kill More Reds in Vietnam, 1966

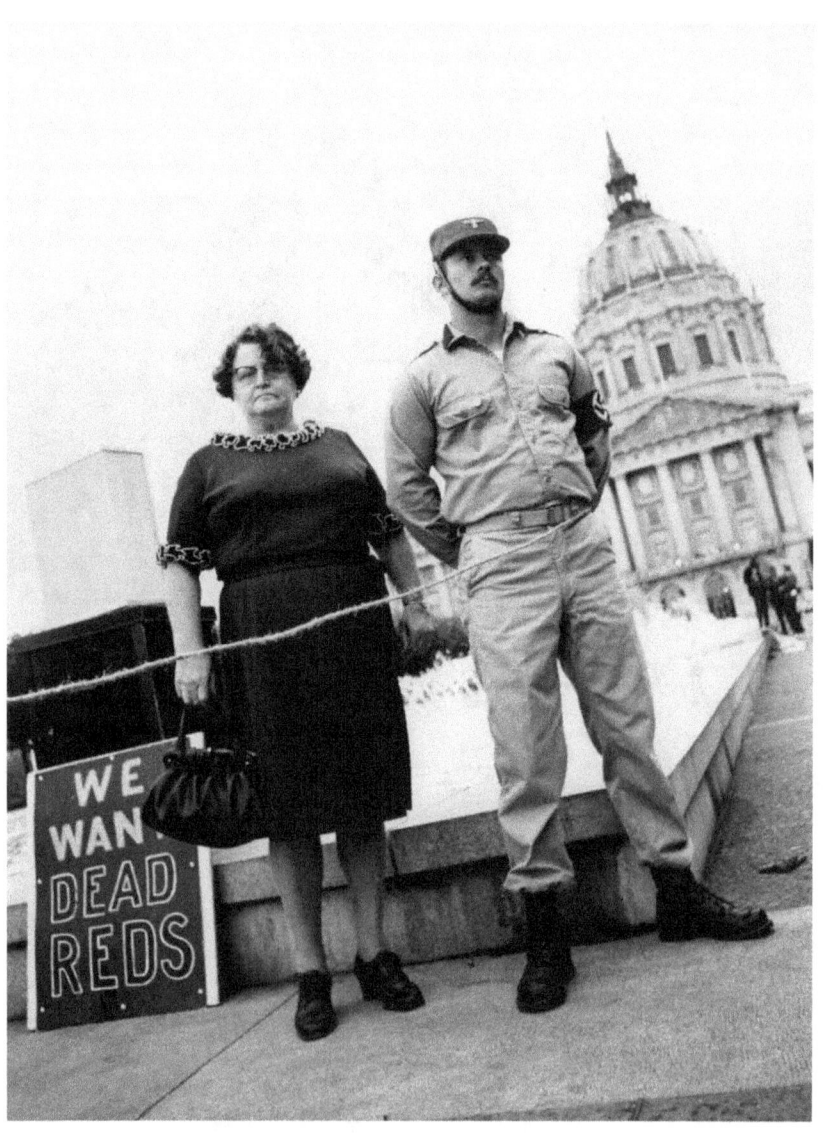

American Nazis, 1966

In the last weeks, there had been more dynamitings, and people were beaten up after nighttime antiwar rallies. I suppose the proposed magnificent work of documentation, for me, was the immediate proof of my allegiance to the American Nazi Party. God knows what would follow with these monsters.

In Berkeley, Jerry Rubin appeared at the Nazi demonstration in front of us. He had his usual halo of hippie hair that stood eight inches above his ratlike features.

Five minutes earlier, I'd seen Rubin circling around. He'd given me the beady eye. I felt the same way about him as I felt about that cockroach, Bill Graham, at the Fillmore.

I watched Rubin very carefully. Was today the day the students finally decided to turn the American Nazis into victims of intolerance?

I looked behind the Nazis.

At that moment, a group of very husky-looking 250-pound football linemen appeared. I had the feeling that these people were not Berkeley English lit students. I also had the feeling the peaceful dynamic in Berkeley protests was about to plunge radically downhill.

From what dark fraternity corner of Cal did Jerry get these guys?

I decided then that I didn't want to be the filling of another protest sandwich.

As I hurried down Telegraph Avenue on my cowardly way, I simply marveled at the lieutenant's brand-new plans of political discourse. In his last whispered sentence, he said his masterstroke was his Ku Klux Klan cross burning.

By the time I got two blocks down Telegraph Avenue, I was hurrying toward my own future. I decided it was time for me to leave California. My occupation was getting too dangerous.

A friend of mine later described what happened, and I heard what befell the Nazis that afternoon.

It took place in less time than a glance behind you. The pockmarked lieutenant almost made it back to his storm troopers.

The Nazis simply vanished as the giant-sized students surged in a huge pile of bodies over them. My friend said it looked like the Nazis were taken out by a gang of lumberjack NFL football linemen in hobnailed boots.

When the Nazis began to pick themselves off the concrete, they got a second helping of realpolitik. They were given a rousing, old-fashioned, outlaw Hell's Angels stomping.

Broken bones. Crushed ribs. Broken heads.

For months, the Nazis had been taunting the anti–Vietnam War people, calling them "pussies" and "gutless faggots."

Big surprise. The lieutenant and his storm troopers were carted off to Alta Bates Hospital for repair work.

Jerry Rubin was clever, I must say. The students had waited until no press was around.

The Nazis couldn't press charges because no press covered the attack, and they had no evidence of the attack. The cross burning never took place, or at least I never heard of it. I remembered as well the fragile truce between the police and the Vietnam War protestors. When would that end in both San Francisco and Berkeley?

Over the last two months, Cary Welch and I had exchanged letters. A week ago, he'd again invited me to come east and join his household of four children and his wife, Edith. His house was a slow ten-minute walk to Harvard, down streets bordered by huge 200-year-old elms.

As I crossed over the Bay Bridge on the F train to San Francisco, I thought about fleeing California before this whole slide-zone landscape disintegrated.

I decided it was a good time to leave California before dope or madness moved society towards more effective methods of mayhem. It had become very clear to me that the other part of photography was that you were always in the middle, and the pay was terrible.

***

Thirty minutes of the longer film I made on California can be seen on YouTube under its title:

CALIFORNIA: MANUFACTURING THE FUTURE

CHAPTER THREE

Cambridge, November–December 1966

Nothing in the Welch house appeared to ever be put away inside closets or bureaus.

After I arrived, I was offered a large third-floor bedroom at the front of the house. It had a huge four-poster bed, circa the seventeenth century, which was set against the far wall, away from the windows. I was told by one of the children that Cary's grandmother, a wheezing ancient, had expired under her bedcovers in this relic a few seasons before. Alternatively, I could opt for a smaller bedroom down the hall with a less macabre history.

On the second floor were the bedrooms of the Welch family. The ménage on Channing Street was infinitely curious.

It looked as if an entire family had just returned and unpacked from a long journey. Clothes were scattered everywhere: on beds, on furniture, and underfoot. Occupying the house were four children, ages five to thirteen: little Edith, Thomas, Samuel, and Lucia. They appeared to be normal children, but this was not a normal house to grow up in.

In Cary and Edith's bedroom, as an example of the Welches' domestic chaos, there were huge, tottering piles of art books. Sometimes there were shifting passageways between the books. At other times, perhaps depending upon the season, books lined either side of the bedroom, where they appeared to grow outward from the walls like some kind of incrustation.

Welcome to the treasure house. But then this was New England, and Cambridge was only twenty miles from Salem, where they used to drown their witches or crush them with huge rocks. I'd soon find out that New Englanders wore their history like a horsehair shirt.

In the basement, Cary had equipped a study room with a good library of India-related books. He also had a set of McIntosh amplifiers, with a foursome of goosed-up KLH speakers, which were on the scale of the ones in San Francisco's Fillmore Auditorium.

Set into an alcove beyond the speakers were three Kodak Carousel slide projectors. The slides for these projectors were part of Cary's archive, which eventually included 60,000 photographs, and they documented his self-made, fantastical, and perpetual around-the-world art tour.

This was where Cary worked, if you could term what he did work.

***

A horribly cold street. Late afternoon. The wind moved snow devils through the black trunks of the trees, up and down the deserted Cambridge street behind Memorial Hall.

I had finished the final cut of my Indian movie on the Bhil tribal people of Western India thas I'd made in the 1961-1962 period. I was hugely grateful for the completion money put into my film by Robert Gardner. At Harvard, I had a moment of fragile patronage that I hoped would help rescue me from more years of trying to scrounge up money for my photography.

At Harvard's Peabody Museum, I needed to see someone named Cora Du Bois. Professor Du Bois was an anthropologist with a specialty in India and a long list of Indian government contact. I had to put work into an eventual thawing, and I hoped for reconciliation with the government's Ministry of External Affairs in Delhi.

Inside the museum the wind rattled the windows of the Peabody. I closed the front door to the museum, and to my left was the closed door of the director's office, then another office beyond. Inside this second office was a humorless, dour-looking woman in her fifties, laboring away at an eight-inch stack of index cards.

"Is it possible to see Professor Du Bois?" I asked.

The woman looked up, then through me. With machine-gun delivery, she said, "Not here. She's always busy and seldom graces us with her presence here. Thursdays at 3:00 p.m. In her office once a week. Leave her a note."

With deliberation, never making eye contact, nor losing her place in her stack of cards, this dour creature returned to her depressing work.

I wondered how long she had worked in this office. Decades? Half a century? Two hundred years?

Across the room, someone else occupied a desk near a rear window. She looked up and gave me an expression that was almost a smile.

In contrast to the drab across the room, this woman was utterly bewitching. Long legs. Long fingers. A long torso. She had long ginger-brown-gold hair. She seemed to be staring at something on her desk. I crossed the room and looked down over her shoulder at an engraved wedding invitation.

She looked up and simultaneously pushed the invitation under a pile of papers.

"Yes?" she asked.

I was stunned. She was otherworldly. She was so lovely. Her legs went on forever.

I mumbled, then coughed and finally got out my question: "Do you know where Professor Cora Du Bois has her office?" I swallowed only with great effort.

The woman was perhaps twenty-eight. She had on bluish eye shadow, and as she stood up, I saw that she was wearing a greatly abbreviated leather miniskirt. She moved across the room and beckoned me to follow her with a wave of her hand.

In the hallway beyond the office, she pointed along a corridor.

"Down there. Climb the stairs. On the second floor, it's the third door down on the left side of the corridor. Leave Professor Du Bois a note. Whatever you want, you've been warned—she's elusive and uncooperative."

"Thank you," I managed. "Could I borrow a piece of paper and a pencil?"

I wondered how long this bewitching woman had been working here? I also wondered if she looked forward to Friday, and not having to work at the Peabody Museum.

Back in her office, the woman handed me a pad of paper and a pen. I sat at an empty desk and wrote Cora Du Bois a note.

Turning, I took a picture of the young woman at her desk. She was reading some names on a list. She heard the camera shutter, and she sighed and looked up at the ceiling. She didn't turn to look at me.

"Could you put my note into Cora Du Bois's mailbox?" I asked.

Slowly, the woman turned her head toward me.

She nodded without speaking. It was unnerving and extremely odd. She tilted her head to the side, and it was like a little girl bending her head to get a different view of the world.

I left the note on her desk and beat a hasty retreat out the door, with the woman still watching me. The Peabody and its inhabitants were unnervingly weird. I fled.

***

At dinner that night, I asked Cary if he knew any of the people in the director's office of the Peabody Museum. I described the young woman I'd met. What I didn't say was that I couldn't get her out of my mind. She kept slipping in and out of my thoughts.

Cary thought about this. He said he'd think about whom he presently knew at the Peabody. "I don't think I actually know the person you're talking about," he said. But then he added, brightly, "But I can, and will find out for you!"

Everyone at Harvard apparently knew everyone else, somehow.

I thought that everyone in Boston had known one another from dancing class, then boarding school, and they'd all been in one another's weddings.

I had learned that East Coast families knew one another for countless generations. As I became better acquainted with the Welches, I thought that Cary and Edith probably knew everyone of a certain societal group on the East Coast. They knew their collaterals, their parents, and their grandparents.

Cary left the room.

Across the table, Edith looked at me. She smiled and shook her head at this waste of a perfectly warm meal. "When he gets an idea, it's very hard for him to give it up," she explained.

I heard Cary talking on the telephone. Two minutes later, he was back.

"She's the Myrle's sister-in-law," he said to Edith. "Isn't that frightening? It's absolutely frightening."

Cary turned to me.

"The person you spoke with at the Peabody is named Joan Mitchell. Her brother-in-law was in my class at St. Paul's School, and then with me at Harvard. For twenty-seven years Hankie, also known as the Myrle, has been one of my very best friends." He paused, then stared into his dinner, shaking his head. "How ingrown and close together everyone is around here."

I began to see how Cary might sometimes be exhausted by his social obligations.

"Anything more about Miss Joan Mitchell?" I asked cautiously.

"There is actually lots more. According to her sister, whom I just spoke to, she's supposed to be going to a place called the Carpenter Center. For some reason, there's a dance next Tuesday at 7:00 p.m. In the basement of where you work."

Cary threw his arms wide. "Though I shouldn't mention this, as I recall Joan was actually in our wedding. I should have remembered that. Edith handles all my corollary social associations and my life's journeys. Sorry."

From across the table, Edith was watching Cary stonily. I thought about that. As things go between married couples, I'm sure Edith would tell Cary later how pleased she was with him.

For the moment, though, Cary beamed at me happily. On second thought, was his look childishly malevolent?

"If this basement meeting develops into a larger interest of yours," he advised, "I hope that you can devote quite a lot of time to Joan Mitchell. Let me tell you, the mating process of East Coast ladies is…how to say this, Edith?…a very long, unnerving, complex, and exhausting undertaking, with an always uncertain ending. Am I right, my dear?"

Edith looked at Cary as if she were very far away from this conversation.

***

The lights in the large concrete room were dimmed.

Everything in the Carpenter Center was concrete. A set of speakers was turned up to a deafening level. I felt right at home in this basement, since I'd been working here for the last three months. My editing room was four feet away, behind a concrete wall lined with filing cabinets. It was tucked inside the largest basement room in the building, where the dance was now being held.

Tuesday of next week came.

I saw Joan Mitchell with a consumptive man in a leather jacket. He looked very frail, almost translucent.

I approached. I asked her to dance.

Joan smiled at her consumptive friend across the room. The music was so loud that one could hardly speak. She moved toward me.

In those days, you never, ever touched your dance partner. We danced in the fashion that everyone did during those wild dancing days. This consisted of wrenching your body around, then jumping up and down in close proximity to your partner. If you could manage it, you threw into the dance a group of quick jerks.

Around us whirled Cambridge's finest.

Presumably, they'd known one another from the time they were three or four years old. There was a scattering of New York people who were in the arts at Harvard. A salt-and-pepper mix of differing ethnicities leaped and whirled around us.

Joan Mitchell was poised.

She was terribly controlled as she whirled and jumped. Tonight, at least, she didn't stare at me from odd angles. At least I didn't have that to unnerve me. What did unnerve me, however, were her short, short miniskirt and her very long, thin torso.

The consumptive moved toward us through the crowd. He smiled wanly and cut in. Then Joan Mitchell and her problematic, tubercular companion whirled off together into an absolute wall of opaque sound.

I wondered how it was possible to start a relationship with someone you couldn't talk to.

In frustration, I left by the rear door of the basement room as the dance continued behind me. I didn't have to go far to work on my film this night. Sinking down at a table over a stack of unedited photographic proof books, I shook my head. So far, Joan Mitchell's communications with me consisted of directions to Professor Cora Du Bois's office on the second floor of the Peabody Museum. I laughed when I wondered, "Could this fragile moment be the beginnings of a long-term relationship?"

That night, I arrived back at the Welch house after having worked hours on editing California photographs.

Everyone had gone to bed.

I fell asleep that night reading Cary's first edition of *La Storia do Mogor,* which recounted an eighteen-year-old Italian boy's trip to India in 1654. It was an unbelievable story. As a military mercenary in India, the writer fought in the Mogul empire's wars of dynastic succession. It was the story of a lost soul, and was a staggeringly wonderful book. No matter how hard I tried, I couldn't shake India out of my life. I fell asleep dreaming of a beach at Varkala, on the palm coast of Malabar.

***

My winter at Harvard was spent printing my photographs of California. The new year came; it was 1967.

I'd been appointed as the first research fellow in film and photography at Harvard. At that point, Harvard was one of the few universities in the world that had classes in photography and film. I set my own hours.

I arranged to get the keys to the back door of the Carpenter Center. When it had been constructed next to the Fogg Museum, it was connected to the Fogg by a subterranean passageway. No one used the passageway, and few people had keys to it except the janitors of the two buildings.

I obtained keys to both ends of the passageway from my new friends, the nighttime janitors.

At night, when everyone left the Carpenter Center and the Fogg Museum, I'd wander the galleries of the Fogg looking at astonishing paintings. In the basements where Cary stored his art, I'd pull out pieces and look at them. Perhaps someday I could find a film subject to do with the Fogg and Cary's collection. I could remove art from the Fogg, film it on the huge Oxberry animation stand owned by the Carpenter Center, then finish the project at the Carpenter Center. I imagined this project being done with these two leading institutions one hundred feet from each other.

At the Welches' house, I put blackout shades on the windows. I slept all day and worked all night.

The work I did at night consisted first of editing my California pictures. I'd stare at my proof books, at the tiny contacts of my negatives. In the lavishly equipped Carpenter Center darkrooms, I'd then print the negatives I'd marked, taken in California between 1960 and 1966. I was the only occupant of the darkrooms. I printed my pictures, and I listened to hundreds of hours of rock and roll over the months.

In the darkness of the lab, I found out that there were basically two ways to make movies. The first and easiest way was to have lots of money, in which case you hired people to do all things that you didn't want to do. The second way was immensely more difficult. You took your greatest asset, your own time, and did grueling scut work on the film by yourself. The advantage of the second approach was that every mistake was your mistake. It was a brutally efficient way to learn how to make movies.

I took off a few nights a month. I was entertained, delighted, educated, and entranced by the ever-surprising Cary Welch.

The more I came to know Cary, despite his self-absorption and competitive foibles, of which there were more than anyone should have, the more I came to think of him as part genius and part willful, spoiled child.

It was fascinating the way his mind worked. It was almost otherworldly, what he saw in art.

It was amazing to me that Cary survived both his childhood and his years in boarding school. His mother had been deeply involved in her social obligations in Buffalo, New York, which, apparently, never included Cary or his sister. Cary had been brought up by nannies, and then he was packed off to St. Paul's School in Concord, New Hampshire, when he was eleven years old. Did his parents ever pick up their children and hold them when they were young? Probably not. The result was the person who became Cary Welch.

In life, with luck, you will always stand upon the shoulders of others. In the months I spent with him, I came to think, that I owed Cary a debt I could never possibly repay. But in a way, I did repay him.

Cary was fascinated by the strangeness of the life I'd lived, in contrast to his life, bound by the East Coast societal straitjacket of the world he'd been born into.

The more I knew him, the more I thought of Cary Welch as a man bent on escape. He was intrigued by my solitary journeys in India. He was fascinated by my solitary collecting life and my photography. He seemed a man lost in the mysteries of his own life and survival, plus his attempt to somehow escape from four children, a concerned, brilliant wife, and a life that had been validated both by the establishment and the trustees of Edith's and his own fortunes.

***

Cambridge, January 1967

In all honesty, I had to say my pursuit of Miss Joan Mitchell was not going well. It was not going well at all.

She seemed to have disappeared. Perhaps she never went out in public places? She appeared each day at the Peabody Museum and then suddenly disappeared. Apparently, she was untraceable. It was a mystery.

With difficulty, I was learning what Cary had said in regard to the mating rituals of East Coast establishment ladies. His observations had been devastatingly correct. They were shy, retiring beings. They rarely appeared in broad daylight. In pursuit of one of these rare creatures, I decided that the only way I'd ever meet Joan Mitchell socially would be with a suitable introduction.

At the edge of desperation, I threw the Welches and all their connections into the fray.

In the past months, I'd learned a few biographical facts about Joan Mitchell.

Edie Sedgwick was Joan Mitchell's cousin. Edie was an American actress, a socialite, and a fashion model. At that moment, Edie was one of Andy Warhol's film "superstars." Warhol, the silently boring man whom I'd photographed in San Francisco, had anointed Edie Sedgwick as his Girl of the Year.

I asked Cary if he could arrange a suitable introduction to Joan Mitchell. He looked at me and said, "Difficult going? I suppose so. Over the generations, Joan comes from an extraordinary family." Then he continued, "I told you this was going to be difficult with these sorts of shy luminescent beings. For a quarter of a century, her ancestor Edward Stotesbury, who died in 1938, was the senior partner of J.P. Morgan. He was the most powerful banker in America. You know she's Edie Sedgwick's cousin, don't you? When you meet Joan, for god's sake don't mention Edie. It's a very difficult family."

Cary thought for a moment. "Also, don't get into a conversation about Edie's father, Fuzzy Sedgwick. A monster. A difficult conversational cul-de-sac."

Families. Cul-de-sacs. Tangled histories.

In Cary's narrative I quickly became submerged in the thickets of East Coast tribal American stories.

Joan and Edie were also descended from the family that provided both the idea and the first land in central Manhattan to create Central Park. Additionally, in the 1850s the family owned the famous clipper ship the *Flying Cloud*. In the next century, during World War II, the most important paintings and treasures of the Metropolitan Museum of Art were removed from Manhattan. They were placed for safekeeping far away from possible German air raids inside the family house outside Philadelphia, which was also one of the largest houses ever built in America.

After hearing these chronicles, I walked alone through the nighttime streets of Cambridge. I spent much time thinking about where I came from. I was born in California. Both sides of my mother's family had settled in the first decade of the Massachusetts Bay Colony. Before that, my mother's family was descended from one of the last Norman knights who held Rouen Castle in 1205, during the Angevin Empire.

My father's family, the Worswicks, possessed one of the earliest British surnames. It was an eleventh-century name, forty generations removed from the present day. Seeded over the American West were hot springs and small towns named after my family in the nineteenth century. These were facts that no one in my own family seemed to notice or care about. In America, who cared about the family cobwebs, fading pictures, and burials that had turned to dust? In America, my family lost its history.

Cary invited Joan Mitchell to one of the Welch dinner parties. Miss Joan Mitchell agreed to grace a gathering of the semi-famous, who appeared now and then in Cambridge.

The night arrived.

Again, like so many other nights, it was snowing. A fourteen-inch blanket of unbroken fresh snow covered the driveway at Cary's house at 15 Channing Street.

I listened to the knocker rapping at the front door. Edith hurried through the hall to the front of the house. As usual, the doorbell didn't work.

Joan Mitchell stood there after Edith opened the door. Edith kissed Joan on the cheek.

Then Cary appeared, and he kissed Joan Mitchell on the cheek.

"How long have we known each other?" Cary asked Joan.

"I think eleven years," she replied.

Joan stood back and shrugged off her coat, which Cary took. He pointed in my direction.

"Clark, meet Joan. Joan, Clark."

I approached, and Joan Mitchell stared at me as she was turning in my direction.

Standing there, she gave me a quick, polite smile. I wondered, could it be this easy to meet someone in a correct, if calculated, meeting place?
She put out her hand. In my own hand, hers felt like ice.

"I'm always cold in this terrible weather," she said. "I'm sorry my hand's so cold."

I shook my head in confusion.

In the dim light of the hallway, I couldn't stop myself from staring at the woman in front of me. The central female figure of a very famous tapestry at the Musée de Cluny in Paris, titled *La Dame à la Licorne (The Lady and the Unicorn),* looked precisely like Joan Mitchell.

In this work, one of the greatest works of medieval art in France, the lady had the same narrow face. She possessed the same clear, bright eyes, set above a long, straight nose. More startlingly, she had an identical high, medieval forehead, which pitched back and upward to her hairline.

For a brief moment, it was as if I'd been transported back centuries. I stood there.

At the door down the short hallway, Cary turned and waved us both toward the living room. Joan followed him in her suede miniskirt that enclosed impossibly long legs. The living room was in semidarkness.

On the sofa sat James Ivory, the usually mute film director.

Next to him was the semi-famous Desmond FitzGerald, the twenty-ninth and last Knight of Glin, who held one of the more curious titles in England. FitzGerald was descended from a personage named Seán Mór na Sursainge, and a twelfth-century Norman family. He was trying, at that moment, to obtain a fine-arts degree at the Fogg Museum. More prosaically, Ivory, at his end of the sofa, was just then trying to set up a film in India called *The Guru* with 20th Century Fox.

We had drinks.

Edith and Joan disappeared to deal with the children in the kitchen. A few minutes later, I heard the children being herded upstairs to bed.

At the edges of the living room Ivory, FitzGerald, and Cary talked about India. I was lost in the mysteries of this evening, half there and half not there. In the spirit of the evening and my exceedingly brief meeting with Joan, I only half-listened to the conversation.

Thirty minutes later, the ladies came downstairs into the dining room, and we settled down to dinner.

Cary loved to talk. FitzGerald also loved to talk.

The assembled dinner party received the art gossip first from London, then from New York. Habitually, Ivory never spoke unless he was answering questions about himself. For their own parts, FitzGerald and Cary settled into a discussion on the art criminals who ran the Drouot, the great Paris auction house, and the recent spate of fake classical Indian paintings that seemed to be coming onto the market from a yet undiscovered link to the Drouot.

During the meal, Joan had settled on staring at FitzGerald. I felt she didn't harbor tender feelings for him, or, perhaps. she didn't harbor happy feelings for people of his class in Britain.

At the end of dinner, Edith faded away into the kitchen and Cary rose from the table. He led Ivory and FitzGerald back into the gloom of the living room to look at Indian paintings under a single bright light.

Joan and I remained at the table in the dining room. I began speaking about the strange things that were then happening in England, where people seemed to be body-surfing drugs along with mushrooms, speed, and everything else you could swallow.

I asked Joan if she knew London lately, or previously?

"I haven't been to England for eight years," she answered in a controlled and measured voice.

Leaning across the table, she looked at me carefully then said, "In London, I studied with the great Viennese art historian Dr. Ernst Gombrich, and I haven't been back since. I once attended the Courtauld Institute of Art."

Joan paused. She ran a thin hand slowly across her forehead, thinking, then began speaking in a distant voice. "In London, I shared a tiny bed-sitting room with my best friend, Cynthia Ryan. During the very cold year we were in London, we spent a lot of time trying to keep warm and feeding shillings into a wall-mounted water heater in a seedy bathroom down the hall. During my year at the Courtauld Institute of Art, all I was was horribly cold."

Joan stared through me, no doubt reliving her carefree days in London.

Leaning forward, she peered around the doorway into the living room at FitzGerald. She shuddered as she looked at him.

"Cynthia and I were the first two American women to ever attend Britain's most famous art college. We both developed a keen knowledge of the British upper-middle and landed classes. All of them are like that awful beast FitzGerald, sitting there in the next room."

"They aren't what you think they are," she whispered. "They're hateful. They're vile people. They absolutely *loathe* Americans. And when it's convenient for them, they come over here to freeload and grace us with their oh-so-clever company."
Joan took a deep breath.

I sat there, thinking about this ordeal that had gone on for a year.

"I'm not finished yet," Joan continued. "During class break, both Cynthia and I went off to Florence. In Florence, glorious Florence, whom should we discover but our whole class from the Courtauld. They were completely different in Florence. Weeks drifted into more weeks of parties, and dinners, and confidences. We had jolly lunches. Ribald dinners. During the day we studued the glories of the high Renaissance. In the narrow streets, all of us were the greatest of friends. Then we all returned to London, and guess what?"

She turned to stare at the twenty-ninth Knight of Glin for a long moment. I was surprised he didn't burst suddenly into flame. Abruptly, she turned back to me.

"After class break in London, after our wonderful weeks-long visit in Florence, not a single dismal person in our class at the Courtauld spoke to either Cynthia or myself for the entire rest of the class year."

Joan then asked quietly, "You're really quite shy, aren't you?"

I felt I was sinking. This was not going well. I nodded. I took a deep breath. I was absolutely unnerved.

Joan gave me a quick, wonderful smile. It was the first time in the night she'd genuinely smiled. "So am I. Shy, I mean. And I'm talking much too much. It's unladylike, isn't it? What do you do?" she asked suddenly. "Tell me. Is it exciting and interesting?"

For the next few minutes, in the dining room at the back of Cary's house, for the first time in a very long time I talked about my photographs. I said that I did films, and I took photographs. I said I also sometimes traveled.
Joan simply watched me. She didn't speak.

Finally, she asked, "Edith said you were very nice and that you're a kind person. Are you a kind person?"

The conversation suddenly had gotten very dense. This evening had gone far beyond the mind games people played on each other in the Haight-Ashbury, or the power trips of the psychedelic world in Los Angeles. I opened my mouth to answer, but I thought better of it.

I had the feeling that Miss Joan Mitchell had been very wounded, and she'd been terribly beaten up. Perhaps that was the reason she was so elusive.

Finally, after what seemed interminable moments of thinking about the complicated question of kindness, I ventured an opinion.

"I think we both need kindness," I answered. I looked into her eyes and nodded to myself. "I think both of us probably need much more kindness in the worlds where we each live."

Joan leaned forward as a smile lit up her face. She swept back her long, almost reddish blonde hair.

"Cary said that you collected art. I'm still an art historian of sorts."

Whatever had made Joan pensive passed. I began telling her about my travels and where I'd been.

I told her about my journeys during the last seven years. I told her of years when I'd had no fixed address. I told her about the Himalayas, about the Balochistan desert and the transcontinental travelers who moved from India to Europe and who were lost to the indefinable expanse of Asia.

I told her about the Buddhist cave temples of western India that had been forgotten in the low jungles. I told Joan about the killing winds of the Karakoram passes beyond Chitral on the edges of Afghanistan that turned a man to ice where he stood. I told her about the Indian art I collected. I told her how a small group of us had begun collecting art and how we bought our art off the pavements of Bombay near the Chor Bazaar for the price of the scrap metal contained in a tenth-century statue.

I told her of my strange arrival in Cambridge. Of being taken in by Cary Welch and Robert Gardner.

For the first time, in the darkness, it was my turn to stare at her. I was haunted by Joan. She was the exact image of a woman born eight centuries before. She had the same long, stunning face; the same impossibly high forehead; the clear, direct eyes.

"You're staring," she said softly.

"I was thinking of something else. I'm sorry."

The evening came to an end.

The other guests left. Cary and Edith retreated upstairs.

At the front door, Joan spent another of those infinitely long moments staring at me. Then, without another word, she turned and left.

At the end of this strange and wonderful evening, I was totally shaken.

Not even a goodbye. I heard a car start in the driving snow, then it moved off down the street.

I didn't know if I'd ever see her again. Probably not. The whole evening had been a bungle. I felt empty.

Twenty minutes later, I left the house. In the cold, driving snow, I stood there outside on the street watching the snow clouds rip the moon into pieces in the winter sky. I felt like I was breaking.

I walked into the storm, and I didn't know why I'd told Joan the things that I'd told her. I felt cold tears on my cheeks that were freezing in the wind. I'd met too many people in my years of travels. I'd said too many goodbyes to friends I'd never seen again. I never expected to see Joan again.

Through the nighttime snowing streets of Cambridge, in the growing storm, I returned to Channing Street an hour later.

Everyone was asleep. I crossed into the darkened living room and stood there. In the shadows of the old house, I could almost feel the ghosts whispering, but it was only tree branches creaking in the storm. It was as if the whole dinner party had never happened.

At the rear of the house, in the kitchen, the telephone began to ring.

I moved through the house and found the receiver wedged between stacks of disordered cookbooks. I picked it up.

A voice said, "How about coffee tomorrow? I wanted to ask you.... Say, 5:00 p.m. in the foyer of the Carpenter Center?"

I didn't answer.

"Are you there?" Joan asked.

"Joan?"

"Is that alright? 5:00 p.m.?"

"I'd like that very much," I said slowly.

"See you then. Bye...."

The telephone disconnected.

I stood there in the half-light of the kitchen. I thought of a place that had vanished 800 years ago and the people who'd vanished with the centuries.

I thought of the *Lady and a Unicorn* tapestry in Paris.

Outside, the wind shuffled more silently between the trees as the storm began to die. I went to my room.

That night, I thought of the woman I'd just met. I thought of her otherworldly beauty from another time. I thought of her beauty that had vanished into the darkness of 300,000 nights.

I thought of something the Buddhists called *wa*. *Wa* is a Buddhist's spirit that never perishes.

"*Bon nuit,*" I said in the darkness.

***

Cambridge, March 1967

Six weeks later, I still lived at the Welch house.

On a separate track, Joan and I had become friends. We liked each other. Cary was right about East Coast ladies being shy creatures.

What seemed to have happened in our era was that women lost any trust they'd ever had in men. From my own point of view, after my experiences in San Francisco and the brief period of flower power, by 1967 it was an outright war to get any woman's trust when it entailed a relationship. I wondered in this new world of women's liberation, whether all women hadn't suddenly become shy creatures.

We went for trips to Nantucket or the Cape for the day. We went to war protests, to dance halls, and again and again to the Welches' basement to listen to Cary's huge record collection or hear his unbelievable Ph.D. seminars on art history. Joan lived on the top floor of 108 Marlborough Street, in a six-story townhouse. In the first weeks I'd known her, I'd never once been in her apartment.

When I'd been in India, I learned that if things are going to happen, in time they will happen.

I gave Joanie, as I now called her, one of my cameras. During the past few weeks, I had taught her the basics of photography.

There is no middle ground in photography. One either has talent, or one doesn't. Joanie had a great eye, and she was a superb photographer.

In the Carpenter Center darkrooms, I taught Joanie how to print photographs.

As we drove back and forth between Boston and Cambridge, we both noticed something odd was happening in Boston. It seemed that in their infinite and unyielding wisdom, the municipal fathers had enacted a plan to improve their city. This entailed tearing down much of the seventeenth-, eighteenth-, and nineteenth-century city of Boston. Presumably, this vandalism, which was costing billions of dollars, would bring the city to a point where it could share in the manifest superiority and glories of the twentieth century.

The more we looked, the more we wondered if there would be anything left of old Boston after progress had leveled it.
And so we both began taking photographs of "the redevelopment" of Boston.

The North End of the city, a quarter of a mile away from the Old North Church where Paul Revere had once signaled that the British were approaching, was the first victim of this cultural obliteration. Similarly, another quarter mile northward, a new six-lane highway was being clear-cut through historic Charlestown, where one of the first battles of the American Revolution had been fought on Bunker Hill.

In Charlestown, we were offered by its owner a Federal house from 1790 with all the interiors intact for $4,000. The next week, we went back to see the house again. The the impatient landowner had torn the house down to make it into a parking lot paid for with a federal subsidy.

**

A film I'd pitched on the Kotah Rajputs in Rajasthan seemed to be coming together. If it did, I'd shoot it the following year in India.

The John D. Rockefeller III Fund had agreed to look at a proposal to fund production. John Kenneth Galbraith, the former U.S. ambassador to India, had agreed to do the narration. It would take four or five months for the proposal to wend its way through the foundation's committees; however, I still was not much liked by the Indian government.

Hopefully, since I was now working with the most notorious, or the most famous, U.S. ambassador to India, Galbraith would put his Indian friends to work on my "government problem." One of Galbraith's best friends in India was Madame Pandit, the sister of former Prime Minister Jawaharlal Nehru. That gave me six months to work out my own problems with the Indian government.

I was now working at Harvard on a different schedule; I started at 1:00 p.m. and worked until 9:00 p.m. And, I must confess, I was falling in love with Joanie Mitchell.

By mid-March, Joanie was picking me up in Cambridge at 9:00 pm after my work. We would go to her apartment on Marlborough Street for dinner. After dinner, we would establish our emotional bonds more firmly. I had given up on returning to Harvard after dinner, then working on my films until 6:00 or 7:00 in the morning.

In April, for Easter, Joanie went to visit her mother's house in Bryn Mawr, Pennsylvania. She telephoned to tell me that her mother was alarmed and appalled by her exhausted, run-down, and wan physical condition.

Her doctor was called, and Joanie was told that she was suffering from nervous exhaustion.

***

It was May.

I finished the final cut of the Indian tribal film I had started so many years before, and I'd sent it off to the Indian consulate in New York. Former ambassador Galbraith agreed to send his compliments along to the Ministry of External Affairs in New Delhi, giving them notice of my film's completion and his interest in my well-being.

Joanie's schedules and my own didn't quite mesh.

I think I needed a rest from emotional bonding with Joanie.

I told myself that I had to go shoot some projects in Mexico. I told Joanie that I'd be gone for one month.

Joanie gave me one of her searing long looks. I had to back away from a long-term relationship. I needed to get out and onto the road again. Joanie was completely silent when I walked out the door of her apartment.

My month long absence from Boston, and from Joanie, proved to be a terrible mistake on my part.

In the last eight years of my life, I'd made too many farewells to people I'd never seen again.

I spent thirty days of my month long trip to Mexico regretting my decision. On the thirty-first day, I was back in Cambridge.

***

Boston, June, 1967

In Cambridge, I moved out of the Welch house on Channing Street. A mile away, I rented a room in an eighteenth-century house, and thanks to my minimalist lifestyle, all my possessions fit into three cardboard boxes.

In the room I'd rented, I wondered what to do about a difficult personal problem: Miss Joanie Mitchell.

I stared at the walls of my room for an hour. I wondered how I'd answer the "Did you have a nice trip?" question Joanie would ask.

I'd written her only a few postcards. I was devastatingly lonely without Joanie. I wondered if she'd ever talk to me again. In the end, I phoned her at the Peabody Museum.

I swallowed with difficulty. No answer. Joanie was out, or she didn't want to talk to me. A half hour later I phoned back and left a message. I'd be at her apartment at 6:30. "

***

In the late summer afternoon, I walked from the subway toward Joanie's apartment. I climbed the stairs to the top floor of 108 Marlborough Street. I knocked, and the apartment door opened.

In front of me was Joanie. She was immaculate. Gorgeous.

Looking at her, I decided I'd left too many pieces of myself in too many places around the world during the last nine years.

Joanie frowned. She stared at me with one of her forever looks.

I bent forward slowly and kissed her.

"I'm sorry. I had to go. I had to settle some things...with myself."

"Did you settle your things?"

I nodded, slowly.

She stood there. From behind her back, she produced one of my two postcards that I'd sent her. I looked down at it. There were tear stains on my card.

"I missed you. I missed you very much," she said. "I never thought you were going to come back."

I wrapped my arms around her. The only place I wanted to be was with Joanie and for a long time. I knew I'd traveled a very long way.

We had dinner in the apartment.

I went to the window an hour later and looked out.

The trees had leafed out for summer on Marlborough Street. Along the whole street was a long, long line of lovely bow-fronted five-story brick buildings, which stretched two blocks one way and seemingly to infinity down the left side of the street.

In the small kitchen, Joanie watched me warily as I stood there looking out the window. She brushed her long hair to the side. "Stay here with me, alright?" she asked.

"I have to tell you that I've moved out of the Welches'." I turned to face her. I stood there. I closed my eyes. Then I opened them. "I promise. I'm back."

***

For the next three months, Joanie and I lived together without a cross word between us.

I looked forward to each morning when the night ended, and then we could spend another new day together. That was all I wanted in my life.

Joanie seemed content.

The Rockefellers gave me a grant for the film project on Rajasthani Kotah painting in India.

The Indian government had agreed via Galbraith that I could pick up my visa in Rome. My film on Indian aboriginal people was removed from the Indian blacklist. My former art-collecting and film transgressions had apparently been forgiven. Although I wondered about picking up the visa in Rome, I had Galbraith on my side now, so why worry?

In August, after a walk at dusk around Fresh Pond, I asked Joanie if she'd like to go on a trip with me.

The wind blew her hair. She looked startled. "Where are we going?" she asked. "I hate the Cape or Nantucket in August."

"I think we should go to Iceland."

She looked baffled. "Iceland? Why do you want to go to Iceland?"

"That's the cheapest way to get to Europe. By Icelandic Airways," I explained. "We get to stop in Reykjavik for as long as we want. Then we'll go to Luxembourg, France, Austria, Italy, and Sicily…before India."

"Anywhere else?" she asked cautiously.

"Maybe we'll spend some of the winter in Pakistan and then go to India. No one goes to Pakistan, and it's a place you'll never see again like it is now. It's incredible."

Joanie wrapped a long strand of her hair around her index finger nervously. "Are you certain?" she asked. "You really want me to come with you?"

I ran my hand down the contours of her face. "I don't want to leave you. Ever. Never again."

Joanie put out her hand and rested it on my neck. "Thank you," she said softly. "I think I'd love to go traveling with you forever and ever. Then both of us can make pictures. We can travel in strange places. We can climb mountains together. I want to go all the places you've been and see them."

"We leave together." Joanie kissed me.

I'd been absolutely dreading this moment. What would I have done if she didn't want to come with me?

My world was suddenly perfect.

***

Joanie sublet her apartment.

I had a long talk with Robert Gardner. He was preoccupied with his own films. Things were not going well in West Africa for him. It seemed that for the large Smithsonian–Harvard project he was working on, he couldn't find any nomads to film. His African project was on hold.

The only cloud on the horizon, and my last problem, was Joanie's mother. She was a traditional sort of East Coast–establishment lady. As Joanie recounted her conversation with her mother, she roared with laughter. "Are you ready for this, you sinful man?" she asked.

"First, my mother's reaction to our planned travels as an unmarried couple was alarm. Then she said, and these are her exact words, 'Checking into hotels, which you might propose to stay in, my dear, let me tell you will be put under lock and key'."

"She then said that in every hotel, in every country that we travel to, we'll be arrested because of our unmarried condition."

Joanie paused and smiled, even maliciously. "I was told that in India, they are particularly strict. Unmarried couples attempting to stay in a hotel are regularly carted off by the police. Rules are rules. Until very recently, you know, India was part of the British Empire."

I'd never met Joanie's mother. It was something to look forward to.

***

CHAPTER FOUR

Bombay, April 1968

Filmmaking. The final journey into darkness.

My promised Indian visa had not appeared in Rome, nor in Karachi or Lahore. At the end of half a year of waiting for this visa, Joanie and I took a Middle East Airlines flight from Karachi to Bombay. Two hours after we landed at Santa Cruz Airport in Bombay, we were both placed under supervisory arrest by the Indian Criminal Investigation Department, or CID.

Upon conclusion of the lengthy negotiations concerning our freedom, at the end of our fourth week under house arrest, Professor Galbraith worked his magic. We were both released from the constraints of surveillance in the seedy Rex Hotel in Colaba.

I received a telegram from Galbraith at the American Express Company. The message went: *"You didn't tell me how much the CID absolutely and totally disliked you. Naughty lad. I had to go all the way to Nehru's sister to get you off the hook, boyo. Best regards, Ken"*

A day later, at the same letter drop, another message awaited me.

It was an unexpected communication from Addis Ababa with an Ethiopian stamp on it. I stared at the sender's name.

I suddenly remembered a sort of half-invitation extended the year before.

This letter contained an invitation from Robert Gardner to film in East Africa and take part in an expedition to Ethiopia.

I must confess, I'd never thought much about Ethiopia until that moment. It wasn't a country I'd ever considered traveling to. I had only the vaguest idea of who lived in Ethiopia, besides the fact that they were a strange subset of very early Christians.

A sort of dance list was enclosed with the invitation, which included the making of both films and photographs of Ethiopian tribal groups. These groups had never been filmed or documented before. I wondered if Gardner had yet substantiated that these groups existed?

I showed the letter to Joanie. To ponder this invitation, we retired to Colaba to our favorite Parsi restaurant, Leopold's, on the Colaba Causeway.

"What do you think this is about?" Joanie asked.

"I don't know," I answered slowly.

After we'd ordered our afternoon tea, I tried to work out what had happened to Robert.

"I think Robert's expedition to West Africa was abandoned, and this is after he's worked on and off for two years trying to find African nomads to film. I suppose Stuart Cody, the Carpenter Center sound technician that Robert was supposed to bring with him from Cambridge, has fled Ethiopia, leaving Robert in the ditch."

Joanie knew Robert's reputation. She said, "If you need credit and validation, don't hang out with Robert. You might expire from holding your breath."

Joanie had worked at the Peabody Museum for four years. In academia, reputations simmer to a boil. Joanie explained that Robert had the reputation of a prickly, intrusive taskmaster who never thanked anyone for anything they might have done for him. He sounded like every other filmmaker I knew.

"What do you want to do?" Joanie asked slowly.

"I think that no one I know or have ever heard of has done any photography in Ethiopia. Most of it is impossible to get into. Do you want to go to Ethiopia?"

Joanie fell silent and didn't answer.

"I'll have to record his sound. We can take our own photographs that will be ours, since we'll have to pay our own way to Ethiopia. I don't think Robert said anything about our tickets." I thought about this, "I don't honestly think that either of us will ever again get an invitation to go to Ethiopia, but the rest of this expedition should be a free ride, courtesy of the Smithsonian Institution and Harvard."

Joanie unfortunately knew Robert better than I did. She'd grown up with Bostonians. Her mother was from Boston, and I remembered that she'd once said her grandmother had been in Robert's mother's wedding.

"And of course," Joanie said, "He'll ride us around Ethiopia and show us a good time?"

I laughed. Joanie had come a very long way from Boston. Before I met Joanie, she'd never been beyond Europe. Nothing had prepared her for India. Nothing had prepared her for being under house arrest in the brothel that was the Rex Hotel in Colaba. She was fascinated, appalled, and intrigued by India.

Joanie was very tough. Very determined. Very sharp. She was exceptionally talented as a photographer.

"We'll go," she answered.

I thought about a journey to Africa after India.

Joanie thought about what she'd just agreed to. "It should be riveting, being in a place so few people have gone. Even with

R.G.G." The initials referred to Robert Grosvenor Gardner. Robert was related to the people who had started the telephone company.

By telegram, we both committed to join the first-ever Harvard–Smithsonian film-and-photography expedition to Ethiopia.

What we volunteered for was pledging our warm bodies and too many weeks and months of work in the bush. Little did we know, but we'd just signed up for startling travels to places we might never return from.

***

Cambridge and New York, November 1968 to 1973

After Ethiopia. we returned to Harvard and to Boston. For five years, Joanie had lived on Boston's Marlborough Street in an area of great prosperity. We moved to the slums of Somerville, which offered a four-bedroom hundred-year-old apartment for $75 a month.

In our new apartment building on July 20, 1969, as the first man walked on the moon, on the floor below us an off-duty policeman pulled his service revolver and shot at his wife, who was running out the door.

Joanie went back to work at the Peabody; I went back to work at the Carpenter Center at Harvard.

I had an exhibition of my Indian photographs taken between 1959 and 1968, at the Williams College Museum of Art. When my films *The Changing Rains* and *Manufacturing the Future: California,* were finished, I left Harvard, and Joanie and I went to New York to make feature films.

***

Joanie and I were married in September of 1970 in Bryn Mawr, at Joanie's mother's house in her garden. Our honeymoon consisted of going to a Chinese restaurant on 95th Street and Broadway in New York. After our travels in 1968, Joanie told her mother that we'd survived a year of foreign travel without once being arrested or evicted for illicit cohabitation.

In New York, during 1971, I started my first feature film. In America, the feature-film world was divided between Hollywood and New York. Filmmaking in Hollywood entailed huge crews sometimes with hundreds of people engaged in a "shoot."

In New York, filmmakers used small crews of only five to ten people. In Hollywood, it usually took multiple hours to set up a shot. In New York, by contrast, a certain style of gritty filmmaking had emerged. You usually set up a shot with lightweight equipment in ten to fifteen minutes.

In interviewing my final selections for the star of my feature film, I came down to two actors. One was named Sylvester Stallone, the other, Tony Page.

Page's acting credentials, given the era, were impeccable. He'd done eight years in prison for attempted murder, drug dealing, and white slavery. Given the genre of my proposed movie, he seemed to be completely irresistible. My film entailed the murder of an Italian policeman by a local mafioso. The plot then revolved around a revenge killing of the mafioso by the policeman's son. In my film, Tony Page played the murderous policeman intent on vendetta. After living through a few years of Afghan vendettas that spanned whole generations, I saw my film as a similar sort of Italian family story.

My production partner and producer was an extraordinary man named Louis Pastore. Pastore had grown up in the Bronx, inside the milieu we were describing in our film. He had lately worked for the management-consulting firm Booz Allen, where he'd organized the ZIP code program for the U.S. Postal Service. After successfully putting five digits on every envelope, letter, and package mailed in America for the next half century, Pastore had been assigned to reorganize both Paramount Pictures and Columbia Pictures.

In a lateral career move, after reorganizing both companies, Pastore left the most famous management-consulting firm in America to become my movie producer.

Amazingly, we finished our film. Considering the milieu of independent, non-studio-affiliated feature films made in New

York, this was a feat akin to climbing Mount Everest without clothing or crampons.

Our film was released under the title *Family Honor,*and distributed by Cinerama–ABC Films in America.

***

During the early 1970s, opportunities for doing New York independent feature films seemed to evaporate in front of me.

Stallone had deserted New York and gone to live in a garage apartment in the Hollywood Hills to write spec scripts. My lead actor, Tony Page, had devoted himself in New York to a massive growing dope habit, fueled by industrial quantities of alkaloids. My partner, the ever brilliant Louis Pastore, also deserted New York for Hollywood. In late 1973, after three years of trying to get feature films funded I realized that I had to invent another life for myself if I wanted to stay in New York.

I began to examine the photography world more closely. I remembered my conversations with Cary Welch in the mid-1960s. I wondered if *now* wasn't the perfect moment to start collecting photography. The idea was almost outlandish.

Who collected photography in 1973? Very few people.

I turned my mind back to art collecting. It seemed to me that for photography, something altogether remarkable might soon be happening.

By 1973, I'd been taking photographs for fourteen years. I was in danger of repeating myself. It was time for me to turn toward new things.

In that year, photography didn't register as anything in the art world.

In New York, there were hints that this might change. In 1969, Lee Witkin opened a photography gallery in New York. across the street from Bloomingdale's, and it had slowly gained a following.

As I thought about the idea of collecting photographs, I realized the only parallel I could think of to reference was the classical Indian art world of 1959.

Unfortunately, I'd sold my Indian art a year or two before the prices for it had begun to rise astronomically. If I ever found another art of emergent curatorial interest, I could form a second collecting career.I thought back to what you could buy during 1959 in the thieves' market of Bombay.

What I'd learned from art collecting in India was that you did your own research. You put your bets down on what you bought, and you forged your own path in forming your collection. Finally, you held on to that collection for decades if that's what it took to get your art recognized.

As 1974 came around, I felt I needed something large in my life to replace what I'd personally lost in my first collection of Indian classical art.

I came to the conclusion that by collecting photography, I would reinvent myself in a new persona. It would be an opportunity few collectors ever got. I had the feeling that somehow, out there in the world, there were seismic shifts looming in the photography world, and these would be changes one could hardly think of—or believe.

In New York, I began to buy extraordinary nineteenth-century photographs of Asia, the Middle East, and India for a dollar apiece. I found these pictures in the used-book shops just north of Astor Place.

At the same time, I set out to visit both universities and libraries in an attempt to find who had major holdings of photography. Most important was determining what was rare in this new collectors' field. It seemed to me, as I did my rounds, that most rare in existing collections were the pictures I was already collecting of the non-Western world.

The other glaring omission, besides collections devoted to a single country, were collections of photography as art. In the early 1930s, the Metropolitan Museum of Art had been offered Alfred Stieglitz's personal collection of art photographs from the Photo-Secession period, formed at the turn of the twentieth century. Stieglitz had become so alienated from the art establishment, he'd threatened to throw out his collection. At the last moment, sponsors found a way for the Met to acquire the collection, not as art itself, but as a research adjunct to its print collection. Forty years later, at the beginning of the 1970s, the collection was still hidden away in the print department of the museum and remained almost invisible.

The discovery of this sort of neglect evolved over months of visits and thinking about photography as a collectible art. Libraries and universities had diverse, uncataloged collections of photographs filed under subject headings like architecture, geology, the Middle East, or China. *National Geographic* had recently culled its collections and thrown out most of its century-old archive of historical photographs, accrued since the first days of the magazine.

Similarly, Harvard had disposed of its social ethics collections, which included the earliest views of the Himalayas, and thousands, or tens of thousands of photographs of immigrant groups and social conditions.

Who would know what they threw out? No one would ever see these pictures again.

As I visited museums up and down the east coast, I had a growing feeling that I was the sole occupant of a marvelous desert island, even though I was living in the middle of New York City.

***

London and New York, 1974–1976

The mid-1970s was a very bizarre time in the art world.

The financial world seemed to be trembling. A sudden rise in oil prices had completely gutted the stock market.

In the art world, Modernism needed a rest. We seemed to be between things.

I realized that this interval in the Western art markets was a time that appeared perhaps once a century, when a collector could buy particular types of art and absolutely no one else wanted it. It was like buying thirteenth-century Gothic sculptures in the middle of the French Revolution, when the cathedral of Notre Dame had been turned into a stable, when the churches of France were looted, and when those incredible Gothic sculptures were burned for firewood.

My thoughts turned again and again to photography.

In the mid-1970s, people seemed to be waiting for something new in the art world.

Photography had existed since 1839, when Frenchman Louis Daguerre commercialized the first photographic process. In the intervening 135 years, there had to have been extraordinary pictures created. But where were those pictures today?

I remembered Cary Welch's faded albums of nineteenth-century Indian photography in Cambridge. Once upon a time, those albums had held wonderful photographs, but now they were mostly faded wrecks. What had happened to cause this destruction and neglect?

I asked myself other questions: What photographs survived from nineteenth-century America and Europe? Did any photographs in good condition survive from the worlds beyond Europe and America? In the non-Western world, one could almost pinpoint the moment millennial cultures ceased to exist with the advent of the Industrial Revolution. It was also when the medium of photography documented the last moments of worldwide traditional cultures.

Considering my own experience in the nascent world of photography collecting, I knew about the history of photography when few people in the world knew that photography *had* a history.

In considering photography as an art, I was certain that an entire submerged archipelago of unseen extraordinary pictures existed that were masterpieces of the genre.

It seemed to me that the ultimate achievement of photography was both exactitude and precision never equaled by any other art.

I also felt that photography possessed a sublime artistic presence as an art-document in the last moments before a worldwide consumer society began to emerge in the 1970s. This was a time when much of the world was being homogenized in mankind's cities, and even the landscape itself changed with the necessities of our growing billions.

I asked myself as a photographer and a documentarian, "Why don't people collect photographs of a world that has become irretrievably lost?"

And so I did what collectors do: collect.

I'd missed collecting. I missed the chase. I'd finally come around to the idea that collectors are probably not ordinarily sane people. I missed the ecstasy of finding a grand object.

I started out trying to discover important photographs, using the single criterion I'd used for collecting paintings of India in 1959, fifteen years before. I looked for great photographs.

Once, I had asked Henri Cartier-Bresson what his photographs were about. He answered, "I collect time."

So this is what I started to collect. I began to gather great photographs of all sorts of subjects that were art-documents of vanished time.

***

In the summer of 1959, inside a tiny, dark photography shop called Johnston and Hoffmann in Calcutta, off Chowringhee Road, I'd seen my first nineteenth-century photographs of India.

By the late 1950s, the firm of Johnston and Hoffmann, founded in 1888, was still in operation. I bought my 35mm film there. I had my negatives developed by the firm. A wasting, thin Bengali clerk of indeterminate age sold me a few of their remaining nineteenth-century prints in stock. For the next three decades, I tried to buy more nineteenth-century pictures made by the firm, but such was their extreme rarity that more were unavailable.

From time to time, I wondered where similar photographs of India, China, Burma, the Middle East, and Southeast Asia were, and what were the names of the firms that made them.

In 1975 in New York, on East 64th Street just off Park Avenue, I met a man who helped me answer these questions.

My introduction had been arranged by the president of one of the Rockefeller foundations. At that time, the core group of Asian and Western Asian academics and their collaterals, who controlled cultural access to Asia, was not more than ten people in America. The man I was introduced to, Allen Wardwell, had just become director of the Asia Society Gallery. He was part of this small handful of people in America interested in Asia.

The director's office was on the fourth floor, in a building built by the Rockefellers and donated to the Asia Society. This was where I first met the complicated, shy, and very brave Wardwell.

Wardwell was looking for an exhibition similar to one mounted a decade before, which was the first full-scale exhibition of imperial Indian Mogul art in America. The exhibition was extraordinary, and it broke new ground and created a great stir in the New York art world. In many ways, it put the Asia Society on the cultural map. Titled "The Art of Mughal India," it exhibited mostly unknown sixteenth- through eighteenth-century Indian paintings and objects from the Mogul imperial ateliers and was curated by the then-unknown Cary Welch.

I explained to Wardwell that it was my hope that the Asia Society might sponsor an exhibition I had and that the first book on nineteenth-century Indian photography might possibly emerge from this work.

Previously, in 1965, I'd had an exhibition of my Indian photographs at the Santa Barbara Museum of Art, in California, and the Smithsonian had recently circulated my exhibition of photographs of Ethiopian rock-cut churches to twenty American museums.

Wardwell knew I had extensive connections to India through our mutual Rockefeller Foundation friend. In 1966, I'd pitched a similar exhibition on Indian photography to Gordon Washburn, then head of the Asia Society Gallery, who had no interest.

I showed Wardwell some examples of nineteenth-century Indian photography I'd collected. I told him that British museums and libraries possessed these types of photographs in remarkable quantities. I liked to think the idea wasn't exactly a lie; it was more an informed hope. Although I had visited a dozen or so American universities and libraries, they were devoid of nineteenth-century Indian photographs. Yet these pictures had to be somewhere. Why not England?

I told Wardwell I had to get funds to go to England in order to firm up loan requests for Indian photographs held in the British Museum and other institutional collections. I had to make requests of British collections which formed the last visible remnants of the imperial British Raj. I knew that no one had yet made an exhibition on the British Raj in India, and it could prove very important for the Asia Society.

"Do you know someone named Cary Welch at Harvard?" Wardwell asked.

I said I did.

Wardwell was much taken with the pictures I showed him. Moreover, he agreed hesitantly that this might be an interesting idea for an exhibition. He said he would be in touch.

It was a most curious meeting. Wardwell was a buttoned-up man of the East Coast establishment. As I walked down Park Avenue, my feeling about this meeting was that Wardwell was reserved almost to the point of invisibility. He had not given me any idea what he thought.

As I walked across Central Park, I wondered if my meeting had occurred or if I'd imagined it.

Two weeks later, I received an unexpected phone call from Wardwell. He said in his hesitant way that he was greatly taken by the pictures I'd shown him, and he couldn't get them out of his mind. He suggested that if an exhibition was done at the Asia Society, could I possibly consider doing a book of this work for them? At that point, I'd approached at least twenty publishers with the idea of a book. Each of them had turned the project down.

I said that doing a book of the exhibition might be an interesting idea.

The result of this conversation was that Wardwell proposed to sponsor both a book and a monthlong research trip to London in order to generate loan requests from British collections.

After I hung up, I took a deep breath. I was absolutely flattened by this phone call. My next call was to Cary Welch.

Everything in England hinged upon an introduction. Without a good introduction, you couldn't even buy a hat in London to get into Lock & Co. on St. James's Street.

On the telephone Cary said he'd give me an introduction to Maggs Bros. booksellers on Berkeley Square in Mayfair, and then to one of his best friends in England, Robert Skelton. A keeper at the Victoria and Albert Museum in South Kensington Skelton was then an emerging doyen of British-Indian art studies. From those two introductions, Cary said I could unlock anyone in the British museum establishment.

In the kitchen of our small apartment on West End Avenue in Manhattan, I put down the telephone. I explained to Joanie what had transpired with the Asia Society.

I then told her that I didn't know if collections of nineteenth-century Indian photographs even existed in any British museums, let alone whether they existed in quantities that warranted an exhibition.

After I told her this small problem regarding my proposed exhibition, Joanie voiced her confidence by covering her face with her hands and shaking her head. Suddenly, I was having a wonderful time!

"My God," she whispered.

For myself, I was just then thinking I'd start with the Victoria and Albert Museum, then I'd go to the Queen's Collection in the Round Tower at Windsor Castle. From there, I'd start on the large society collections, like those held by the Royal Geographical Society and the Royal Asiatic Society.

***

London, 1975

London was incredibly dreary; the whole place reeked of poverty and neglect.

Garbage bags were piled everywhere on every street corner. The streetlights went on at 4:00 p.m. to try and cope with the gloom that had subsumed an entire country. I checked into the Gresham Hotel, a few blocks from the British Museum. A week's lodging was forty pounds.

Before I went to see Robert Skelton, I visited the British Museum. Their Indianist, Douglas Barrett, answered my query by telling me that nineteenth-century Indian photographs were "not art". Personally, he loved Indian photography, and he himself collected nineteenth-century Indian photography. He said he was a bit "handy." This I supposed meant that he made things in his basement for "home use." In fact, Barrett claimed to have made a lovely decorative fire screen interleaved with marvelous nineteenth-century Indian photographs for his fireplace.

This was promising. The leading Indianist in England had developed a program to incinerate his own Indian photography collection. I fled the British Museum.

In our next telephone conversation, I dreaded telling Joanie how, exactly, I'd describe my first research in London.

Before I met Robert Skelton at the Victoria and Albert Museum, I visited the museum's library to look at its nineteenth-century Indian photograph catalog entries. In the 1800s, the Victoria and Albert had been the main venue for the cultural and artistic exchanges between the British and their Indian empire. During the nineteenth century, the empire included Burma, Ceylon, and India, with an additional 560 Indian princely states. Half of the

Persian Gulf, now known as the Emirates, was also until very recently part of the British Indian Empire.

Curiously, the extensive museum catalogs of the Victoria and Albert didn't appear to have a single Indian photograph from the nineteenth century, apart from a set of 470 small copies of photographs. These were brought out in eight volumes and published between 1868 and 1875 under the title *The People of India*.

If there was a single museum in Britain that should have possessed truly vast quantities of Indian pictures, it was the V&A. Apparently, photographs of British India during the nineteenth century had been lost or discarded after World War II. Or perhaps, according to the Victoria and Albert librarian, somehow they'd been inadvertently miscataloged or perhaps sold off as scrap paper.

This was a terrible moment.

***

The day after my disastrous V&A library visit, I called on Robert Skelton.

Skelton was a legend in British Indian studies. He'd literally climbed his way through layers of the caste-bound British museum establishment with the determination of a man climbing the deadly and dangerous frozen seracs of the Himalayas.

As a 16-year-old, Skelton had first worked at Sotheby's as a teaboy, then at the V&A as a carrier. His new job was moving objects from one place to another place in the museum.

At night, he began to study Indian art. Then he managed the nearly impossible task of teaching himself Brahmi, the oldest written script used on the Indian subcontinent. After Skelton's self-directed studies of Indian art, no one came near him in erudition, even at Oxford or Cambridge.

On the top floor of the museum, Skelton welcomed me into his modest office, which was a ten-foot-by-ten-foot space wedged into a freezing corridor.

I couldn't believe this was the office of one of the greatest experts of the British-museum and English-intellectual establishments. I also wondered what this dismal office was like in the freezing depths of an endless, rainy British winter?

We had 10:00 a.m. tea. I gave him my introduction chit from Cary Welch, which he read and then folded carefully.

Through Indian friends, I knew Skelton had been a good friend of David McCutcheon, my tutor at Santiniketan University in Upper Bengal. Cary's introduction, and our friendship, was not nearly as important to Skelton as my relationship with McCutcheon. It cut through Skelton's measured, distant reserve.

In 1973, McCutcheon had received the most senior appointment in Indian studies at Oxford. It was the crowning achievement of twenty years spent at the center of the Bengali intellectual establishment, which equaled Skelton's unbelievable career at the V&A. McCutcheon was fluent in Bengali, as compared to Skelton's mastery of Indian art, and perhaps the most brilliant mind in Indian cultural studies. McCutcheon was also the teacher of a generation of Bengali writers, and for decades he'd composed English subtitles for the films of the great Bengali filmmaker, Satyajit Ray.

When McCutcheon died of polio in India a week before he was supposed to leave for Oxford, it was a tragedy for Indian studies. He was irreplaceable the field was then so small, the loss of this single scholar would require a generation or more to overcome.

I told Skelton that in my last letter, ten days before he died, McCutcheon had told me he'd taken delivery of the only Calcutta-made Western-style suit he'd ever owned in his two decades in India. He never got to wear that suit.

Across his desk, Skelton seemed lost in thought about the subjects of this very strange meeting. Then I explained my project to Skelton. I told him of my problem of finding Indian photographs .

Wordlessly, Skelton rose from behind his desk. He beckoned me into the hallway and pointed down the corridor in front of him.

Quite mystified, I followed him through the frigid top-floor corridors of the museum.

After many twists and turns, Skelton arrived at a locked door. We stood in front of the door, and then with a key, Skelton opened the room.

Deliberately, he stepped inside and switched on a light. Skelton then turned, smiling broadly. He still hadn't said a word.

I stepped into the room.   It was literally stuffed to the roof with pictures of nineteenth-century India. Floor to ceiling were rows after rows, then more rows, of Indian photographs.

Skelton explained about the contents of this room and how they got here. From 1955 to 1975, while the museum universe regarded photography as an unwanted nineteenth-century curio, Skelton had pursued his own guerrilla campaign of useful work inside the corridors and basements of the V&A. In a period when most museums culled their collections of photographs and then threw them out, at the V&A, Skelton rescued an entire corpus of nineteenth-century Indian photography from the loading-dock trash bins.

His thought had been that someday, at some time, someone beside himself would recognize the worth of these pictures.

During two decades, he'd filled this room with the work of some of the greatest British photographic artists working during the 1800s. Contrary to every academic and museum curator in the world, he'd installed in his solitary rooftop kingdom the century-long photographic gatherings of one of the world's greatest museums.

"I almost died getting all these pictures up here," Skelton said. These are my little artistic orphans."

***

For a week, I returned again and again to the V&A.

In the awful Gresham Hotel I'd lie awake at night thinking about Skelton's pictures, which swam through my mind. Skelton's eye was as good in Indian painting as it was in photography. Both Skelton and Cary had the eye. Instinctively, they knew what was transcendent in an art object.

What photography had been able to document on the Indian subcontinent in the nineteenth century was extraordinary. What was more amazing, perhaps, was that not only had these pictures been forgotten, but so, too, had the names of the artists responsible for this gigantic undertaking.

Quite separate from British-made Indian photography was the work of Indian photographers who had documented the courts and state activities of the 560-odd princely states of India. The footnote of this astonishing work was that the dominions of the maharajas and princes of India comprised 40 percent of the land area of the British Indian empire.

Skelton's archive was unimaginable in its scope.

In the V&A collection, there were pictures of the great Hindu religious *melas,* or religious festivals, and invariably the pilgrimage sites of India. In group photographs, which verged on the unbelievable, there were sometimes, literally, half a million people.

There were photographs of famines and wars now barely remembered. The subjects covered by the nineteenth-century photographers of the Indian empire were encyclopedic. Other photographers had documented the scenery of the Himalayas during grueling journeys that must have taken place over decades in some of the most remote regions on Earth.

There were also photographs of Indian architectural masterpieces created by the Hindus, the Buddhists, and the Muslims, as well as photographs of century-in-the-making cave temples and entire ruined cities overgrown by jungle.

In all of these discoveries, my feelings never wavered about Skelton. If there was ever a great hero immured inside the museum scene of Europe, it was him. He had undertaken a self-taught career, and then a lifetime of work, against the grain of an entire nation's museum establishment. For this work, he was later given a well-deserved OBE (the Order of the British Empire. by the Queen,

To this day, even decades later, I'm not sure that anyone realizes what Skelton salvaged.

He was, and will always be, my hero.

***

In the weeks that followed in London, I began to discover incredible pictures.

The collections in England were operatic in their breadth. It was dizzying. No one had seen these pictures for a century or more. Inside the backs of closets and locked room, in a score of museums and societies, I discovered singular collections of nineteenth-century Indian photographic work.

The locus of these pictures went on and on: they were in the V&A, the Museum of Mankind (part of the British Museum), the India Office Library and Records Office (now part of the British Museum Library), the National Army Museum, the Royal Asiatic Society, and finally the Royal Commonwealth Society, now housed at the Cambridge University Library.

The scope of these collections spanned the non-European world. In addition to pictures of the nineteenth-century British Indian empire, I found wonderful, staggering images of Southeast Asia, China, Japan, and the Middle East.

In time, I came to believe that on the basis of this single visit to Britain, I could do similar exhibitions of nineteenth-century work that would make new benchmarks in the history of photography. More importantly, the artists who created these pictures would challenge the history of photography.

In London, I was seized by a kind of photographic mania.

I'd taken a gigantic chance in promoting my idea to the Asia Society of the worth of unidentified and unknown nineteenth-century photography. I'd used up every ounce of credibility I had in the small world of Asian studies and shoved it into one last bet. But now this wasn't just my bet, it was also the bet of an entire lost archive of forgotten pictures and a gallery of incredible artists. Above all, I'd discovered that, despite its difficulties in creation, photography of the non-western world was one of the greatest miracles of the nineteenth century. Consider the making of a single photograph during the 1860's in the distant reaches of the non-western world, thousands of miles away from Europe or America and sources of glass, chemicals, and camera supplies.

This miracle entailed coating a clean glass plate with a light-sensitive collodion mixture. In intervals from minutes to hours, the photographer had to then expose his negative before he took it to a nearby dark tent to develop it. Obtaining fresh water was perhaps the greatest difficulty of a photographer's operation. If he was exceedingly lucky, a photographer in the field could perhaps expose two plates in a complex morning's work.

The preferred printing process used by photographers from 1860 to 1895 was the gold-toned albumen print. In this printing process, the photograph was chemically cauterized permanently from the elements with a gossamer coating of gold.

In London, it was bitterly cold. I fled down rain-spattered streets for a week and then a second week of searing winds. Each day, I returned to different museums and looked at pictures for eight hours. Many of the collections began in the early 1850s, when photography was only in its second decade.

I kept phoning Joanie in New York. I kept telling her I'd be delayed in coming home.

I had the growing feeling, as I looked at photography as a collector and not a curator, that not only would photography become *the* art to collect, but this was also possibly the last opportunity to buy a large quantity of art of any major importance.

***

New York, 1976

On East 64th Street, my brave but inhibited friend Allen Wardwell included my exhibition, *The Last Empire: Photography in British India, 1855–1911*, in the summer program of the Asia Society Gallery. Curiously, no one I'd spoken to was aware of any summer exhibition program there. Their members generally left the city during the summer.

In terms of the notice my exhibition would receive, then, I thought it would likely disappear the moment it opened, with the pictures swiftly returned and buried for another century in their respective museums.

The exhibition opened. It continued on for a few days with only scant people appearing in the galleries. The summer exhibition program was proving to be worse than anyone had thought, with a year of my life wasted on people who were instead sunning themselves on the beach in East Hampton.

Then, quite unexpectedly, the writer Paul Theroux took up my book and the Asia Society exhibition in an extraordinary review on the cover page of *The New York Times Review of Books*.

The day after Theroux's review appeared, there were 104 people in the previously deserted summertime society galleries. The next day, there were 275 people. By the end of the week, there were hundreds of people visiting the Asia Society each day.

The last British Viceroy of India, Lord Mountbatten, had written a brief text for the exhibition's catalog. His second cousin, the Queen of England, attended the exhibition without any publicity during a brief New York visit. Word of this got out. After a few weeks, thousands of people were now passing through the galleries daily. Today, thirty-nine years later, the *Last Empire* exhibition is the best-attended exhibition ever staged at the Asia Society.

Nineteenth-century Indian photography had been abruptly hurled into the art-world firmament. The exhibition's catalog became one of the best-selling photography books of the past two decades and is still in print. It generated a reappraisal of the period and, when coupled with Paul Scott's titanic four-volume cycle of *Raj Quartet* books, which take place in the last decades of the British in India, suddenly the Raj became in vogue in the literary world.

For me, there was one lasting effect: scores of collectors of nineteenth-century Indian photography have told me that they took up collecting thanks to this single exhibition.

After *The Last Empire* closed, I wondered if it might be possible to do similar first-time work on China, with a nineteenth-century photography exhibition and accompanying book. Alternatively, it might be possible to focus on photographic work done in Japan in the late 1850s, the approximate time the country opened to the West.

In the four small and modest Asia Society galleries, I began the first steps of having the work of nineteenth-century Orientalist and Asian photographers recognized. During the next decades, I would build my own collections, featuring a constellation of artist-photographers. These included W.W. Hooper, Colin Murray, Samuel Bourne, Raja Deen Dayal, Charles Scowen, Felice Beato, Kusakabe Kimbei, Suzuki Shin'ichi, Lai Afong, and scores of other photographers.

***

Millbrook, New York, 1975.

In the mid-1970s, both the British writer Bruce Chatwin and I owed a huge and probably unpayable debt to Paul Theroux, who was the first person to acknowledge our work. For me this allowed my family's escape from the endless, grinding maze of trying to live and work in Manhattan.

The first morning I woke up in the village of Millbrook, New York, I was amazed by the silence.

There were no sirens and no garbage trucks loading their wares at 2:00 a.m. There were no sounds of bullets being fired on neighboring streets. A block away from our apartment in the city, two policemen had been killed by a machine gun. I had the feeling New York was about to burn.

For four years, Joanie and I lived in a two-bedroom apartment. We then moved to Millbrook, into a modern house built on ten acres and designed by a Yale architect. Minutes after sunrise each day, the birds began to sing. How could anyone not like this, I asked myself on my first morning. All this pastoral quiet and near silence seemed unnatural, unnerving, and very strange.

Twelve generations of my family were buried ten miles away. After migrating down Connecticut during the seventeenth century, they'd settled in Dutchess County, New York, in the 1760s. I told my mother when I moved to Millbrook to tell her many relatives who lived in the area I was extremely unsociable. Perhaps she could say I had a wasting disease, and I needed complete rest.

We planted a garden. First, the deer ate the tomatoes; then, leaf blight killed the rest of our vegetable crop. I was glad I hadn't moved to the country because I wanted to become a farmer. Next, a huge tree fell across our driveway. I decided I had to buy a chainsaw to cut myself out of my driveway.

The decade suddenly became very tough. During the mid-1970s, in both Europe and America, severe economic shocks shook the world causing near financial collapse. What one did in order to survive from 1973 to 1979 was to live more simply. We hunkered down in the country. We waited for things to get better.

My own world became exceedingly difficult. It was almost impossible to make movies or find work on museum or book projects.

The year 1971 America abandoned the gold standard, while in Europe there occurred the near financial dismemberment of Western society during decade of the 1970's.

1973 marked a world oil crisis when the price of oil quadrupled.

From 1973 to 1974 was a stock-market "break" and a severe market collapse, with one of the worst market downturns in modern history. There were gas lines and long lines in supermarkets. In America, there was gas rationing for a brief period; for a longer time, there were wage and price controls on every consumer staple.

On January 1, 1974, e British Prime Minister Edward Heath declared a three-day workweek to ration electricity usage, and commercial users of electricity in the United Kingdom were limited to three specific consecutive days of consumption.

In the U.K., coal miners went on strike. Then the garbagemen and transportation workers voted to strike.

During the winter of 1974, England stayed at home. Piles of rotting garbage filled the cities. Union actions caused multiple catastrophes.

Across the U.K., it became difficult to hold on to family property and collections gathered over the centuries.

Increasingly, the wealthy and solvent were targeted by the new Labour government, which held the government by a majority of three seats. Draconian new inheritance laws effectively confiscated inherited property in the United Kingdom.

In a series of spectacular house sales, everything went to auction. This included old master paintings, Chinese antiquities, ceramics, rugs, furniture, family portraits, and, barely noticed, century-old collections of photography.

In the frigid darkness of the auction rooms, photographs that hadn't been seen in a century or more were laid out on long, badly scared trestle tables. In London, at Christie's auction house in South Kensington and at Sotheby's in Belgravia, buried among the country-house accumulations, were masterpieces made by photographers of huge technical virtuosity and talent. These were pictures heaved in disheveled bundles into the maw of the auctions.

In the great United Kingdom house sales of the 1970s was revealed a new vision of the medium of photography during the nineteenth century. As a collector, you had to be there for the whole course of the 1975 through 1977 London auction seasons. It was a brief, once-in-a-century moment to collect.

There were nineteenth-century photographs from Europe, America, and South America. But more interesting to me were the photographs that turned up from India, the Middle East, Southeast Asia, Japan, and China.

These were pictures that had been absolutely forgotten. Particularly striking was work by extraordinarily accomplished artist-photographers, most of whom were unknown and unpublished.

The range of photographic masterpieces from worlds beyond Europe and America seemed unending. These pictures had been quietly accumulated by discerning travelers during the 19th century, who had apparently gone everywhere in the world.

I could not believe then, and I still can't today, what I found in those auction viewings. It was as if I'd stumbled into the world's greatest treasure hunt.

I began writing four different books on the history of photography in the non-European world of the nineteenth century. These were books on India, China, Japan, and the Middle East. I felt like a character marooned in a W. Somerset Maugham short story, traveling to places in far Asia a century after these pictures had first been made. In these auction sales, I traveled through these pictures from Yokohama to Bombay, to Hong Kong via Saigon and Singapore, and to Colombo and Cairo. In my hands, I held images made by light that had disappeared a century before.

Foolishly, I'd given up and dispersed my collections of Indian classical art. But now those collections were simply a warm-up for a much larger collection I began buying. I was first into a rediscovered field of art and photography.

In the auction rooms, I was one of the few people in the photography world who had traveled in the non-Western world. I'd faced the winds of the Karakoram Mountains and felt the burning heat of central India under my feet. What I discovered were art documents of cultures that were rapidly disappearing everywhere on Earth.

As I looked at tens of thousands of pictures, during an epoch of auction cycles in London, I trained my eye to determine the art and veracity of a photographer's vision. I sorted the good, the bad, and the excellent in intervals of brief moments.

It was a time when so many photographs were coming onto the market, the British auction houses of Sotheby's and Christie's had created six individual annual sales solely dedicated to photography.

Auction week was an exercise in Zen-like concentration, where you looked at impossible numbers of photographs. In all my years of collecting, London during the mid-1970s, during these auction weeks, was the supreme period of photographic collecting.

The great photography dealer, Harry Lunn, once described the two-year period between 1975 and 1977 in the London auction rooms as "the insanity and mania of the pictures." It was a moment when great photographs were dumped in literal bales onto the market.

***

PHOTOGRAPHS

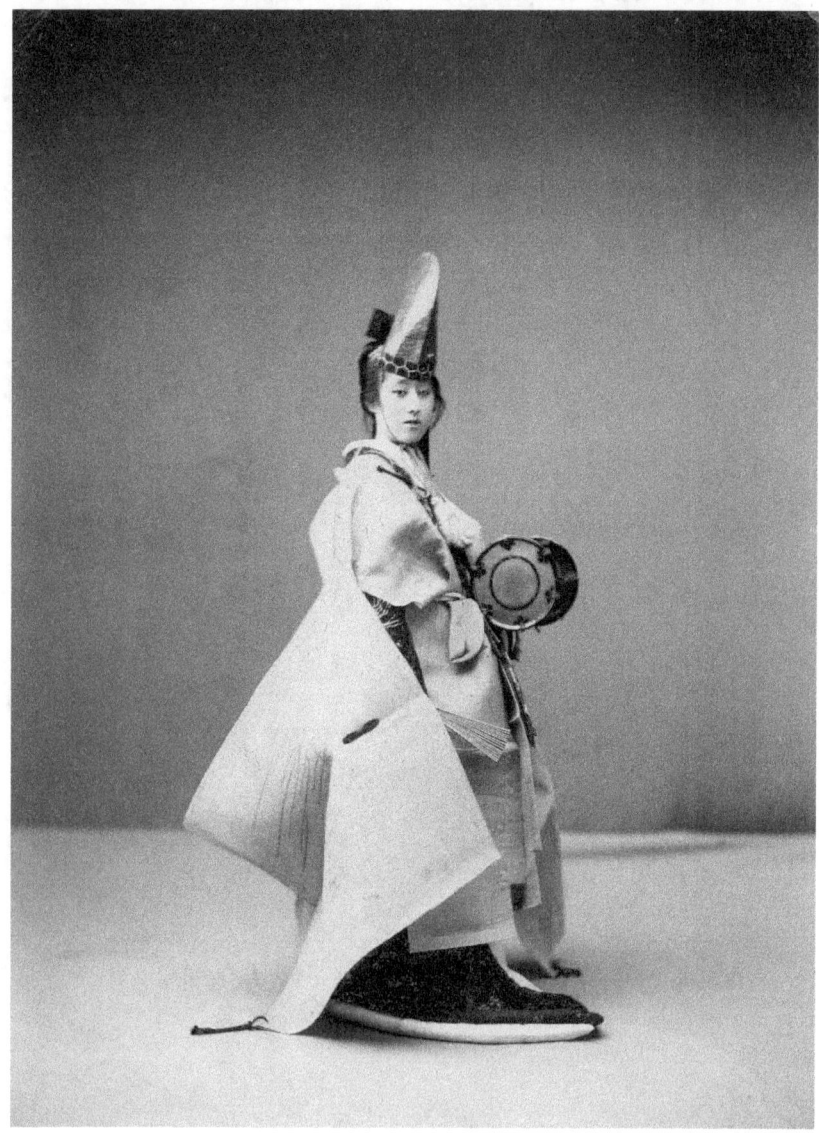

Japanese Dancer, 14the century Costume, Ogawa Isshin

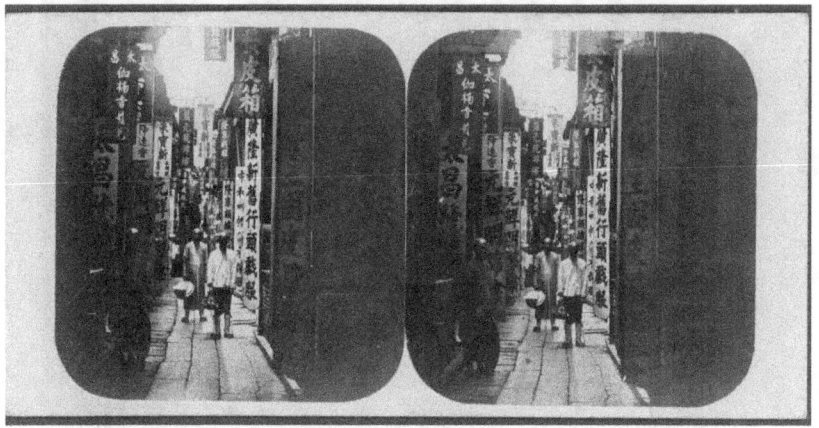

Physic Street, the First Photographs of Canton, 1858,

Pierre Rossier

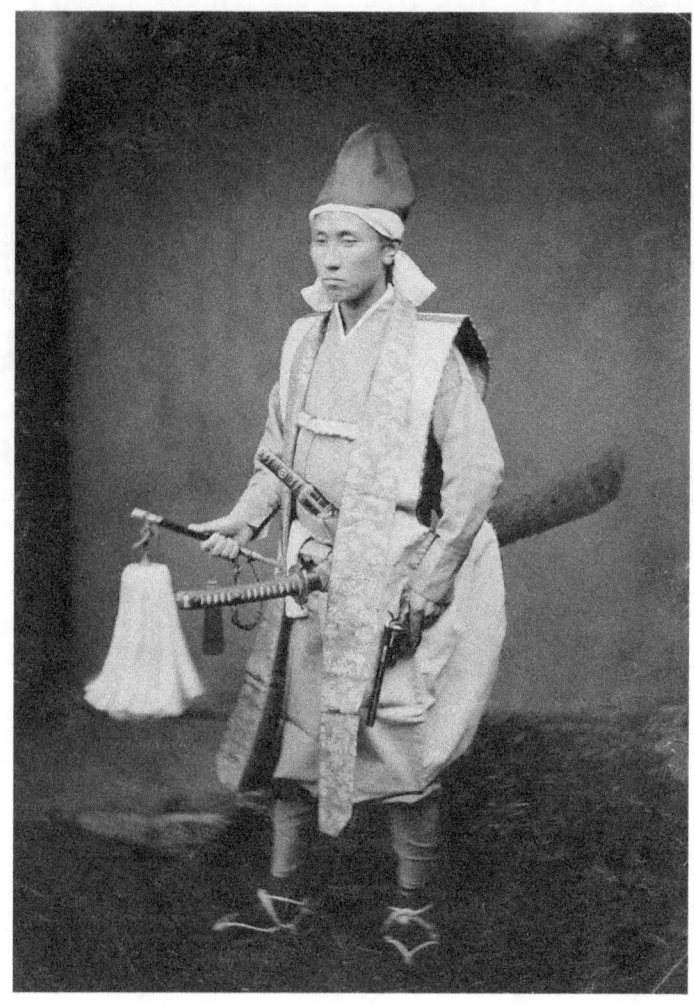

Samurai, Satsuma (Japan) 1864,

Felix Beato

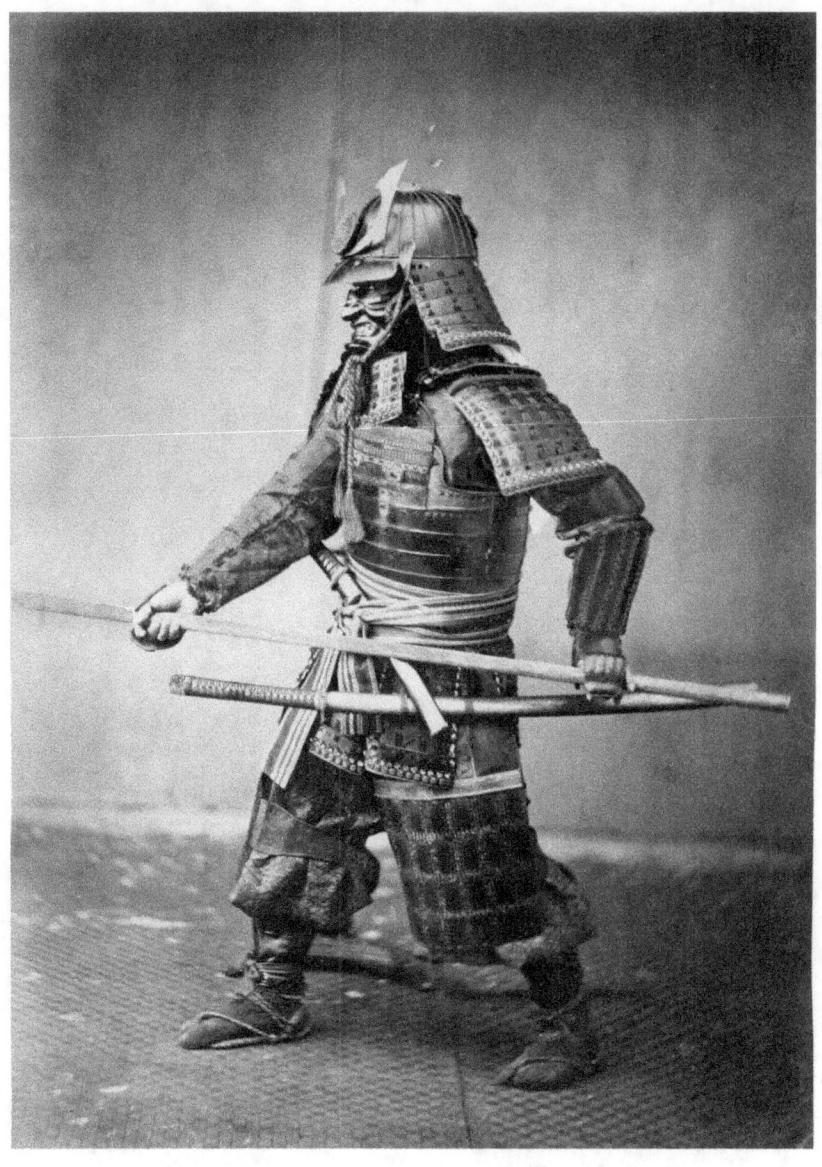

Koboto Santaro, Chief of the Shogun's Bodyguard, Killed Defending the Shogun in 1868.

Hand Colored by Charles Wirgman, Photograph Felix Beato, 1864

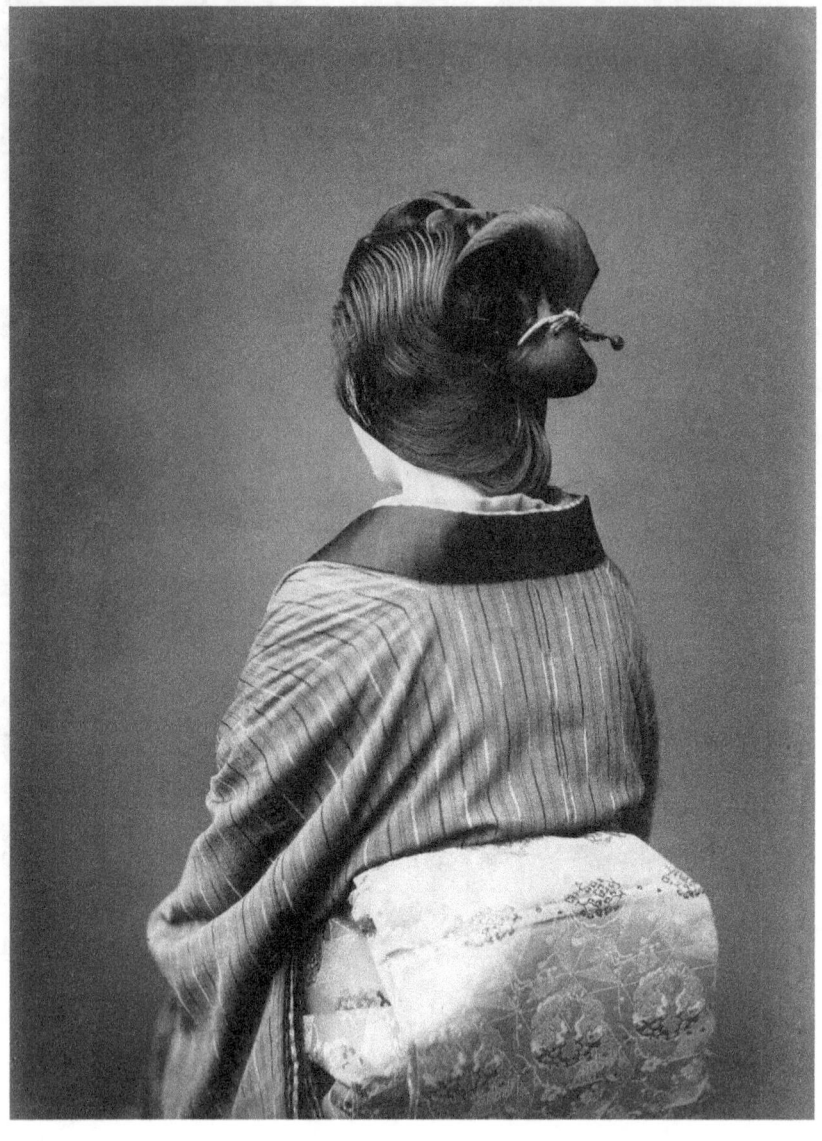

Geisha, Obi and Hairstyle, Japan, 1880's

Kusakabe Kimbei

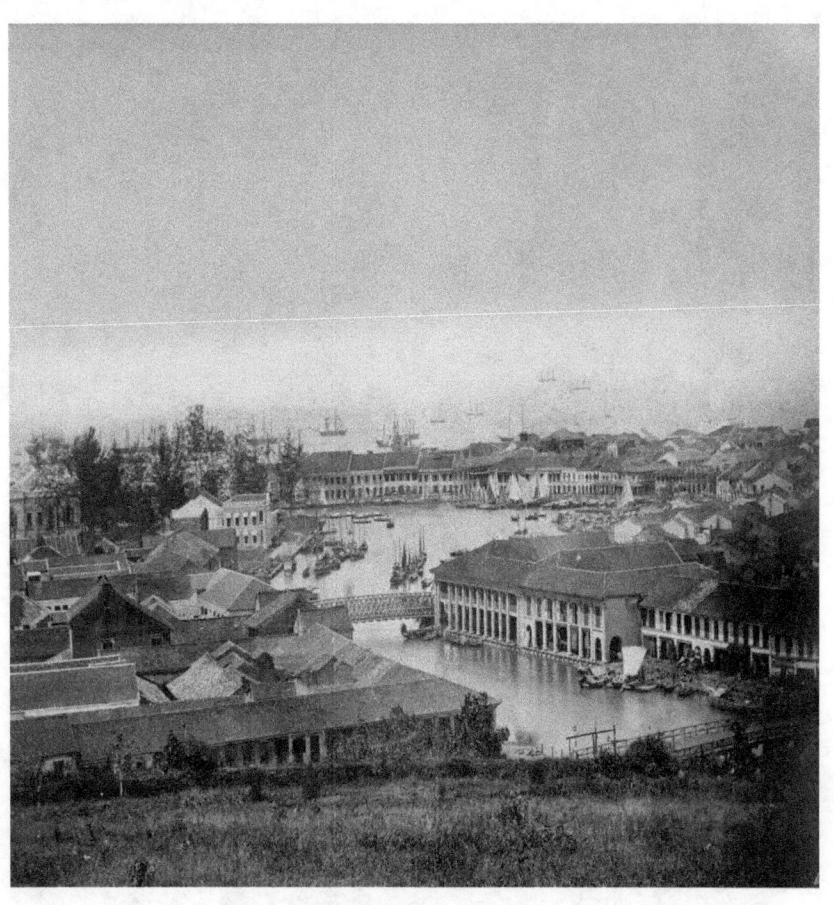

The Harbor, Singapore, 1861

Hermann Sachtler

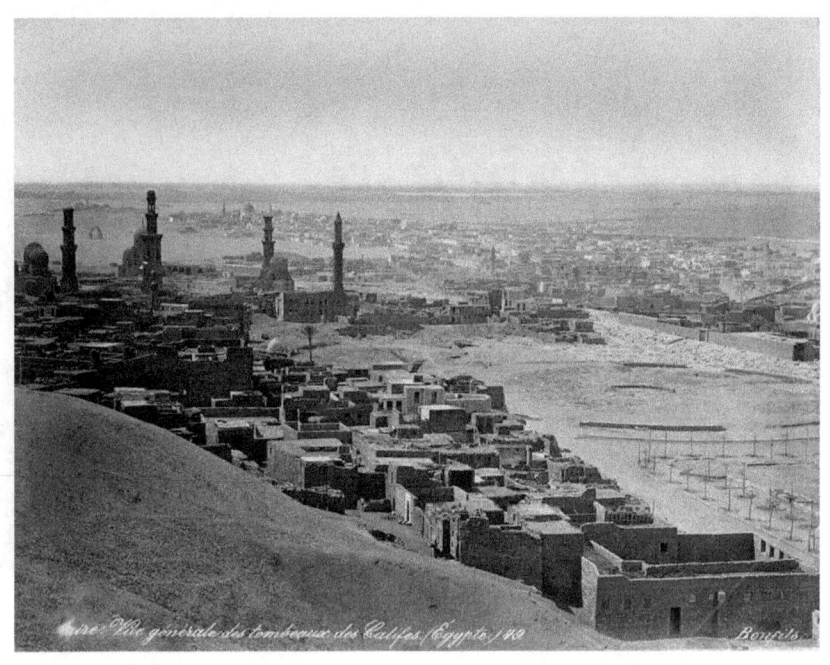

Cairo, Tombs of the Caliphs with the Pyramids in the Distance,

Felix Bonfils 1868

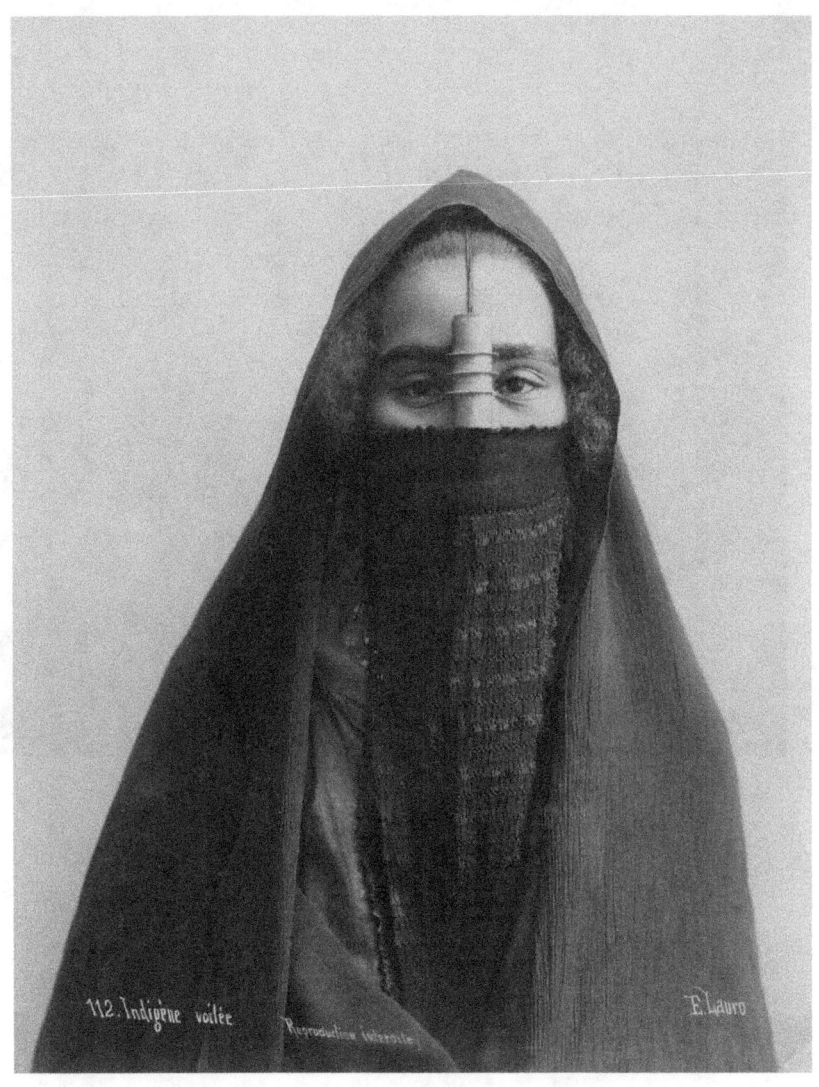

Indigene (Young Woman), Cairo, 1890's

E. Lauro

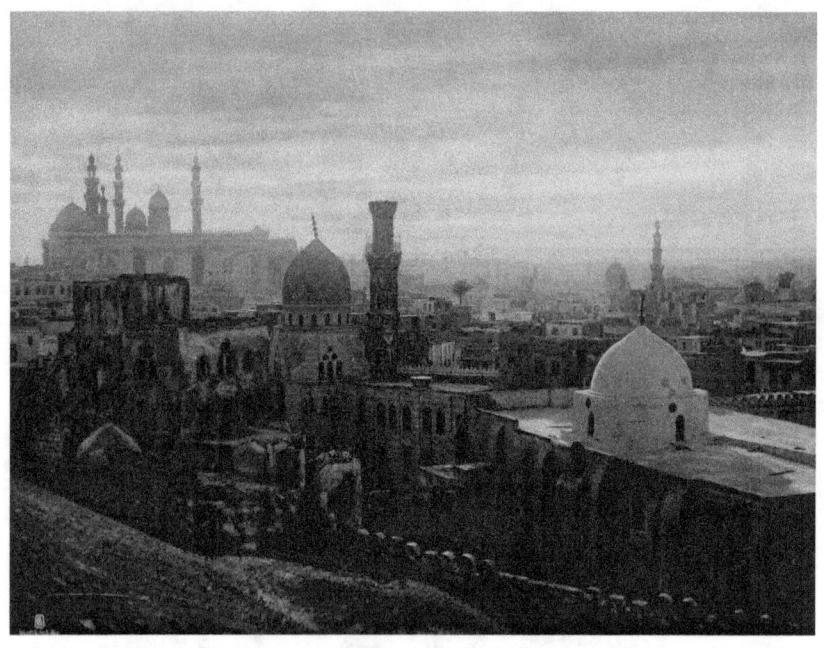

The Mosque of Sultan Hassan, Cairo, 1905

Lehnert & Landrock

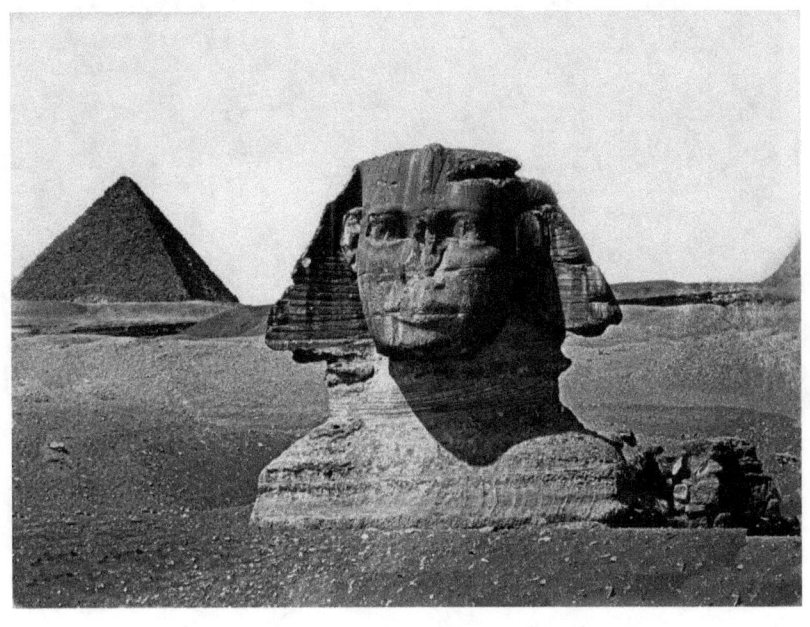

Sphinx& Pyramid, Egypt, 1859

Willhelm Hammerschmidt

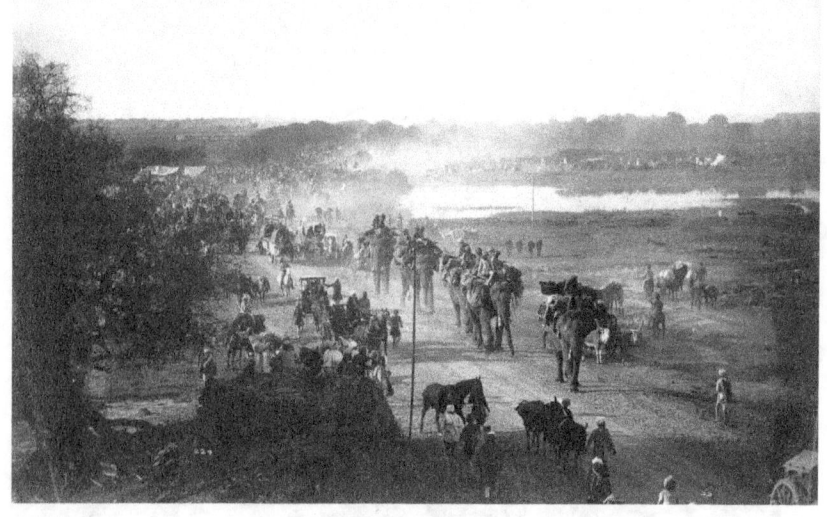

The Last Photograph of an Indian Army on the March, Panipat, 1886,

Raja Deen Dayal

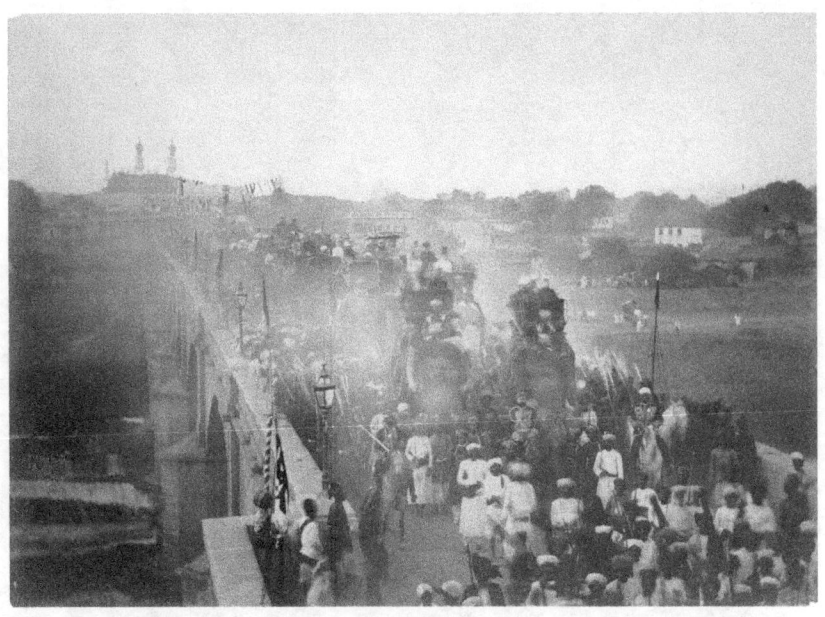

The Archduke Ferdinand's Visit to Hyderabad, 1890s,

Raja Deen Dayal

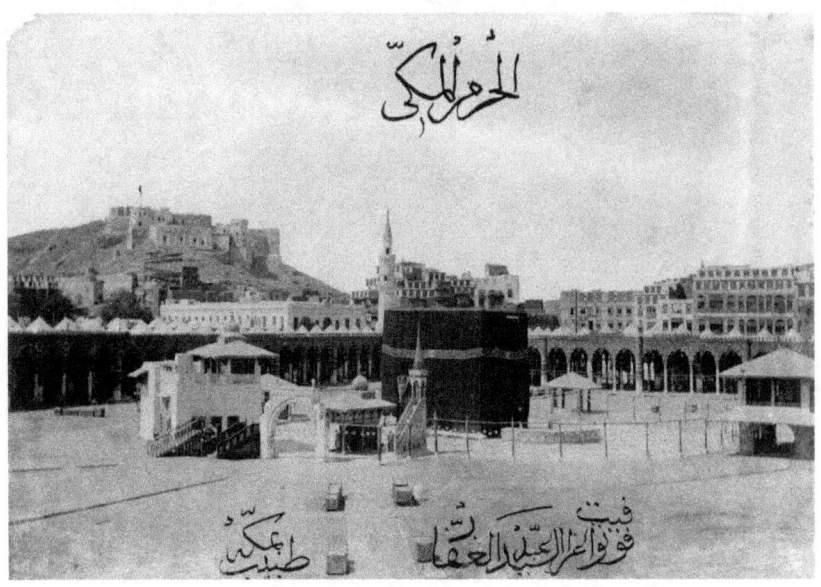

الحرم المكي

Arabia, The Ka'aba Mecca, 1886

abd al Ghaffar,

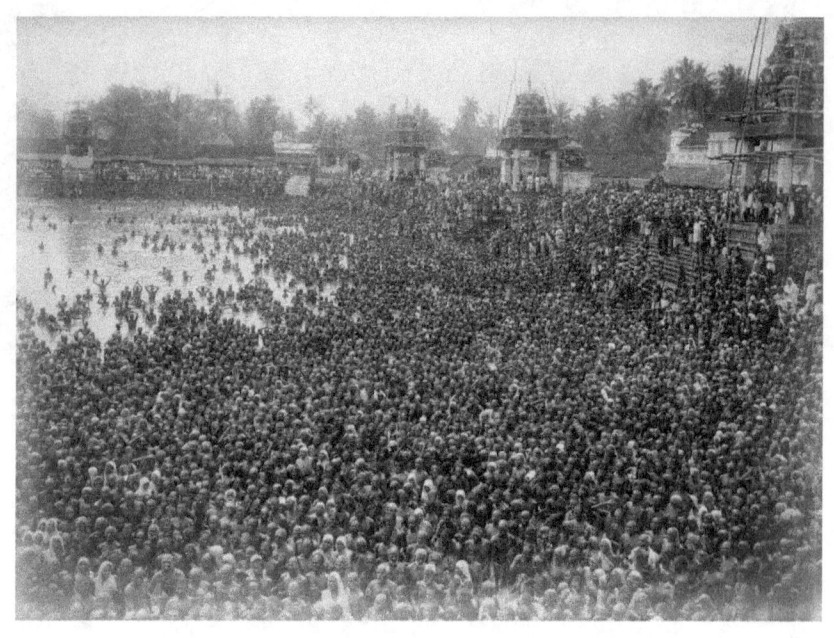

Bathing Ceremony, Kumbakonam, South India, 1880's,

Nicholas Brothers

331

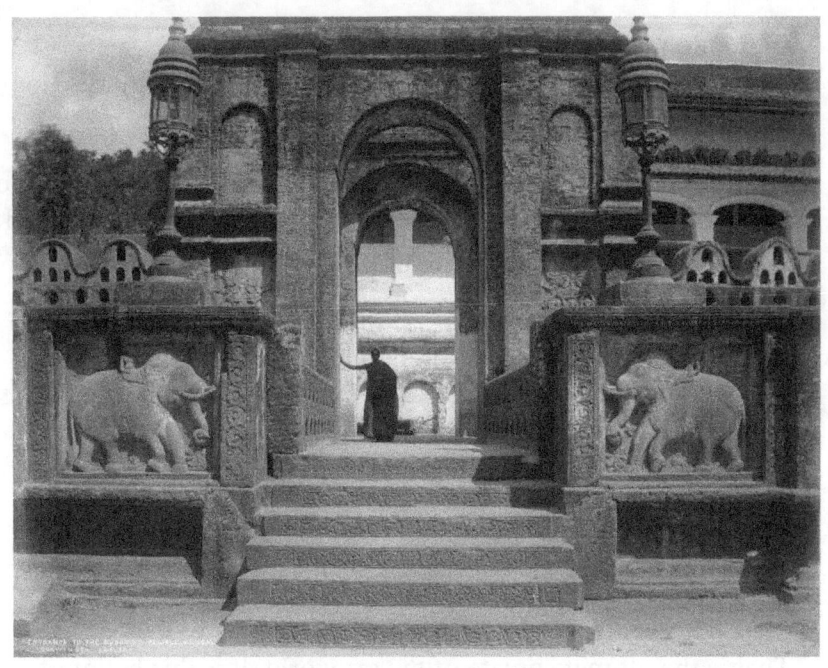

Entrance to the Temple of the Tooth, Kandy, Ceylon. 1870s.

Charles Scowen

London 1975-1977

In London, I became a different person. I was obsessed with pictures. Nothing else mattered. I wanted more and more. The photographs at auction became a sort of drug.

During auction week in London, I kept waking up in the middle of the night with pictures floating through my brain. At the end of these weeks, I felt as if I'd been damaged.

The gold standard in collecting was a sense of connoisseurship and the belief that in the brief moment when you first saw a picture that was great, it sprang out from hundreds or thousands of other photographs.

In my world of collecting, I believed with certainty that connoisseurship was the sole criterion for acquiring art. Either you believed great art existed, and there was such a thing as a great picture, or you didn't.

That is the ultimate opiate of the art world. It is this belief of one's own recognition of what a great object is when one first sees it. Then, if one is very lucky, one buys that picture.

In the hearts of those of us who loved pictures, we knew the photographs we bought would someday become the core collections in the great museums of the world.

We collected the work of artists that no one had heard of before. It had taken Impressionism at least sixty years to gain traction in the public mind and become hugely sought after in the art world. From 1975 to 1977, in just two years, photography that had started the decade in the subbasement of the art gulag established itself as a major art form.

I don't think there has ever been anything like this in the art world since. It was a 732-day sprint toward collecting glory!

During the rest of the 1970s, photographs began to emerge from attics and closets. They were dragged out of museum basements. They appeared out of the drawers of antique furniture shops, from locked and forgotten storage rooms, from historical and art societies, and from ethnographic museums.

In India, I was able to buy the entire studio of the greatest Indian photographer of the nineteenth century. For twenty years, Raja Deen Dayal had been the appointed court photographer to the Nizam of Hyderabad. The Nizam, then the richest man in the world, personally controlled the market of the diamonds of Golconda. Raja Deen Dayal photographed his court, his palaces, the archaeological sites of his kingdom, his stud, his railway system, and his armies.

In a closet of the Royal Asiatic Society in London, under the brooms and mops, I discovered the greatest album of nineteenth-century China coast photography ever put together. .

***

The Rise of the World's Greatest Photography Dealer

As the 1970s began, the art photography world slumbered onward as it had slept for the past hundred years or so. In the art world. photography was irrelevant.

During the period from 1973 to 1975, there were still only a few collectors of photography. For the few dealers in the field, photography was not a highly remunerative endeavor.

When both the British and New York photography auctions began to catch on, a few dealers and a group of fearless collectors emerged from the forests of indifference.

You could buy everything in the field for modest prices; Walker Evans, Edward Weston, and Eugène Atget pictures were $125 each. Take your pick. Few collectors showed up to buy any of these artists.

But then something quite extraordinary occurred: in 1974, a vividly improbable man entered the scene.

Few people took this man, Harry Lunn, seriously. However, after Lunn and I compared notes, and spoke over a period of months in on and off conversations, I began to take him very seriously. He asked me my opinions about photography and where it would go. In turn, I listened to his ideas about who was important in photography and what would happen in the field.

From 1974 to 1998, the year he died, Lunn and I had a series of ongoing conversations and arguments. At one point I didn't speak to Lunn for a year.

In retrospect, there has been no other career in the art-dealing world as unlikely as the completely outrageous success of Harry Lunn.

Between 1974 and 1980, Lunn came to single-handedly control 85 percent of the world's photography market. Think about that. It was staggering.

When I remember Lunn, I try to measure the scale of his unlikely, untoward success. In the ups and downs of the art world, I don't think any art dealer has ever come close to having such control over the entire spectrum of a single art market as Lunn did. Not Joseph Duveen, not Frank Lloyd, not Paul Durand-Ruel, not Ambroise Vollard or Leo Castelli, nor even Larry Gagosian.

Lunn and his restless soul brought unique gifts to the art world. What other art dealer has ever had his previous life as a CIA agent exposed to the blinding light of publicity by *Ramparts* magazine?

I suppose in some small corner of his mind, Lunn felt bad about being forced to give up a life of public service.

Only in America could there be such a success story of redemption and repurposed talents. Lunn was able to take his hard-earned training as a government employee into the private sector. After all, what had he been doing for an entire decade before he was exposed by *Ramparts*? He had been a spy. A provocateur. A character assassin. It had been Lunn's hard-fought and useful work to destabilize and subvert the European art world in order to further a CIA-based vision of American cultural exceptionalism.

With Gore Vidal based in Rome, and Lunn based in Paris, these two American CIA-sponsored bon vivants spent their time in the mid-1960s roving around Europe. They whispered lies and innuendos as they wove a poisoned net that came eventually to span the European literary and art worlds. Years later Lunn and Vidal would meet in the Rizzoli bookstore on 57th Street and have delighted whispered conversations *sotto voce*.

Lunn's trajectory in the world of private commerce was like an octopus intent upon sucking the life out of an unsuspecting bed of clams. Once retired from government work, thanks to his unique on-the-job training, Lunn drifted inexorably back to the art world and the continental places where he'd thrived during the 1960s.

In retrospect, as I watched Lunn over the decades, I came to think that he was so spiritually flaky, so unconscious of the havoc he created in suborning every person and opportunity he ran into, that he was able to achieve a position in the art world that was nearly metaphysical.

He was especially adept at something called bilocation. Somehow, Lunn could occupy two places simultaneously.

The first place he occupied was the world of art deals, misinformation, and more or less day-and-night spying on the competition in his particular sphere. The second place he occupied was his carefully assumed role as the outsize champion of photography, with his no-holds-barred boosterism of the individual photographic talents of the artists he represented.

The remarkable thing about Lunn was his absolute sparkling brilliance. His mind was like a steel trap; he remembered all things.

Everything he ever learned went into his giant embrace of photography, as he surrounded and enveloped an entire art field.

As my final and largest gambit in collecting, I decided to carefully study Lunn's stock of American photographers.

As he built up this stock, I came to believe that by some unknown process, he'd managed to identify and define many of the iconic careers of American modernist photographers.

After observing Lunn, I decided to acquire photographs from what I considered the medium's most vibrant, if unlikely visionary during the years when photography was rediscovered by the art world of the twentieth century.

The photographers I mainly chose to collect were Walker Evans and Berenice Abbott.

These artists knew one another. They had photographed from the 1920s to the 1970s. They shared the same darkroom at one point, and both were at the center of Lunn's emergent art-dealing work. I'd also collect the Photo-Secession and Abbott's heroic reprinting of Eugène Atget's negatives of Paris, which she'd undertaken from the 1930s to the late 1950s, using silver-rich paper. In my own opinion, Abbott's forty year "edit" of Atget's work, from the thousands of negatives she'd acquired, is the best and most important selection of this extraordinary artist's work.

Both Evans and Abbott work, along with my non-Western nineteenth-century pictures, formed the two polarities of my growing photography collections.

Unlike 99 percent of the photography collectors beavering away at forming collections of artists' most important works, I collected in a different manner. I'd limit my twentieth-century collecting to two, or perhaps three, careers in photography. Then, I'd try to collect work from the beginning to the end of the artists' oeuvres, buying as many pictures as I could afford.

Instead of gathering a few photographs to represent the great artists in the field, I'd gather scores of pictures. I'd collect in massive depth. To me, as a photographer, what was important about an artist's work was both his evolving vision, and preserving his oeuvre intact so that one could view the totality of his vision.

To my mind, the two most important museums in the world are the monographic Van Gogh Museum in Amsterdam, and SK Stiftung in Cologne, Germany. Both museums are dedicated to a core purpose, which is preserving the life's work and evolving visions of two towering artists of modernism. The artists around which these two museums have been built are the painter Vincent Van Gogh and modernist German photographer, August Sander.

My thoughts about a second collecting career in the art world were quite simple. If I'd been a collector of Impressionists in nineteenth-century Europe, I would have watched what the great Parisian dealers like Paul Durand-Ruel and Ambroise Vollard sold.

Similarly, in the 1970s, all I had to do was watch what Harry Lunn sold, and be lucky enough to buy scores of pictures, then hundreds

***

It became fascinating to watch as the greatest masterpieces of photographic modernism moved into the market, many of them passing through Lunn's hands.

The 1970s was *the* period when photography began to ascend into the artistic stratosphere.

At heart, Lunn's business plan was simple. He ran a gigantic wholesaling operation that provided one-stop shopping to the world's retail photography dealers.

As the decade developed, behind the curtain there was Lunn, who more than happily (and quietly) supplied enormous amounts of stock to the entire trade.

Allied to his carefully crafted business plan, Lunn set out to absorb huge collections of Ansel Adams, Robert Frank,

Berenice Abbott, Diane Arbus, and Walker Evans photographs. He then spent decades building both the markets and the reputations of these photographers. Witness the results that you see today—the aforementioned photographers are now the beating, vibrant, and pulsating heart of photographic modernism.

As the prices paid for photography rocketed higher and higher into the 1980s and 1990s, out there in the fast lane was Lunn leading the pack around and around the speedway. His trips across the Atlantic on the Concorde began to resemble a daily commute.

Since everyone who was anyone in the photography world now collected pictures sourced from Lunn or his dealing collaterals, there emerged a consensus of what was both sublime and important in photography.

With the passage of time, it has been forgotten that these masterpieces were first and foremost Lunn's pictures. They were his artists.

I must say, as I watched this art miracle unfold, the world of Harry Lunn became more and more mesmerizing. The only word I could use to describe both Lunn's work and the building importance of his artists was *bilocation*.

Lunn was everywhere and nowhere. At one point in the late 1970s, he controlled almost the entire photography market. As a dealer if you wanted pictures you went to Lunn. He was, in aggregate, the photographic dealing world. *The source.*

Harry Lunn was like the Hindu god Shiva, the creator and simultaneously the destroyer of the world.

***

Collecting Photography: 1970 to the Present.

Perhaps the most interesting corollary to the rise of photography as an art collectible in the 1970s was the determination of what was, and was not, rare in this emergent field.

By the end of the 1970s, a price structure in photography collecting began to be determined by the scarcity of particular photographic prints.

In the decades that followed, both the collectors and dealers in this new field fought their own corners for purposes either noble or base. As they fade away and are forgotten over time, what remains of interest to the historian is how, quite by happenstance, the issues of value and rarity were arrived at.

This problem of defining an established base of monetary values, both with the dealers and in the auctions, was complex. Nothing was set in stone. Prices went up; prices declined. Slowly, as price discovery occurred, ideas of rarity and monetary value were grafted onto other ideas about the exceptionalism of a few of the most important "iconic" artists of photography.

What emerged from this process, which dealers like Lunn engaged in, was an almost monastic set of monetary and aesthetic values for particular artists and prints. Increasingly, the photography market came to center itself upon the idea that particular photographers towered above their contemporaries in artistic importance.

Such as it was, in this layering of photographers' work, one witnessed great careers become grander, while lesser careers faded away into an oblivion of the darkest night.

If you were a collector of twentieth-century photography, you could actually miss the new photography boom altogether if you incorrectly guessed the particular importance of an artist wrong in this emerging market.

If you want proof of this economic layering, look only at a single, hugely famous collection for the devastation of a bad guess, or in this case, thousands of bad guesses. What is hot in one decade is more often cold in the following decades.

From the vantage point of the twenty-first century, consider the collection formed by the Polaroid Corporation during the 1970s and '80s. The corporation collected hundreds of modernist photographic careers, with literally millions of dollars lavished on these artists. Today, as one looks at this collection, one gets an intimate, ground-zero look into the different seasons of collecting.

The Polaroid Collection contains approximately 30,000 photographs. Excluding the pictures of Ansel Adams, who worked for Polaroid for decades, the work of the hundreds of photographers represented in the collection are probably not worth as much today as a set of Cindy Sherman photographs.

The triage of twentieth-century "art photography" reputations was grim.

The task of any collector in the 1970s was to divine what career an artist had presently, and whether he or she would still be important in forty years. I always believed that the most risky bet any photography collector could make was buying the work of an American modernist photographer.

Most artists are never recognized, and their work disappears into an artistic black hole. Of the few artists who are recognized during their own lifetimes, fewer still are collected in the generation after their deaths.

For myself, in the course of looking at huge numbers of pictures over decades, I decided I would try to collect the rare vintage prints of the one photographer who was my standout favorite of the twentieth century.

As my friend Sam Wagstaff, the great collector, once said, "Think with your eyes, and buy with your heart." He also said "Dig."

"Dig?"

The artist I collected was Walker Evans. I collected as many Evans prints as I could find.

For years, I'd studied Evans', career. He worked during an astonishing moment in twentieth-century American modernism: between 1927 and 1973. During that forty-six-year period, he was able to reinvent himself decade after decade, creating incisive pictures as a new kind of documentary artist.

Most people who collect Walker Evans to this day collect his iconic year of 1936. This was the year when Evans photographed rural America and the American South for the government-sponsored Works Progress Administration. Looking at Evans' work for only this single year of 1936, his posthumous reputation remains enduringly strange, given the longevity of his 46 year career, and the importance of his vision over the shifting artistic sands of almost five decades as an artist.

Even odder to me than this is that in the twenty-first century, no other photographer of the twentieth century has had the international breadth of influence as Evans. From the Dusseldorf School and the work of the Bechers in Germany, to the work of Robert Frank and a host of other artists in both Europe and America, Evans' work is *the* iconic career in twentieth-century modernist photography.

I had the feeling that collecting a single year of Evans' lifelong output totally missed the point of his entire oeuvre.

In 1936, Evans was the subject of the first monographic exhibition of a photographer's work at the Museum of Modern Art in New York. Thirty-six years later, Evans was given another monographic exhibition at the MoMA. The latter exhibition reinvigorated and reinterpreted his career, but for the most part it plowed the same set of mid-1930s pictures that everyone knew.

What I could not understand was why no one collected the work of Evans' entire art-document project, which took up most of his life. I asked myself, "Was Picasso's long career, s he worked his way through his seven decades as an artist, just his Cubist Period or his Blue Period?"

When I excavated the hagiography of Evans' anointed career, I discovered that outside his 1936 work, his prints were exceedingly rare. For me, as a collector, it only got better. In most cases, the unknown part of Evans' oeuvre existed only in single prints. Through the long arm of time, perhaps just a few collectors see, what no one else sees.

Today it is by general agreement that Walker Evans was one of the most influential photographers of the twentieth century. It has become unquestioned canon. To me, however, it is nothing short of breathtaking that in both the collecting and dealing worlds, two generations have walked past 97 percent of Evans' career outside his work done during two years in the Depression.

As things go in the art world, the last words on this issue and Evans' posthumous artistic reputation will be negotiated on issues of rarity. During the 1980's when Walker Evans prints became available on the market only three people put down sizable wagers on the posthumous reputation of Walker Evans. They were the photography curator of the Getty Museum Weston Naef, and the collectors Joan and Clark Worswick. Between us we own over fifty percent of the "vintage" Walker Evans prints extant.

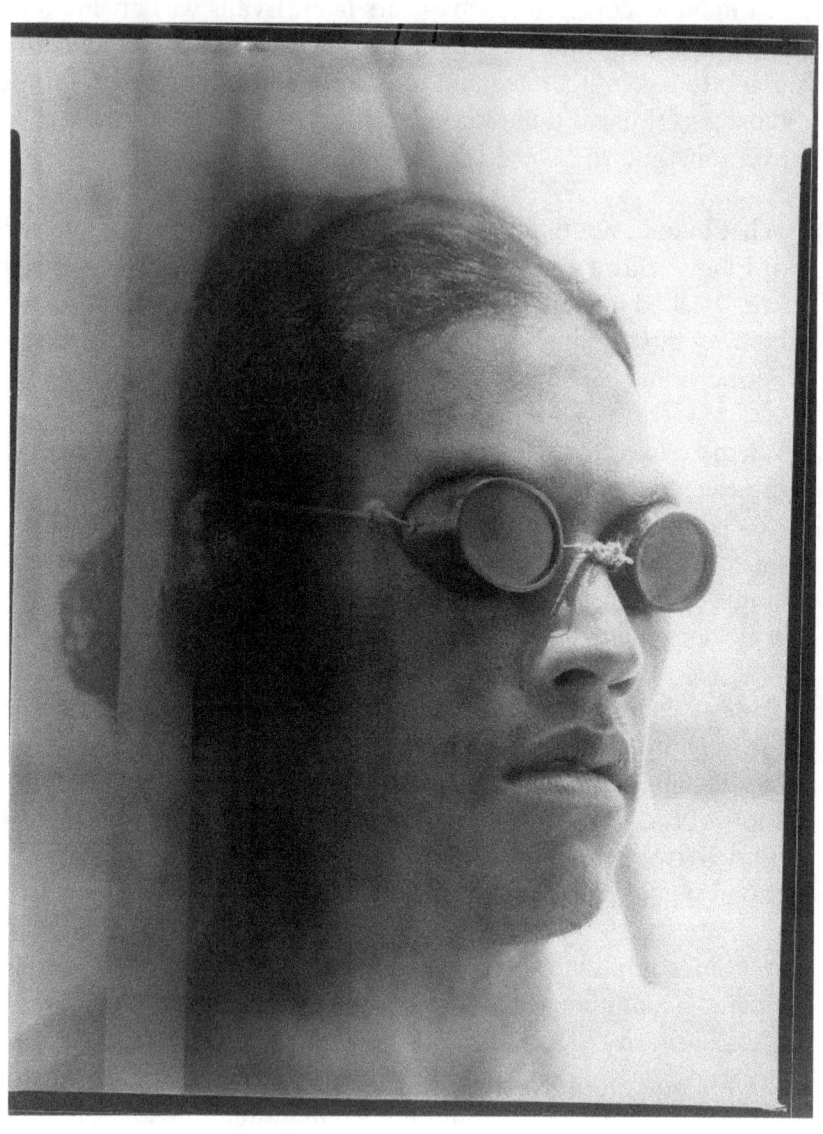

Tahitian Pearl Diver, 1932

Walker Evans

Like all decades, the 1970s passed.

By the end of the 1980s, one marveled at how many pictures had tumbled to the forgotten places where people had buried their pictures for generations. Because I'd witnessed classical Indian art dry up, then disappear in the late 1960s, I never took it for granted that manna from collectors' heaven would last forever.

At some point, it would end.

In London and New York, the great pictures of the nineteenth century that you once found in the auction salesrooms appear in vastly abbreviated numbers.

During the 1980s, the museums discovered photography. The new excitements of discovery slowly leaked out of photography. In the new era of the 1990s, dealers dealt in vintage prints of the great masters of photography. New collectors came into the market with massive amounts of money and bought the iconic masterpieces.

It seemed to me that these new collectors were equipped with grocery lists of art. In their cold-blooded earnestness, they reminded me of bankers trying to find some upside in a defective corporate balance sheet. As more and more people began to collect photography, there were fewer and fewer great pictures to collect.

Ironically, now that photography was Art with a bright neon capital *A*, you displayed it in a frame. Then you put it up on your wall.

Unfortunately, what the newly minted collectors didn't yet know was *the absolute very worst thing you could do to a photographic print is to give it a daily bath of sunlight.*

Large numbers of very expensive pictures began to quickly auto-destruct and then completely fade out.

In the future, the only people who will have impressively rare photographs will be collectors who live in small apartments with limited wall space or in basements with low light levels.

Pity the rich with lots of wall space and vast, sunlit apartments.

***

The first generation of photography collectors began to fade away.

An example of where these collections went was the work gathered by Sam Wagstaff, one of the great collectors of photography during the 1970s. At the beginning of the 1980s, he sold his collection to the new Getty Museum for millions. The brilliant young photography dealer, Daniel Wolf, who brokered that sale and the sale of six or seven other large photographic collections to the Getty, sold much of his own collection to the Getty and also to the Denver Art Museum.

Without anyone taking much notice, the first-generation collectors of photography had stopped collecting pictures by the middle of the 1980s. Many of these individuals had grown older, and their collections were either dispersed or bought by museums.

At the beginning of the twenty-first century, photographs are now worth a great deal more money than they used to be.

In the 1960s and 1970s, one collected at a moment when great daguerreotypes cost five dollars apiece. During the 1960s, I occasionally bought a great photograph for a dollar. I remember asking Robert Lebeck, the transcendent German collector, how much he'd spent for his greatest daguerreotypes during the 1960s. These pictures are now in a German museum and considered national treasures. Lebeck thought for a moment.

Then he answered, "Until 1975, I never bought a daguerreotype for more than five dollars."

During 1971, the New York dealer Lee Witkin had sold Eugène Atget duplicates, deaccessioned from the Museum of Modern Art, for $125 each. In 2002, the MoMA deaccessioned another group of similar Atget duplicates. The pictures sold at auction for $10,000 to $60,000. Today, they are worth much, much more. Recently, an Atget print of Paris sold for $550,000. The world changed on us. Vanished from photography was a generation of extraordinary collectors who collected with an unbelievable passion that posed high-wire risks of acceptance by the art world.

It has now been decades since the 1970s.

For everyone involved in photography—whether one worked in an auction gallery or one was a collector—it was an incredible journey. Collectors took giant chances on their individual eye prevailing in a world where there were absolutely no measures of quality except for passionately held connoisseurship. For a photography collector of the 1970s, everything was about risk.

If one didn't collect passionately and bravely, one missed the nearly unbelievable moment when the extraordinary imagery created in photography over the previous 130 years appeared in the market, a chance that happened only once.

I remember something Henri Cartier-Bresson told me in the early 1980s. We were editing a book and exhibition of nineteenth-century photographs I'd collected of the distant, far-off places of the non-Western world. As he looked at the pictures, he said quietly, "These pictures are a miracle of great art. Everything today is now derivative and much the same."

If I'd listened carefully and understood what he'd said at the time, I'd have heard the pitter-patter of little footsteps on the path to the future.

With the appearance of *Facebook*, and its growth into an image-laden behemoth, the likes of which the world has never seen before, people now daily share over 850 million photographs.

Is photography now a toy for the masses? Alternatively, can photography even have a future as art? In the first decades of the Internet, both questions are legitimate. The very bedrock of photography is now being defied in a way that no other art has ever been challenged.

In this new world, everyone *and everything* has a camera—even telephone poles and street corners.

What photography lacks at the moment is an appreciation of what the field has achieved in its almost two-hundred-year history.

Some of the smartest people in the world invented photography, and its inventors were obsessed, *in the 1840s,* by a single question: What is it that makes a photograph unique?

A single phrase is the answer: Photography excels at both preserving and recording the physical artistic differentiations of time.

In no other art can one make an exact, irreplaceable art document of time itself. A photographer of conflict can bring his own viewpoint to his photographs of war or famine. Similarly, the artist photographer brings his own inspirational vision of a fragile fragment of time that can never be repeated.

Every generation has invented, then reinvented, this miraculous medium to fit its own moment. Each photographer's measurements of his world are uniquely his own.

We have forgotten photography's ambition from its earliest days: without bending a knee to anyone, photography is now the people's art.

Were I to stake a wager on the future of this startling medium, I would say that the most important art form of the twenty-first century will be photography. The glory days lie ahead.

***

CHAPTER FIVE

The Road from Baco and Jinka to Lake Rudolf, Southern Ethiopia, August 1968

There is one last problem in this book.

I have absolutely no idea how Joanie and I survived Africa.

I remember the precise moment when I gave up my life of more or less constant travel. It was the moment I also decided there were no old, bold travelers.

It seemed to me that after a decade of almost constant travel, anyone who'd survived on the road had the odds stacked against him hugely. At some point, your time just ran out. Your exit could come by toppling off a cliff when a road suddenly collapsed under you. Alternatively, you could be murdered or perish from poisoned food, a snakebite, or pestilential insects, drowning, freezing, dehydration, or being crushed like a gnat in either an airplane crash or a truck wreck.

You could also be spirited away in a place like Africa by a nasty encyclopedia of tropical diseases like bilharzia, sleeping sickness, eye diseases that left you blind and helpless, or gangrene. The most dangerous thing of all was pushing your last lucky day of travel into a tomorrow that would never come.

In the windswept heat of Lake Rudolf's northern shore, Robert Gardner came up to me.

He pointed down at the lake in front of us, baking like some foul, fetid, terrible soup, with an offer of more foreign travel.

"A few miles to the north, on the Omo River, we can get across," he said. "What I propose to do is cross the Omo near the point where it empties into the lake. Then we can all drive down to Nairobi through the Kenyan highlands."

"Drive to Nairobi?"

I looked at Robert like he was completely mad. The year before, paleoanthropologist Richard Leakey's expedition on the Omo had nearly been destroyed by an attack of gigantic sixteen-foot-long crocodiles.

I stared up at the sun. It was over 110 degrees. I stood there, letting the sun cook me.

But there were other problems with driving to Nairobi.

Across the Omo, and across Lake Rudolf, the deserts were filled with *shifta* bandits. If the *shifta* didn't cut us into pieces, then the desert would barbecue us alive. Beyond the river was a trackless desert where there was a strong possibility of losing our way.

Another small problem cropped up: we didn't have a single map.

I wiped a hand across my cracked, chapped lips.

It was utterly useless having these kinds of conversations with Robert. By the time he presented an idea as a suggestion, it meant that he'd already made up his mind what we were going to do. Then, of course, I remembered the previous day when he'd almost killed Joanie.

Yesterday, Robert had come up to me at the exact spot where we now stood, having this conversation about African travel.

With his best Boston Captain Ahab voice, he had said, "I think I've discovered a nest of cobras. This is, I believe, a unique opportunity."

I remembered staring at him. This expedition had become very strange. Inside my heat-hazed head, I drifted back to yesterday.

"These snakes are very rare," he had said. "This moment is absolutely unequaled in all my time in Africa. Imagine! Just imagine being able to film a rare nest of Ethiopian black-necked spitting cobras."

"I don't like snakes," I said. "In India, I adopted a rule. My rule is that I want nothing to do with snakes. Ever." With my voice absolutely emotionless, I continued, "I hate to tell you this. I don't do things with people who play with snakes."

I settled down in the shade of my Toyota Land Cruiser and rested my back against one of the tires. I looked up at Robert.

Twenty feet away, Joanie looked over at me. Then she stared at Robert.

As I watched him, he unloaded his tripod from his Toyota.

Next, he extracted his smaller Arriflex film camera from its aluminum trunk. Picking up his tripod, he hefted the Arriflex and began walking toward a bluff a quarter of a mile away, overlooking the lake where he'd discovered his cobras.

Joanie hitched up her own Nikon cameras in front of her.

She was wearing her bush hat, short pants, and a bush jacket. She looked like she'd just stumbled out of a copy of *Vogue* magazine.

Without saying anything to me, Joanie began to walk after Robert toward the lake.

"Have fun!" I called in parting.

Both of them hurried toward their distant and exciting discovery of a nesting cobra family.

It was my feeling that if cobras, in general, were bad enough, an East African spitting black cobra nesting on her young would be a difficult-to-match party treat on this sunblasted day. I decided the heat and our terrible journey had frizzled Robert's brain.

In the distance, Robert put his camera down on the desert. He stepped forward. He seemed to be studying how to provoke a whole nest of somnolent cobras into becoming wildlife actors.

As I watched him, I said to myself, "Un-god-damned believable."

Robert began energetically poking the cobra's nest with the legs of his tripod.

Then, suddenly, he yanked the tripod into the air.

Robert began to run, and he seemed to be running as if he were suddenly possessed by Saint Vitus' Dance.

From my vantage point in the shade of my Toyota, the scene was grotesquely, if morbidly comic.

On his long legs, Robert was now doing the hundred-yard dash, shaking his tripod even more vehemently. The cobra, or her children, appeared to have somehow wedged themselves into the tripod's legs. Dodging left and right in the distance, Robert did a magnificent job of broken field running over challenging ground.

My last sighting of Robert occurred when he disappeared over the lip of a hill, running in the direction of the welcoming shores of Lake Rudolf.

Joanie had gone the other direction, and now she circled back toward me. I watched her from where I sat.

Breathing hard, she approached and stopped in front of me.

"That looked like fun," I said. "Did you get any nice snaps?"

A still-panting Joanie narrated what I'd just seen.

"I began to shoot. I couldn't believe it, but Robert took his tripod and began poking the cobra nest trying to get the serpent to wake up."

"The serpent? You mean serpents."

Joanie stopped to shudder.

"The mother was absolutely, exquisitely supine. Then, suddenly, two or three baby cobras sprang out of the nest at Robert. I don't know how they did it, but they wrapped their little wormy poisonous bodies around his tripod. With a lunge, the sleeping mother woke up and flung herself at Robert. All I saw when I began running was Robert trying frantically to shake all serpents off his tripod. I think he trampled his camera in his retreat."

I settled on covering my eyes with my hands, trying not to laugh at the comedy of Robert's unplanned misfortunes. Both of us had spent way, way too much time with Robert Gardner.

"Of course, what you didn't see from this distance, Clark, was that we both had to run for our lives. Close up, this serpent was absolutely gigantic. What you also probably missed was that Robert narrowly avoided getting struck by the mother."

I patted the dirt and gravel next to me and indicated that Joanie should sit in the shade of the car.

"Snakes are just always splendid fun, aren't they?" I said. "What I love about them most are those little unrehearsed improvisations."

Joanie sat. She reached out and put her hand in mine. Her hand was burning hot.

A moment later, Robert appeared over the hilltop in the distance. Warily, he approached the spot where he'd left his camera. I noticed he didn't have his tripod with him. He looked down at the expensive camera he'd recently trampled.

***

That was yesterday.

In the heat and humidity of the nearby lake, Robert adjusted his Abercrombie & Fitch bush jacket. He'd gotten his creases just right. Four of the buttons were undone, and you could see his manly chest. Deep sweat stains pooled in the armpits of the jacket.

At that moment, Robert seemed to be waiting for my reaction to his previous invitation to die of heatstroke, or become a victim of mutilation and homicide, on our joint journey together toward hell in the wastelands adjoining Lake Rudolf.

"I want you to think about this," Robert said. "It's easier to get from here to there, that is, from Lake Rudolf to Nairobi, than back to Jinka or Addis Ababa."

"I really don't think so," I said.

Personally, what I thought about Robert's suggestion to navigate one of the most fearsome desert landscapes on this planet was that he'd had a genetic meltdown and lost his mind.

It was in that desert, populated by the *shifta,* where Louis Leakey had discovered the oldest fossilized remains of mankind, which had originated in this place millions of years ago. But for decades Leakey had done his reconnaissance surveys of this desert by airplane.

One of our two Toyota Land Cruisers was in fine shape. This was, of course, Robert's vehicle. My own Land Cruiser, on the other hand, was in a state of near total collapse and disintegration.

I'd only been told lately that my Toyota was actually a used vehicle. This was by way of an offhand and tardy explanation, months into our journey, that described its sickly state.

Robert's Land Cruiser, by contrast, was purchased brand-new.

I turned in the heat to look across a landscape completely barren of life. This place was the end of the world.

The largest permanent desert lake in the world, Lake Rudolf was also home to enormous numbers of formidably large Nile crocodiles. At maturity, they weighed half a ton. Three years before, in 1965, the photographer Peter Beard and his companion, Alistair Graham, had shot more than 500 Nile crocodiles as part of a census survey of this lake. They didn't make a dent in the population of these monsters. A later census of the lake counted 42,000 Nile crocodiles they hadn't been able to shoot.

For a moment, I studied the man who'd brought us into this place.

The journey he was proposing for himself was a one-man suicide pact. But it also guaranteed Joanie's destruction and my own, along with that of our translator, Abdullah, and our Ethiopian cook, Tekle. I wondered where Robert's death wish had come from. Had it been nesting in his psyche since he'd gone to St. George's boarding school?

"Do you think that's a good suggestion?" I asked finally.

"I think that is a sensible suggestion."

After three months of hell in Ethiopia, I wasn't interested anymore in Robert's film agendas. Nor was I at all interested in his demented ideas about his own immortality.

I shook my head.

Patiently, Robert explained again. "We cross the Omo River on two open canoes lashed together onto wooden planks. We balance our cars on the planks. We ferry one car across, then the next."

"It's just a moonlight drive across the desert, and in no time at all, we'll be having a lovely breakfast at the Gymkhana Club in Nairobi." Robert cracked a half smile and stretched languorously. Our leader had spoken. As far as he was concerned, the decision was final.

I watched as he put on his Ray-Ban pilot sunglasses after blotting the sweat on his forehead.

It was now my time to smile. "The only trouble with your plan is that I'm not going with you, Robert, and neither is Joanie."

"What?" He stared at me in surprise.

I repeated what I'd just said.

"You can't do this," he answered, agitated. He was trying to be civil, but it was a great struggle.

He repeated, "We have to go on. We have to cross the Omo and get into the desert."

"I think perhaps you've forgotten one thing."

In the extreme heat, Robert was beginning to get angry. "I haven't forgotten one thing. I haven't forgotten anything."

"The last time I thought about this, I had changed four tires and my spare tire all by myself. Do you remember that? It was four days ago. I wondered why you didn't ever have any flats, but then you have a vehicle with new tires that actually works."

I brooded about that a bit more.

A few days before, I had discovered that all five of my tires had deflated. The wheels of my vehicle were resting on their rims. No one had helped me as I took the tires off the car. No one had helped as I pried the tires off their rims with two screwdrivers. Huge Ethiopian desert thorns had caused the punctures. I had to patch each tire two or three times.

Finally, I reinflated and remounted the tires. Even the spare tire on the roof of my Land Cruiser had gone flat.

I was too tired to argue about Nairobi. I asked Robert, "How many flat tires have you had on this trip?"

Robert didn't answer.

"Happily, I want to tell you something."

"Happily what?" Robert interrupted me angrily.

"Happily," I continued calmly. "I want to tell you that we don't have any remaining tire patches."

I got up, and without another word, I moved to sit in the shade, which was now on the other side of my Toyota.

In the end, I think that was the only reason we survived Ethiopia. It was because I ran out of tire patches.

Robert didn't care. He'd have killed us all. He didn't even care about himself at that point. In Ethiopia at the end, I think we all went crazy.

Ethiopia, 1968

Joanie and I were in Ethiopia for ninety-three days. For eighty-nine of those days, we were in the field taking pictures.

For nine years, I traveled in the non-Western world. During that time, I didn't really live anywhere. I lived with my projects and my cameras. I lost count of how many times I crossed the Atlantic and how many times I moved between India and Europe.

That day on Lake Rudolf, I stopped traveling.

It was at that moment in the broiling sun in southern Ethiopia that I realized I'd burned up the last of my nine lives.

I had traveled since 1959 with no fixed address.

***

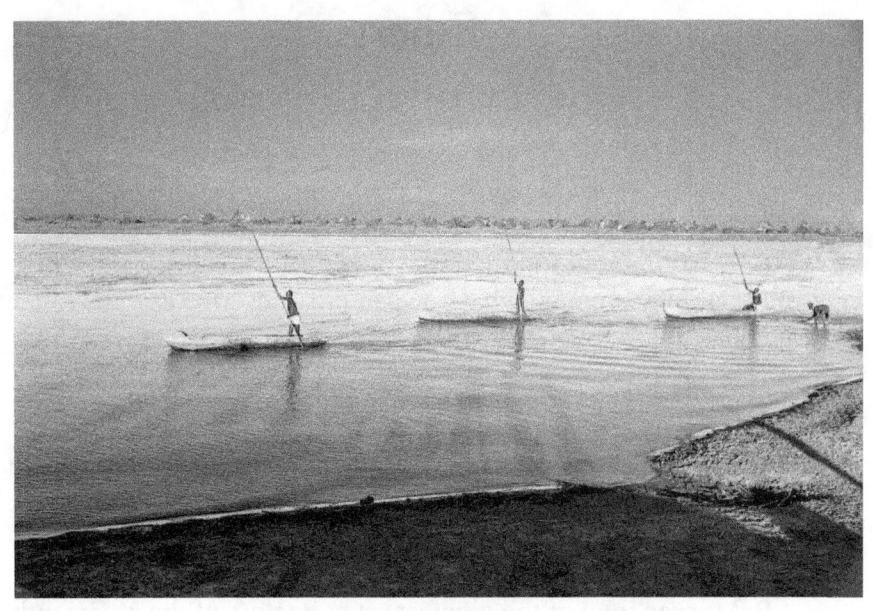

The Omo River, Ethiopia.

The Cradle of Mankind dated 6,500 generations before today,

Joan Mitchell Worswick, 1968

Postscript:
Upon the Moments Photography Emerged
as a Collectible Art

At the beginning of the 1970s, some of the greatest names in photography enjoyed what one can only describe as extravagant neglect.

What follows are a few choice examples of abandonment:

In Boston during the early 1970s, the original plates to make the gravures of Edward Curtis's epic multivolume work *The North American Indian* had been on offer with no purchaser for thirty-five years. A Boston printer was the residuary of the efforts of J.P. Morgan, one of the greatest art collectors of the nineteenth and early twentieth centuries, to publish Curtis's work. I was offered both the original plates to create the project, plus some 280,000 gravures, or 60 percent of the prints created for Curtis's epical monograph.

In turn, I met an ex-CIA operative named Harry Lunn, who had started working as a photography dealer. Even as brave or crazed as Lunn was, he turned down the offer of 280,000 Curtis gravures at a moment when photography had a modest future at best.

In a parallel instance, by 1970 Walker Evans, one of the two or three greatest American photographers of the twentieth century saw his career, begun in 1929, shrivel away when he left the employ of Time, Inc.

For the previous twenty-five years, Evans had struggled to get his last major book, on his New York subway portraits, published. His colleagues in the New York publishing world had apparently lost his telephone number.

Simultaneously, the photographer Berenice Abbott was attempting to divest herself of a burden that she had shouldered four decades before in Paris. In 1927, Abbott had acquired the life's work of the great French photographer, Eugène Atget. Atget's work would challenge and change modernist photography. For forty-two years, Abbott's crusade to have Atget's work accepted had been universally ignored by the American museum establishment. By the beginning of the 1970s, Abbott was exhausted and in precipitously declining health.

But then, something strange began to happen in photography.

In England and America, Germany and France, a group of visionary young art dealers, who regarded themselves as provocateurs, found that they could build galleries and careers selling photography. The first of these intrepid souls was Lee Witkin in New York, with a small gallery across the street from Bloomingdale's, on East 60th Street.

In a handcart outside the Metropolitan Museum of Art, the amazing Daniel Wolf first sold photographs to pay for art college. In Cambridge, Massachusetts, there was Rodger Kingston. In Washington, D.C., there was Harry Lunn. In Paris, François Braunschweig and Hugues Autexier had their shop in the Paris flea market. With the advent of these new dealers, photography lurched slowly toward the mainstream of serious art.

In any postmortem in the branding of photography, as art, I return to a conversation that I had with a curator at the Museum of Modern Art during 1970. In the dimly but tastefully lit corridor of the museum, the paintings curator sneered at me when I brought up the role of photography in art modernism.

"Dear man," he had said, "Photography, you must understand is simply an *industrial* art. It's like manufacturing. It is the idiot of the art world. In its most perfect and daring conception, photography is like the municipal art of sweeping streets." Curators and art historians actually thought like this in 1970.

The truth was that museums, with only a few exceptions, were dragged kicking and screaming into exhibiting photography. Despite all their claims to the contrary today, this is the truth. Art historians were even more recalcitrant than curators in judging photography as an industrial pursuit. Photography, as the canon went, was utterly unworthy of serious art-historical scrutiny.

If one rummages through the dustbins of art history, in a certain sense, the closest comparison to the rediscovery of photography as an art form was the glacial acceptance of Impressionism and Modernism during the late nineteenth and early twentieth centuries. Seen through the lens of history, the acceptance of Impressionism was like the Earth shifting upon its axis. It was an event, in retrospect, which had the grandeur of a spectacular seismic event in the ethos of the art world.

In my own mind, regarding the resurrection of photography in the art world, I go back to a moment in the mid-1960s when I went to a sparsely attended lecture at Harvard College given by Walker Evans. The dozen or so undergraduates present seemed generally uninterested; they had been dragooned into attending by Davis Pratt, a friend of Evans's, who had just lost his job in New York at the Museum of Modern Art, in a kind of art putsch.

Photography like Walker Evans himself, seemed to have fought the long, good fight and both photography and Evans had lost the last battle. Together, both the artist and his medium had been discarded into the trash heap of old things. On that cold winter evening, in a dimly lit Cambridge lecture hall, I wondered if this wasn't Walker Evans last stop in the growing oblivion of an unknown an artist.

***

For decades, I've labored with the question of whom it was that sparked an interest in photography as an important artistic medium. Who championed photography in the art world and finally prevailed?

Furthermore, if art dealers and collectors, art historians and museums, did not stand behind photography, how could photography ever accomplish a Lazarus-like resurrection?

Of course, there were a few crazed and brilliant souls who collected photography. In reality, however, none of these collectors, or the even small, insurgent group of young art dealers, represented the mainstream of anything in the art world.

As it turns out, it was the auction houses that stepped up and stood behind photography. It was the auction houses that introduced the great collectors and dealers to the medium. To be precise it was five people who led A Reinventionof the art of photography in the 1970s.

In London, there was Philippe Garner at Sotheby's and Stuart Bennett at Christie's. In New York, there was Anne Horton at Parke-Bernet, with David Margolis and later Denise Bethel at the Swann Galleries. In the past decades, I have never seen these five names grouped in print, nor their considerable accomplishment acknowledged in establishing photography as a fine art. It was upon the shoulders of these five intrepid souls that photography again gained its place in the art world.

***

Clark Worswick

Hotel Belmares, Puerto Escondido, Mexico
Millbrook, New York

BOOKS

The books below: The Last Empire, Princely India, Imperial China, and Japan were the first books ever written on classical 19th century photography where 70% of the world's population live. These books were of places, and landscapes that, were then unchanged,

***

The Last Empire, Photography in British India, 1855-1911, (1976), Aperture. Introduction by Lord Mountbatten, Additional Text Ainslie Embree. 10th edition in print

Imperial China, Photographs 1850-1912 (1979), Crown Publishers. Additional Text, Jonathan Spence.

An Edwardian Observer, The Photographs of Leslie Hamilton Wilson (1978) Crown Publishers,with, Edwin Newman

Japan, Photogaphs 1854-1905 (1978) Alfred A. Knopf). Additional Text, Jan Morris

Princely India, Photographs of Raja Deen Dayal,1884-1910 (1980) Alfred A. Knopf. Additional Text, J.K. Galbraith.

Walker Evans: The Lost Work (2000) Arena Editions.

Kenro Izu: Sacred Places (2001) Arena Editions. (The Photography book of the Year, 2002)

Edward Curtis: the Master Prints (2001) Arena Editions

Abbott/Atget (2002), Arena Editions

Festival of Lights: Photographs of India at Night (2004)

Paris Changing: Revisiting Eugene Atget's Paris
Photographs of Robert Rauschenberg, 2007

Sheying: Shadows of China, 1850-1900. 2008, (2 editions)
Turner Books, Madrid

Gardens of Sand, Photography in the Middle East 1859-
1900, (2010) Turner Books, Madrid

Walker Evans: Decade by Decade, (2011) Hatje Kantz,
Collaboration with James Crump. Prize as: One of "the
ten best books published in the United States, 2011", The
Library Journal

The Orchid House: Art Smuggling and Appointments in
India and Afghanistan , 2012

ArtMachine : A Reinvention of Photography 1959 -1999, 2016

***

ABOUT THE AUTHOR

Clark Worswick (1940-   ) was born in Berkeley, California. After attending the progressive Verde Valley School in Arizona (1954-1958), he enrolled in Visva Bharati University, at Santinikitan in West Bengal (India). Thereafter, he traveled in the first wave of young westerners to pass though the Iranian and Afghan deserts on their way to India.

His book, *The Orchid House Art Smuggling and Appointments in India and Afghanistan,* recounts these seldom described travels. *ArtMachine* is the second of his biographical accounts of travel. In Calcutta during 1959, he began collecting photographs. His book *Art Machine: A Reinvention of Phaotogaphy, 1959-1999* is the second volume of a biographical series.

The First Research Fellow in Film and Photography at Harvard University his books on Indian, Chinese and Japanese 19th century photography were the first works to identify scores of non-European artists working in the medium. His books have been named "Best of the Year" by *The NY Times*, *The London Times*, *The Washington Post*, *The Sunday Times*, *Newsweek* and *Time Magazine*.

His books on Indian, Chinese and Japanese 19th century photography were the first works to identify scores of non-European artists working in the medium. A book about the Worswicks' Walker Evans collection by James Crump titled, *Walker Evans:Decade By Decade* was named by The American Library Association "one of the ten best books of the year published in America."

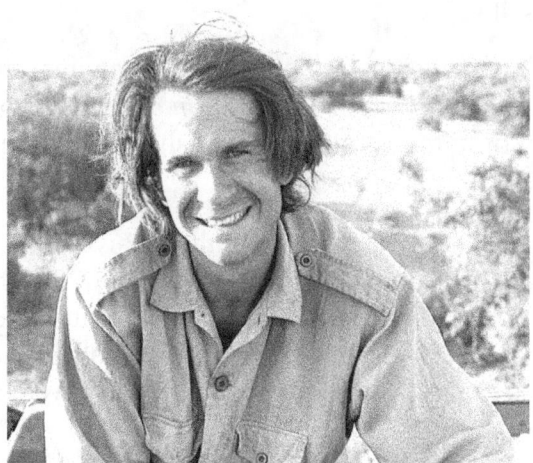

Ethiopia, 1968

BACK COVER TEXT

This book is a narrative of buccaneering bravado, rescue, and the creation of great artists' careers rescued from oblivion. It is a story for anyone interested in photography.

This book is, also, a never told narrative, of the Lazarus-like resurrection of photography against the formidable odds, of the entrenched art establishment, and how photography recreated itself as an art.

At the beginning of 1960's no university anywhere taught a single course in photography. In the whole world only two museums held infrequent exhibitions of photography. Nor did there exist, at that moment, a single photography dealer anywhere on earth. It was not until 1975 that the first photography gallery opened in Tokyo.

But this is also a story of an adventure, love, and dangerous travel ranging across the Middle East, Indian Asia and East Africa. It details the life of a working photographer, who became an "insider" in the decades long battle for the legitimacy of photography.

The startling collision of photography, as an important art, is the subject of *ArtMachine: A Reinvention of Photography, 1959–1999* seen from the point of view of an artist fighting a decades long war.

In 1960, one could purchase from the archive of his life's work, any Edward Weston picture created by one of the emblematic American photographic artists of the 20th century, for $25. The same prints today sell for over $2 million dollars each. In the now global reinvention of photography, there were scores of stories like this.

***

www.ingramcontent.com/pod-product-compliance
Lightning Source LLC
Chambersburg PA
CBHW060820170526
45158CB00001B/38